THE LANDLORD'S HANDBOOK

A COMPLETE GUIDE TO MANAGING SMALL RESIDENTIAL PROPERTIES

THE LANDLORD'S HANDBOOK

A COMPLETE GUIDE TO MANAGING SMALL RESIDENTIAL PROPERTIES

DANIEL GOODWIN & RICHARD RUSDORF

Longman Financial Services Publishing
a division of Longman Financial Services Institute, Inc.

While a great deal of care has been taken to provide accurate and current information, the ideas, suggestions, general principles and conclusions presented in this book are subject to local, state and federal laws and regulations, court cases and any revisions of same. The reader is thus urged to consult legal counsel regarding any points of law—this publication should not be used as a substitute for competent legal advice.

Executive Editor: Kathleen A. Welton
Acquisitions Editor: Wendy Lochner
Copy Editor: Patricia Stoll
Interior Design: Edwin Harris
Cover Design: Salvatori Concialdi
Cover Photo: Jonathan J. Stein
Inside Photos: Rich Rusdorf

Published by Longman Financial Services Publishing
a division of Longman Financial Services Institute, Inc.

Printed in the United States of America.

89 90 10 9 8 7 6 5 4 3 2

Library of Congress Cataloging-in-Publication Data

Goodwin, Daniel L.
The landlord's handbook.

Bibliography: p.
Includes index.
1. Real estate management. 2. Rental housing.
3. Landlords. 4. Landlord and tenant. I. Rusdorf, Richard F. II. Title.
HD1394.G656 1988 647'.92'068 88-8899
ISBN 0-88462-405-6

Acknowledgment

Many people helped put this book together. We especially would like to thank the staff officers and support personnel of Inland Real Estate, without whose time and creative efforts this book would not be a reality: Ronald Balcer, Patti Beyer, William Buckley, Laury Cowell, Patricia Luciew, Sharen Mangiameli, Michael Semprini, Jonathan Stein and Bella Zielinski. We also appreciate the review and suggestions of Elliot Kamenear.

Special thanks are extended to Cathy Caputo, who gave us her insight into property taxes; to Delores Friedman, whose expertise in insurance and risk management permitted us to explain the multitude of insurance terms and types of policies, and to Russell Lenich, for sharing his knowledge of accounting procedures.

Contents

About the Authors

Daniel L. Goodwin is the chairman and CEO of the Inland Group of Real Estate Companies. Mr. Goodwin has 20 years of experience in the purchasing, financing, management and sale of more than 2 billion dollars worth of income-producing residential properties. He has been involved in over 1,200 separate real estate transactions throughout the country.

Richard F. Rusdorf, CPM® has more than 18 years' experience in property management, and supervises a mortgage structuring division of the Inland Real Estate Corporation. A real estate broker, Rusdorf is an NASD member and is a past president of the Chicago chapter of the Institute of Real Estate Management.

The Inland Group of real estate companies is a billion-dollar real estate and financial firm headquartered in Oak Brook, Illinois. Inland, comprised of the largest property management firm in the midwest, manages more than 40,000 units, from two-flat buildings to 1,000-unit complexes in six states. Its mortgage company is one of the largest apartment building mortgage bankers in the United States, and Inland's commercial brokerage company is Chicago's largest apartment seller.

1

Managing Income-Producing Properties

***Carol Ann McMillion** is a writer and teacher. She owns and lives in a 60-year-old three-flat in an innercity neighborhood.*

"One of the smartest things I ever did—I didn't know it at the time—was to buy this building. Rent from the apartments pays the mortgage, taxes and insurance with some left over for improvements and maintenance. I get the usual tax benefits and the building has appreciated in value.

"The rental income enabled me to live on a graduate student's stipend for seven years while I was earning my PhD. When my daughter and son graduated college, I was able to offer them a place to live while they established themselves in careers.

"People assume maintaining the building is difficult; it's not. I do most of the routine maintenance myself. Major repairs—a new roof, electricity upgrade, tuckpointing—are tax-deductible and make the building worth more.

"The real challenge is to choose good tenants. This is particularly important when you live in the building. You want to be able to come home to peace and quiet. Even if you have only one or two apartments,

you should screen tenants thoroughly: Check references and credit, and then rely on common sense and intuition. A family on public aid can be good tenants, and someone who seems ideal can turn out to be a real pain."

Managing Profitable Investment Property

George Benton, 36, lives in a one-bedroom condominium that is ideally located along Chicago's North Lake Shore Drive. Since he bought the condominium, George has changed jobs and now works in a Chicago suburb. He would like to live closer to work in a larger home with a fenced backyard for his collie. But he doesn't wish to sell his downtown condominium, because he still considers it a good long-term investment.

Nancy Oates and Bill Wellbrook are successful entrepreneurs in South Bend, Indiana. Five years ago, they developed an insurance service that caters to the specific needs of senior citizens. Now they are considering renovating a turn-of-the-century six-flat along South Bend's Lincoln Way East.

The Hasbrouck, Kiel and Lippert families of Dallas, Texas, organized the HKL investment club eight years ago. The club investments have proven profitable, except for stock holdings in 1987. Now considering ways to conserve profits, HKL is planning to purchase a 40-unit five-story apartment building on Rodeo Boulevard.

What do these people have in common? Like you, they currently own or are planning to purchase small income properties. And, like you, what they need is a practical handbook, specifically designed for the do-it-yourself landlord. While there are many real estate books on the shelves, they often deal mainly with acquiring property and structuring real estate deals. Generally, these books do not provide you, the average real estate investor, with practical, usable techniques and suggestions that help you to manage your investment property more profitably on a day-to-day basis.

This book is designed to share property management expertise with you in clear, everyday language. Based on experience of successful property owners and managers, this book clearly explains the importance of attracting and keeping good tenants by using good management techniques. It discusses how to form a business relationship with your tenants based on mutual respect.

The techniques, forms and worksheets were developed and are used by Inland Real Estate Corporation, a billion-dollar property manager based in the Midwest.

Real estate always has been considered a good investment. However, the recent combination of tax reform and low mortgage rates has made small income-producing properties one of the best investments of the 1980s. Real estate was and is a purchase that stands the dual tests of time and cyclical economies.

Owning and operating small investment properties has made many people financially independent. As a real estate investor, you have the pride of ownership coupled with a hedge against inflation that serves to protect your asset from losing value. As a property manager, your chief concerns are to maintain your property and increase its value. Regardless of your specific goals, effective management is the key to achieving them.

Simply owning rental property will not guarantee financial independence, because good properties do not generate cash flow by themselves. To make money, you need to know good property management techniques. You need to know how to keep good tenants, how to collect the rent on time, how to maintain the physical structure of your property and, most importantly, how to deal with people.

Owning a Home Versus Managing Rental Property

To some extent, owning your home has prepared you for owning other buildings. However, managing rental property is not the same as managing a home. For example, decorating schemes that might be perfect for your home–say, a soft gray carpet framed by emerald green and geometric wallpaper in the same shades with peach accents–could be a real detriment in a rental apartment if those colors do not go with a new tenant's furniture. In apartments, carpeting and wall treatments should be in neutral colors, and in materials that are easy to clean and maintain.

Kitchen appliances also are different for rental properties as compared to home use. You may choose to buy a range that incorporates a microwave oven for your home, but a tenant who already owns a microwave will consider that option unnecessary. Also, as a property manager you must be aware of depreciation; thus you might choose a different water heater or furnace for a rental property than you would for your own use.

You Don't Need an MBA

Some would-be investors think property management requires a master's degree in management. They've heard horror tales of tenant complaints, problems with collecting rent, mechanical equipment failures, apartment vacancies and so on, and they suspect that, unless they have formal training, managing rental property could be a nightmarish experience.

Property management is a headache if you don't know what you are doing. To maximize your investment property, you must make money while keeping expenses in check. If you let tenants run the property down, if you fail to get regular rent increases or if you mismanage cash flow you might not make a profit; you could even decrease the value of your asset. Certainly, attending managerial and real estate courses and seminars can be helpful. And this book will give you proven methods based on 20 years of experience in dealing with virtually every form of residential property and all types of tenants.

Use Your Management Skills in a New Setting

If you are in corporate management or operate your own business you already have many of the necessary skills for small property management, but you probably take them for granted as part of your daily business routine. You do not realize that the same marketing and management skills can apply in a number of business situations.

Marketing

For example, grocery store management requires attracting regular customers; apartment management requires attracting good renters. To bring customers into the grocery, the manager uses numerous marketing tools, including newspaper advertising, special promotions, and so on. The property manager advertises rental vacancies and highlights special features of the apartment and complex such as carpeting, off-street parking, etc.

Maintenance

Regular maintenance is important to the grocery store and the apartment complex. The grocery store manager may not operate the floor scrubber or wash down the checkout counters, but he or she will check that these jobs are done because customers prefer shopping in a clean environment. The property manager also needs to actively monitor maintenance of apartments, common areas, landscaping, parking areas and so on.

Accounting

At the end of the business day the grocery store manager tallies receipts for each department and prepares bank deposits. These accounting numbers will be tallied weekly or monthly against costs of inventory, spoilage, overhead and other factors to monitor the store's profitability. Similar bookkeeping and accounting skills are necessary in property management to make sure rental receipts cover costs while producing a profit. Anyone who can balance a checkbook can quickly learn the accounting procedures used to control income and expenses of a property.

Customer Relations

The grocery store manager needs to have a balanced combination of diplomacy and judgment when dealing with customers. For example, if an irate customer demands a refund for one rotten orange found in a five-pound bag, a smart manager will replace that $2.99 bag of oranges or refund the purchase price to keep that customer buying oranges and other products in the store. It's a good investment in customer relations.

Diplomacy and judgment are also crucial in good property management. For example, an irate tenant may insist that he or she needs a new deadbolt "because my apartment is too difficult to open." A smart property manager will promptly and cheerfully apply a little carbon to the keys and locks; this will probably solve the problem, and the cost in time and materials is about the same as for that five-pound bag of oranges.

Managing Time and People

Properly done, the management of small rental properties can be a rewarding experience. And you don't have to make property management a full-time job.

Obviously the amount of time you will need to manage your rental property depends on your knowledge and resources and the size of your building.

Once you've mastered the techniques offered in this book, you should be able to handle a single condominium unit in 30 minutes a month, while a typical four-flat will require about four hours of your time. Most of this time will be spent dealing with people, so how well you deal with people is one key to effective management.

How This Book Can Help

The information and forms in this book provide you with valuable tools to help you increase your cash flow and creative financial independence. The book walks you through the important management tasks involved from the day you hand over the apartment keys to a new tenant through the day you take them back.

As a new apartment investor and manager you will have to determine the proper rental rate to fit your property and local market conditions. This book deals with rental rates and also shows you how to find tenants and suggests ways to convince them that your rental property specifically meets their needs.

Lease applications and rental agreements can be complicated, but the handbook simplifies them, and even supplies sample form leases and riders. Terminology and contents are defined, along with discussions of prohibited transactions, security deposits, lease distribution and important caveats. You also learn about apartment inspections, lease renewals and subletting and reletting agreements.

Other important aspects of property management include rent collections, maintenance, the different types of insurance required, property taxes and accounting. Each of these is thoroughly addressed, along with sample forms and guidelines.

2

Resident Relations

Ron Vanden Bossche *has a Ph.D. in clinical psychology and practices in the Veterans' Administration. He purchased a three-flat building in 1981.*

"Tenant phobia is not a true psychiatric entity, but it does appear to be a major reason people avoid owning income property. It is a multifaceted syndrome, ranging from our childhood training in avoidance of strangers, to anxious anticipation of being imposed on by pushy complainers, and uncertainty about one's ability to handle the power differential between landlord and tenant.

"It is easy to exaggerate these fears to the point of total avoidance of the role of landlord. But being a landlord is just that—a role. Roles can be learned. The first step is to accept these interpersonal anxieties as normal in landlord life.

"The second step involves the practice of assertiveness training. Simply put, assertiveness is stating the reality of a given situation in a clear, certain, but nonaggressive way. The difference between assertion and aggression is that assertiveness is the giving of information, while aggression is pure power play.

"Although the lease can be seen as speaking all the necessary words for you, at times you will have to restate them to your tenants due to noise, overdue rent and other situations. Do not view this assertive behavior as a confrontation with battle lines drawn and full of explosive potential. It is your right to state the fact of the matter. The reasonableness of the tenant's response will be the guide as to whether or not to continue your relationship with this tenant. Keep in mind that the landlord-tenant power differential means that no friendship or social relationship will be at stake. Nor will the assertive person take the behavior of tenants personally.

"Finally, do not confuse the role of landlord with the role of parent. Responding to tenants as adults who need information, not as children who need correcting, gives the best chance of having good relations and minimized anxiety."

The Landlord-Tenant Relationship

Many people believe that landlords and tenants are natural enemies. Landlords are seen as heartless money grubbers who would trade their mothers for a rent increase; or they are overworked, underpaid drudges who are slaves to their properties and tenants. Tenants are seen as ne'er-do-wells who make unreasonable demands, destroy property and refuse to pay the rent.

There is some truth in these stereotypes: Bad landlords and bad tenants do exist. But the landlord-tenant relationship is basically a business relationship. If you learn to manage rental property efficiently–and that includes choosing good tenants–then landlord-tenant transactions can be mutually rewarding.

It is well worth learning to deal with residents in a rational, businesslike way. When a building is badly managed it becomes an active drain on all resources: the building itself, and your time, energy and money.

Landlords and tenants will often have differences of opinion about their mutual responsibilities. Tenants may think that landlords should do everything in their power to make the tenants happy. Certainly you will want your tenants to be satisfied with their dwelling, but you are not obligated to provide them a garden paradise. If you know your basic obligations as a landlord, you will be less likely to resent a tenant's legitimate request, and will be able to assertively refuse an unreasonable demand.

Most of your obligations are governed and limited by the express conditions contained in a form lease or rental agreement. With or without a written lease, the business of owning and leasing rental property is also subject to state and local municipal statutes and ordinances.

Across the country, local and state governments are beginning to take stronger positions in regard to landlord-tenant relationships. Tenant groups are presenting their cases to city councils everywhere, demanding more favorable treatment from landlords. A new statewide landlord-tenant statute recently came before a vote in the Illinois House and Senate. The bill is representative of national trends in this area and addresses itself to obligations of both parties. The entire real estate industry may soon operate under laws of this type. Sections from the bill are included in discussions of various topics in this chapter.

Throughout this chapter the words *tenant* and *resident* are used interchangeably. *Tenant* refers to the legal relationship between a lessor and lessee; *resident* refers to a person dwelling in a home. In written and verbal communications with lessees it is preferable to refer to them as residents instead of tenants; this takes some of the formality out of the landlord-tenant relationship and puts it on a more personal level.

Landlord and *owner* are similarly interchangeable; they always refer to the lessor. *Owner* is the less formal term.

Landlord Obligations

Landlords must adhere to three widely recognized obligations:

Make Yourself Known

An owner (or other person who is authorized to enter into a rental agreement on the owner's behalf) should disclose to the resident, in writing, at or before the beginning of the lease, the name and address of the owner of the premises, and the person authorized to manage the premises. This is for the purpose of service of process and for the purpose of receiving and documenting notices and demands.

Any person named as agent in a written rental agreement meets this requirement; the agent is also authorized to act for and on behalf of the owner for the purpose of serving and receiving notices and demands.

If tenants are not told who is responsible and has authority to respond to their requests, they may be able to file a valid complaint with the local housing authority.

In some states you might have to disclose the insurance agent or carrier for the property. The purpose behind this disclosure is that, in case of a fire or other emergency, tenants would know whom to call if the owner or agent were unavailable.

Maintain Habitable Premises

At all times during the tenancy owners must maintain the premises in a habitable condition. A dwelling unit is considered habitable if the following minimum standards are maintained:

- Effective weather protection is provided, including unbroken windows and doors.
- Plumbing facilities are in good working order.
- The unit has a water supply connected to a sewage system. If the water supply is under the control of the resident, it must be capable of producing hot and cold running water; if under the control of the owner, it must produce hot and cold running water furnished to appropriate fixtures.
- Heating units and, if provided, air-conditioning and ventilation facilities, are in good working order. If these are under the control of the resident, they are capable of producing heat (or cooling and ventilation); if under control of the owner, they produce heat (or cooling and ventilation) in fixtures provided. Minimum temperatures for heat are usually established by municipal code.
- Gas or electrical appliances supplied by the landlord must be in good working order and properly installed with appropriate gas piping and electrical wiring systems according to building codes, and they must be maintained in good working order and safe condition.
- Building, grounds and areas under the control of the owner must be in a clean, sanitary and safe condition, free from all accumulation of debris, filth, rubbish, garbage, rodents and vermin.
- Adequate and appropriate receptacles for garbage and rubbish are provided. If these are under the control of the landlord, they must be kept in clean condition and good repair.
- Floors, stairways, railings and common areas are in good repair.

- Apartment floors, walls and ceilings are in good repair and safe condition.
- Elevators, if existing, are maintained in good repair and safe condition.

Generally, landlords are not held responsible if interruptions in service, breakdown of equipment or disrepairs are caused by:

- conditions caused by the tenant, members of resident's household, guests or other persons on the premises with resident's consent, or other residents.
- the resident's unreasonable refusal of, or other interference with, entry of the owner or the owner's workers or contractors into the premises for purposes of correcting any defective conditions.
- a lack of reasonable opportunity for the owner to correct defective conditions.
- conditions beyond the owner's reasonable control, including strikes, lock-outs and unavailability of essential utilities, materials or services
- the owner's not having actual knowledge or notice of such defective conditions.

Exclusion or modification of any part or all of these obligations must be in writing and separately signed by the party against whose interest the modification works. If the modification appears in the rental agreement, it must also be typed or printed in a conspicuous place. This means that if you and a tenant have an agreement that the tenant will maintain part or all of the property, it must be specifically spelled out in writing. The tenant should sign an acknowledgment of the agreement.

Honor Express Warranties

If you make a promise to a tenant about the condition of a specific dwelling unit, or the overall premises, services or repairs or replacements to be made, and this promise is part of the reason the tenant signed the lease, you have created an express warranty. This promise is binding whether it was oral or written.

An express warranty may be created even if there is not specific intention to make one. It is not necessary to use formal words such as *warrant* or *guarantee* in order to create an express warranty.

Such statements as: "We plan to replace your dishwasher in a few months," or, "We wash the outside of the windows three times a year," or, "You never have to worry about security around here; this is a safe building," create express warranties, and you might be held liable if someone did have a security problem or if you washed windows only twice, etc.

On the other hand, giving your *opinion* of the relative value of the dwelling unit, premises or services does not create a warranty. For example, you might say, "We have the best maintenance crew around," or, "I think my property is the best building on the block," or, "The view from this apartment is beautiful," without creating a warranty.

It would be wise to consult your attorney for guidance in this matter.

Additional Services

Tenants expect to receive all of the services and benefits your property offers for their rental dollar. They rightfully expect you to live up to your basic obligations as listed above. But most properties also offer additional services to tenants, such as swimming pool, snow removal and so on.

Before the resident moves in, outline exactly what services the property provides: door attendant, snow removal, landscaping, garbage removal, utilities, recreation, receiving packages and so on. Then do your best to see that these services are consistently provided.

Having the swimming pool closed for repairs on the hottest day of the year or failing to provide snow removal after a blizzard are good ways to ruin a landlord-tenant relationship. Residents tend to remember these things when it comes time to renew their leases.

Liabilities of Ownership

Landlords are generally responsible for maintaining the premises and performing the basic services required, and can be held liable for damages caused by negligence (see chapter 9). Owners remain liable until the property is sold.

Unless otherwise agreed, an owner who sells his or her property subject to existing leases, and who assigns the leases in a good faith sale to a bona fide purchaser, is relieved of liability for events occurring subsequent to written notice to the resident of the sale and assignment. The new owner becomes liable to the resident for events occurring after this notice, and for money to which the resident is entitled from security deposits or prepaid rent.

Unless otherwise agreed, a manager is relieved of liability for events occurring after written notice to the resident of the termination of the manager's contract.

Resident Obligations

Tenants are also bound by the lease document and laws governing rental apartments. Unfortunately, most tenants are not knowledgeable or made aware of their obligations. This problem is solved by thoroughly communicating these responsibilities before the tenant moves in.

Standard Tenant Responsibilities

There are six widely recognized tenant obligations. In most states, residents must:

- maintain the dwelling unit, furnishings, fixtures and appliances in a clean, sanitary and safe condition
- dispose of all rubbish, garbage and other waste in a clean sanitary manner in the refuse facilities
- use in a reasonable manner all electrical, plumbing, sanitary, ventilating, air conditioning and other facilities and appliances including elevators
- not place in the dwelling unit or premises any furniture, plants, animals or any other thing which harbors insects, rodents or other pests
- not destroy, deface, damage, impair or remove any part of the dwelling unit or premises or facilities, equipment or furnishings, except as necessary when hazardous conditions exist that immediately affect the resident's health or safety
- not commit waste, make alterations, additions or improvements to the dwelling unit except with the owner's prior consent, nor permit claims to be filed against the premises.

Tenant Restrictions

Unless otherwise agreed, the resident must occupy the premises solely for residential purposes.

The resident and other persons on the premises with the resident's consent must conduct themselves in a manner that will not disturb the neighbors' peaceful enjoyment of the premises, is not illegal and will not injure the reputation of the building or its residents.

Residents must respect the fact that someone else owns the property, and they must respect the rights of other tenants. Common sense dictates that they should not allow or take any action that would hurt the property or disturb other residents.

Landlord's Right of Access

In most states, residents cannot unreasonably withhold consent for the owner to enter into the apartment in order to inspect the premises, make necessary or agreed repairs, decorations, alterations or improvements, to supply necessary or agreed services or to exhibit the property to prospective or actual purchasers, mortgagees, residents, workers and contractors. Owners should not abuse this right or use it to harass residents.

In the event of an apparent or actual emergency, the owner may enter the apartment at any time without notice.

At any time within 90 days prior to the end of the lease term (if such a provision is contained in the lease document), the owner may, as often as necessary and upon reasonable notice, show the apartment for rent between the hours of 7 A.M. and 8 P.M. In some states (for example, Oklahoma and Texas) you must have this right stated within the lease, while in other states, the right is granted to you by statute.

At other times the owner should enter only after notice of not less than 24 hours and only between the hours of 7 A.M. and 8 P.M.

The owner should be provided with, retain in a safe place and may use copies of all keys necessary for access to the dwelling unit.

A landlord has no other right of access except pursuant to court order; during the absence of the resident in excess of 14 days (states vary on the exact number of days) or to remedy hazardous conditons; and/or when the resident has abandoned or surrendered the premises.

Starting out Right

From the moment you meet prospective residents until the day you refund their security deposit upon termination of the lease, you are faced with maintaining good resident relations. The kind of relationship you develop with your residents can dictate how much peace of mind and profit you derive from your investment property.

Your first meeting with a prospective tenant is crucial to the success of the landlord-tenant relationship. You want the tenant to respect you and the property, while keeping your relationship on a strict business level. The image you want to project is one of a professional property owner who is congenial, friendly and welcoming. Above all, you want to maintain control of the relationship at all times.

Tenants expect you to have an office and are willing to come to you, so take advantage of this opportunity. Remember, you own the property and they want to rent from you. If you let them think they're doing you a favor by renting your apartment, you may find yourself as the underdog in the relationship. Of course, you should thank them for renting and you can certainly be appreciative. But remember, you're in business and you must exercise control over who rents your property.

In maintaining positive relationships with all your residents, keep your communications with any problem tenants on a strictly professional business level. You can be sympathetic to their problems but don't let these problems interfere with your sound judgment. Landlords have been labeled as the villain throughout history and you don't need to aggravate a situation by playing that role.

You're proud of your building, and you want the tenants to treat your property with respect. The way to do this is to create a positive image in the tenants' minds. Let them know how you feel about the apartment. Tell them you want them to make it their home. It is in your best interest if the tenants share your pride and maintain the property as if it were their own.

Keeping Good Tenants

Every business involves working with people, and being a landlord is no different. Smart owners recognize the importance of the human factor in a successful business. If all you had to deal with was leaky plumbing, electrical wiring and record-keeping, the job would be simple and everyone would become a landlord.

All businesses need customers and in the apartment business your customers are the tenants. Successful businesses manage to keep their customers satisfied. In the rental business, when you lose customers, you must replace them with others as soon as possible. And when the old customers were especially good, it may not always be possible to replace them with equals. Thus it is better to keep your existing customers than to constantly be looking for new ones.

Resident turnover can be costly. National surveys estimate that a landlord can lose an amount equal to two months' rent every time a resident moves out. This amount is based on the possibilities of losing money from cleaning and redecorating for new tenants; advertising expenses; processing paperwork; damage to common area walls, doors, halls and so on by movers; time spent showing vacant apartments; lost income from vacant apartments and commissions to apartment referral services.

As an owner you won't be able to eliminate turnover completely, but you can minimize it by maintaining a good relationship with your residents. Here is a checklist on developing strong tenant relationships and keeping your residents satisfied:

- Show interest in their lifestyle and needs during the rental interview.
- Follow through on your promises about repairs and decorating. Don't offer something you can't deliver.
- Give residents your work and home phone numbers to use in case of emergencies. Provide them with a list of other important phone numbers for emergency repairs or services.
- Respond promptly to requests for service. Even if you can't meet their demands, let them know where you stand on the issue. Communication is the key to maintaining good relationships.
- Let the residents know in advance what you expect from them and what they can expect from you on such items as rent payment, lease provisions, pets, complaints, services and so on.
- Respect their privacy and right to peaceful possession of their home during their lease period. (*Peaceful possession* is a legal term that means the right to use the premises without harrassment or interruption.)
- If you must enter an apartment when the tenants are not at home, and without prior notice, leave a note stating that you were there and why. In general, do not enter a resident's apartment without giving at least a day's notice.

Dealing with Tenant Complaints

Handle complaints quickly and discreetly. If a resident complains about another resident, your best response is to ascertain as many facts as possible, then contact the other resident to find out if there is any truth to the allegation. If it's a matter of loud, disturbing noises, you can politely ask the offending resident to be more courteous to his or her neighbors. Most tenants will handle this type of problem without contacting the owner.

If you encounter difficulty with one tenant, don't allow it to escalate to a level that might involve other residents. Don't discuss the situation with other residents and don't spread gossip.

If there is a valid resident complaint and the complained-about resident does not respond to your requests, the next step is to send the resident a Lease Rules and Regulations Violation Letter (exhibit 1) advising the resident of the lease provision. This letter should also state your legal options if the problem persists.

EXHIBIT 1: Lease Rules and Regulations Violation Letter

Date ______________________

Dear ______________________:

Our management staff has informed us that there have been complaints about an unusual amount of noise coming from your apartment. This is in violation of paragraph ________ of your lease.

We realize it is often difficult to keep sounds in an apartment at a level that is not disturbing to neighbors. However, we would greatly appreciate your cooperation in this matter. In particular, make every effort to play your stereo equipment at a reasonable volume after 10:00 P.M. [Or refer to particular complaint that was made.]

We trust there will be no more complaints about noise. However, be aware that if the disturbances continue, we will seek remedies as provided by law.

If you have any questions, please call. Thank you for your consideration in this matter.

Very truly yours,

Maintenance complaints should be handled as quickly as possible. If the repair or replacement *cannot* be completed in a few days, tell the resident when you expect it to be done. This eases anxiety and tension between you and your residents.

Handling Claims and Disputes

There may be times when you and the tenants will not be able to agree on matters concerning physical conditions or operating policies and procedures. You may have to serve a termination notice, or even carry out an eviction. In such cases, it is wise to consult a lawyer; however, a number of general guidelines can be helpful.

Legal Counsel

It is wise to consult with an attorney before initiating any action against a tenant that could have the consequence of cancelling or enforcing a lease.

If a resident is not in compliance with the lease, or is the source of complaints from neighbors, a letter written on your attorney's stationery usually influences the tenant to correct the problem. Even if the letter is not effective, you'll have the documentation necessary to proceed with an eviction.

Most states adhere to landlord-tenant laws and ordinances that specify the obligations of both parties. If a local township does not have its own legislation, the state may have a law governing every municipality. At the time of publication of this book, at least 17 states have adopted the Revised Model Landlord-Tenant Act. Probably every state has some form of existing landlord-tenant law. When it comes to who's right and who's wrong, do not assume common sense will apply. Always check with your attorney.

General Guidelines

In the adjustment of claims or disputes, use the following general guidelines:

- Both you and your tenant, on reasonable notice to the other and for the purpose of ascertaining the facts and preserving evidence, should have the right to inspect the dwelling unit and common area premises.

- You and your tenant may agree at the time of any claim or dispute to allow a third-party inspection or survey to determine the conformity or condition of the dwelling unit or premises, and may agree that the findings shall be binding in any subsequent litigation or adjustment.
- If arbitration by a third party is unavailable or impractical, it may be possible, if the dispute involves monetary damages, for one or the other party to file a suit in small claims court.
- You may elect to voluntarily vacate a tenant's lease; that is, you might want to cancel the lease early if you cannot reach a compromise or satisfactorily settle a dispute.

As an example, one tenant registered a strong complaint stating that her kitchen faucet did not have cold water. Normally, you would expect a complaint about hot water, but in this case the tenant expected to have ice cold water running from the tap.

Because the water was supplied to the building from the city and went directly into the apartments, there was little that could be done to make her water colder than anyone else's. She persisted and it became obvious that nothing could be done to satisfy her in this matter. This left two possibilities: The first was to force her to honor the lease and stay in the apartment. The second was to cancel her lease. Since the apartment could be easily re-rented, the decision was made to let her move out under the condition that she would pay rent until another tenant was found, which, as it turned out, took less than a month.

Most states allow a form of constructive eviction. A constructive eviction occurs when a tenant vacates an apartment due to a defect in the condition of the unit, for example, a leaking roof, no heat or hot water and so on. For a constructive eviction to be valid, the tenant must actually move out of the apartment. If you sue the tenant for breaking the lease, and the tenant's defense is that you didn't cure a problem you were properly notified of, the judge may find for the tenant, stating that it was a constructive eviction.

If a tenant is in violation of the lease, other than not paying the rent, and you have not been able to settle the dispute, you may have to proceed with a termination notice.

Termination Notice

When a resident is breaking the rules and regulations outlined in the lease, and the owner's communications verbally or in writing do not obtain cooperation, it may then be necessary to begin the process for eviction. In this case, the notice of termination form (exhibit 2) is used. This form applies to all types of lease violations other than nonpayment of rent, including unauthorized pets, over-occupancy or excessive noise.

EXHIBIT 2: Notice of Termination

NOTICE OF TERMINATION

FOR USE WITH CREB FORM 15 APT. LEASE ONLY

You are hereby notified that your tenancy or lease of the premises situated in ______________ County of ______________, and State of Illinois and known and described as follows, to wit: ______________ ______________ together with all buildings, storage areas, recreational facilities, parking spaces and garages used in connection with said premises, will be terminated as follows:

(A) You have breached or are in default of the terms of your lease for said premises, as follows:

____

____

The owner has elected to terminate your right of possession under the lease, and you are hereby notified to quit and deliver up possession of the same to the owner within *ten* (10) days after service of this notice.

(B) The undersigned elects to terminate your tenancy of said premises, such termination will be effective on the ______ day of ______________, 19____, and you are hereby notified to quit and deliver up possession at that time.

To ______________

____

____

____

____

____

OWNER

____

AGENT OR ATTORNEY

Dated this ______ day of ______________, 19____

1. Box (A) is not to be used as a demand for rent; for that purpose, use the form entitled, "Owner's Five Day Notice."
2. Box (B) is for use when tenancy is not to continue after expiration of the current lease term. Give:
   (a) 60 days notice for terminating year to year tenancy, but do not give notice more than 4 months before the last 60 days of the lease.
   (b) 30 days notice for terminating month to month tenancy, or any other tenancy for a term less than one year, except week to week.
   (c) 7 days notice for terminating week to week tenancy.

FOLD

STATE OF ILLINOIS
COUNTY OF ______________ } SS.

AFFIDAVIT OF SERVICE

______________, being duly sworn, on oath deposes and says
(Served by)
that on the ______ day of ______________, 19____ he served the above notice on the tenant named above, as follows:*

☐ (1) by delivering a copy thereof to the above named tenant, ______________.

☐ (2) by delivering a copy thereof to ______________, a person above the age of twelve years, residing on or in charge of the above described premises.

☐ (3) by sending a copy thereof to said tenant by both (a) U.S. regular AND (b) certified or registered mail, postage pre-paid, at the address for tenant at the beginning of tenant's lease or such other address as tenant may previously have designated by written notice.

☐ (4) (in the event of apparent abandonment only) by posting a copy thereof on the main door of the above described premises, no one being in actual possession thereof.

Subscribed and sworn to before me this ______ day of ______________, 19____.

______________ Notary Public

x ______________

*Identify the method of service used by placing a check in the proper box. Sign on line marked X.

DO NOT USE WITH OTHER LEASE FORMS OR ORAL LEASES

4708

The notice of termination form must be filled out correctly. The chances of winning a case in court for this type of eviction are less than when you are suing for rent because the lease violations need to be well documented.

In section A of the termination form, quote the actual paragraph or clause in the lease that the resident is breaking. Do not use the paragraph number.

Section B of the termination notice is used only when you are terminating a resident that does not have a lease. You must allow a full calendar month for eviction. Thus, for example, if the notice is served on July 15, the date in this space must be the end of the following month, or August 31. States vary on the exact number of days. Some (for example, Oklahoma) allow you to terminate a tenancy in the middle of the month.

Keep the first copy of the termination notice, and deliver the second copy to the resident.

The Affidavit of Service section is self-explanatory. Be sure to have the document notarized. Note that in many states you must deliver a termination notice to a resident or occupant older than 12 years of age. Certain states (for example, Kansas) recognize a notice that was posted or taped on the outside of the apartment door.

Evictions

No one wants one. It's not easy for the landlord, and certainly the tenant isn't looking forward to that day. But evictions are a normal part of managing property and the more you know about them, the more comfortable you will be and the more efficiently you will handle the situation.

Actually having to evict a tenant is very rare, but it does happen and you should be prepared. There are two reasons why you would want to evict someone: nonpayment of rent or noncompliance of a lease provision.

Some general forms for dealing with an eviction are covered in chapter 8.

Eviction procedures vary slightly from state to state and it is best to consult with your attorney prior to initiating any action. Some legal fees can be assessed to a wrongful tenant and you may be able to recover your out-of-pocket expenses.

3

Marketing

Penny Tally *works as an administrative assistant for a marketing company. She started buying income properties a few years ago and performs most of the maintenance work herself. She collects the rent in person by going door to door. Her properties produce a substantial cash flow and currently provide a 12 percent return on her initial investments.*

"When I made my first leap into income real estate, I was working as an office manager and was a single mother of two. I owned a four-bedroom townhome, and I was struggling with a $600 per month mortgage payment. I needed supplemental income, and I didn't want to work two jobs. On the advice of a friend, I invested in real estate and now, four years later, I own 20 apartment units in the city and south suburbs.

"Marketing my apartments has been a process of trial and error. At the beginning, I depended a lot on word-of-mouth from my friends and relatives, and I distributed photocopied flyers in the neighborhood. Then I learned to check the newspapers to determine my rent figures, and began placing more sophisticated ads. My tenants—and my methods of handling them—have improved."

Determining a Rental Rate

In marketing apartments, your task is to present the product in such a way that a prospect will want to rent, and a resident will want to renew. Marketing includes finding and selecting the type of tenants you want, understanding the marketplace, qualifying prospects, preparing your product for presentation, selling the product and following up on leads.

Before you embark on your search for a tenant you must first determine how much rent to charge. If you buy a property that has existing tenants you will not have to immediately face the problem of determining rents, but you will have to calculate how much to increase the rent when it comes time to renew the leases. A detailed discussion of renewal increases is contained in chapter 6.

Break-Even Formula

Determining how much rent to charge is based on two key factors. First, you have to look at the math involved in owning the property. You will want to bring in enough income to cover your costs including expenses, debt payments, taxes and insurance. If your annual projected expenses are $1,200, your mortgage and taxes are $2,400, and you want an annual eight percent return on your initial $15,000 down payment, you will need to generate an income of $4,800 to break even (not taking into account income tax savings through depreciation, etc. See chapter 12).

$1,200 expenses
$2,400 mortgage, principal and taxes
$3,600 total outlay of cash

$1,200 return on investment (cash flow)
$4,800

$4,800 divided by 12 months equals $400 per month

Monthly rent = $400.00 (break-even amount)

Make every effort to purchase a property whose size, amenities, condition and location warrant a rental rate close to your break-even point. The first year or two of operating a rental property usually produces a negative cash flow in which the income does not equal expenses, but the deficiency and loss are made up through tax breaks. Each year, as rents increase, the investment gets closer to producing a positive cash return.

Market Rent

In addition to this break-even formula, you have to consider the second key factor determining rent amount, which is what the market will bear or the law of supply and demand.

Market rent is determined by comparing what similar apartments in comparable locations are charging and then making adjustments for local vacancy factors.

It is not difficult to find out the current market rent. Some time spent responding to "For Rent" advertisements, visiting other properties and reading your local newspaper classified section, will give you a fair idea of what other properties are charging.

You should be thoroughly familiar with your competition. How much are other apartments renting for in the same area? Compare your property to competing properties and adjust for the major differences. Are your rooms larger or smaller? Does your unit have a balcony or patio? How close is your property to schools, shopping and major transportation routes? You must be thoroughly familiar with each of the competing properties and the features of each. With this knowledge, you'll be able to set an accurate rental rate and be ready to respond to prospects' questions as to why your rent may be higher or lower than other properties in the immediate area.

If similar one-bedroom apartments offering similar amenities in your vicinity are renting for $350 a month, you will have a hard time trying to get $450. On the other hand, if your property has nicer qualities, or is better situated, you may be able to command $400 to $450. If the vacancy rate in the neighborhood is low, with few apartments similar to yours being available, then you will be in a position to raise the rent in accordance with specific demand. However, if your apartments are smaller or lower in quality than the competition, you will have to adjust your rent downward; again, this may be offset by a low vacancy rate.

Rental rates vary from city to city, from neighborhood to neighborhood, and from street to street. They even vary between floors and views in a high-rise building. There are too many factors affecting rents to scientfically arrive at an optimum figure. The approach most owners take is to ascertain the general market rent for the area and set a price that is somewhat higher, reducing it slightly if they encounter too much resistance. While this may not be scientific, it does take into consideration competition and the merchandising and sales ability of the landlord.

Selecting Good Tenants

It's difficult to precisely describe an ideal tenant; however, good tenants do have some things in common. They pay their rent on time. They care for the property as if it were their own. They are stable and tend to renew their lease. They will leave the premises in as good condition as they found it, or better.

Therefore, you want a responsible head of household who is and has been steadily employed, earning enough income to pay the rent. You don't want someone with a long history of moving from one place to another or someone with credit problems. Couples with newborn infants often make good tenants. These young families may not be able to buy a house, yet they're upwardly mobile and will want to make your property a home they can be proud to show off to their family and friends. Moreover, they usually move to a larger unit in your building in a year or two.

The elderly also make good tenants. Sometimes these people are retired on fixed incomes with supplemental income from investments or pension funds, and do not move frequently.

Contrary to popular belief, people having pets, especially cats, can be good tenants, as long as the pet is well trained. A pet owner won't want to move, because of the difficulty of finding a building that will accept pets. Sometimes these people have been turned down by so many buildings that they're willing to pay a premium, and will maintain a good relationship with the landlord for the privilege of living in a unit that accepts pets (see pet rider, exhibit 3).

Through experience, you'll learn how to distinguish good tenants from bad ones. For added protection, you can use a credit-reporting company to run credit checks and a job verification letter to verify employment and income. You can also ask applicants for their previous landlord's address and phone number. If they refuse to provide this information or haven't rented before, you'll have to weigh the risks against other factors.

Discrimination

Throughout your discussions and interviews with prospective tenants, remember to adhere to antidiscrimination laws, particularly the Civil Rights Act of 1968, which prohibits any type of discrimination based on race, and

EXHIBIT 3: Pet Rider

PET RIDER

THIS RIDER is hereby made a part of and incorporated as part of a certain lease agreement dated ______ ("Lease") for an apartment (the "Premises") located at ______, Illinois, by and between ______ ("Lessor"), and ______ ("Lessee").

IN THE EVENT OF A CONFLICT IN TERMS, THE TERMS AND CONDITIONS OF THIS RIDER SHALL GOVERN OVER THE TERMS AND CONDITIONS OF THE AFORESAID LEASE.

In consideration of the sum of ______ ($) DOLLARS ("Pet Deposit") to be paid by Lessee upon the execution hereof, the parties hereto agree to the following:

1. Lessor shall permit Lessee to keep **one** ______ (TYPE) ______ (BREED) ______ (POUNDS) / ______ (COLOR) (description of pet) ("Pet") on the Premises for the term of the Lease, and so long as Lessee is not in default of same.

2. Lessee shall clean up after the Pet at all times on the Premises, in all common areas as well as in all areas of the building in which the Premises are situated.

3. Lessee shall keep the Pet quiet at all times.

4. Lessee agrees that the Pet shall not be taken outside the Premises, (including on the patio or balcony), unless the Pet is on a leash. The Pet shall be walked only in the area(s) so designated by Lessor from time to time.

5. Lessee agrees that in the event of any violation of the terms and conditions set forth above, the Lessor shall have the right to demand removal of the Pet from the Premises. Any refusal by Lessee to immediately comply with such demand shall be deemed to be a material breach of the Lease, in which event Lessee shall forfeit the aforesaid Pet Deposit to Lessor and Lessor shall be entitled to any and all other remedies provided by law or equity. However, if Lessee removes the Pet upon demand, Lessor shall return the aforesaid Pet Deposit to Lessee less damages, if any, to the Premises or to the building or to the common areas where the Premises are situated, and the Lease shall continue in effect except that this Rider shall be deemed null and void.

IN WITNESS WHEREOF, the Lessor and Lessee have executed this document on the ______ day of ______, 19 ____.

LESSOR:

______
Lessee

______
Lessee

By ______
Agent

$______ is required pet deposit.

$______ is the required monthly rental amount.

Title VII of the Civil Rights Act of 1968, which prohibits discrimination on the basis of race, color, religion, sex or national origin.

Some states have enacted laws prohibiting adult-only rental policies. Such policies are still permissible in some states (for example, Florida and Texas), but in other states, a requirement by owners that prospective residents shall have no children under the age of 14 years is prohibited. Any owner who attempts to enforce such requirements in a state that prohibits it shall be subject to remedies as set forth by law. Before instituting an adults-only policy, check with your local real estate board to make sure it is legal in your state.

Advertising the Product

There are several ways to find suitable tenants, all involving some form of advertising. You may have the best property in the world, but it won't rent itself. You must make your property's availability known.

Apartment Rental Agencies

If you don't have the time to advertise and show your units, you can use an apartment rental agency or referral service. These companies work on a contingency basis with many owners and will screen residents. They complete all the ground work and present you with a signed lease.

Their fees are usually based on a percentage of the rent, which varies between 50 percent and 100 percent of one month's rent. For example, suppose you retain an agent to rent a vacant apartment for October 1 at a rental of $500 a month. You agree to pay a 50 percent commission for a bona fide signed lease. The agent will locate, qualify and execute a lease with a suitable tenant, usually collecting the first month's rent and a security deposit equal to a month's rent.

In most cases, the agent will deduct the fee from these funds and give you the balance along with the signed documents. In this example, the fee would be $250. Some agents add miscellaneous fees for advertising but this is not a common practice. The agent's commission should cover out-of-pocket expenses.

Using an apartment referral service can save you time. The drawback is that professional rental agencies work for many different owners simultaneously, and thus offer prospective tenants a wide variety of units. Because of the large volume and selection of apartments they represent, it may take longer to rent *your* apartment.

To avoid the expense of retaining a rental agency you can elect to rent the units yourself. If you have some free time in the evenings or weekends or can take time off during normal working hours to show available apartments, you can do an effective job of leasing.

Types of Advertisements

You can advertise in the classified section of your local newspaper or put fliers or signs around the apartment building or complex. Word of mouth referrals are especially effective. In fact, your best source for valuable new leads will probably be other satisfied tenants.

Newspapers

Newspaper ads should include all the necessary information to attract good prospects, including location, monthly rent, apartment size, major amenities and a contact name and phone number. If the property is currently occupied, you should also mention the availability date. Emphasize important selling features such as good views, a high floor in a high-rise building, backyards, patios, playgrounds, nearby shopping, schools and transportation.

A booklet entitled "Copy That Sells," published by the *Chicago Tribune,* 435 N. Michigan Ave., Chicago, IL 60611, offers the following advice for composing a newspaper ad:

> All advertising is highly competitive. And this is true even more so on the classified page, where there are literally hundreds of ads vying for the reader's attention. In order to get the message across, you want your ad to:
>
> - gain the reader's attention
> - hold the reader's interest
> - stimulate a desire for your property
> - persuade the reader to act on your rental
>
> In order to be successful at this, it is important to remember that the property you are writing about cannot be all things to all people. For your ad to get action, you must direct your advertising to a specific market. Before you write the ad, always ask yourself: Who is your likely customer for this property?

To pinpoint the market, you must consider the demographics of the renter. Determine:

- the household income
- size of household
- age, occupation and education of target market

Then—write your ad for that particular group. An effective ad will answer the question: How does the property fulfill the potential renter's needs?

The 24-page booklet outlines the elements of successful ads and includes sample copy of descriptive wordings on various house features and sample ads. The sample ads in exhibit 4 are examples of effective copy that would produce the desired results.

Fliers

Professional fliers can be printed inexpensively. Since a flier provides more space than an ad, you can include more information, such as a floor plan or photo of the property. You can distribute fliers throughout the neighborhood (where permitted by law), and with permission, in grocery stores, churches, Laundromats and other establishments where there is a bulletin board. Fliers can also be distributed to tenants of other apartment buildings in the area—not with the intent to solicit your competition's residents directly, but to make them aware of an apartment available in your building in case they have a friend or relative who needs one.

Note: The United States Postal Authority prohibits stuffing fliers inside mailboxes unless they are stamped.

Signs

Since most people have a preconceived notion about where they wish to live, one of the most effective and cost-efficient means of advertising is a sign. Often, potential tenants will drive or walk around the area they wish to live in and a simple sign advertising your apartment is the least expensive way to attract a customer.

A small handwritten or typed sign (exhibit 5) can be taped in the doorway of the apartment highlighting basic rental information in a neat, legible manner.

A larger and more expensive, professionally painted, permanent portable, wooden or metal sign on the building or in the front of the property can be used. Because of size and appearance this will attract more attention than a paper sign. This sign should state only the type of units available

EXHIBIT 4: Sample Newspaper Ads

EVANSTON 8825 ALBANY
DELUXE 6 LARGE RMS $866 Across from Lincoln Schl. Near beach, shops, subway, NWRR. 555-3456 June 1st 555-7890

6 ROOMS—2nd flr., heated, 2 blocks west of Dan Ryan on 105th St. No pets. Working. $475 + sec. Days 555-2686 or Eves. 555-4974

HYDE PARK—7500 E. 54th Pl. 1st fl., 4 rms., decor., $535. Avail. now, excellent transp. 555-4192

GARDEN APARTMENT
3½ rms., stove & frig. Utilities incl. 8100 W./7600 N. $350 + 2 mo. sec. 555-1136

Newly renovated Victorian. 2BR, owner occ. Walk to train. Immediately avail. $650/mo. 555-2093

Near Irving & Western. 2 bdrms, 2nd flr, 2 flat. Available May 1st. Cable. Will decorate & carpet. Htd. No pets. $425/mo. + dep. 555-2144 afternoons & eves.

DesPlaines—HUGE dlx. 1BR. Quiet 4 unit bldg. New dec., appls. Pkg., ht. incl. Near train. $525. 555-3004

DOLTON—lovely 2 bdrm. apt., modern 4 unit bldg., 2nd fl., w-w cptng., heated, stove, refrig., window air cond., parking avail., laundry facilities. Available July 1st, $500 + sec., working & references. 555-4183

SKOKIE—Spacious Garden Apt., near train, all utilities paid. $420 mo. Call 555-4467

Avail. May 1—Kimball/Sawyer. 2 Flat, 5 Rm., 2 Br. Mod. Kit. $475 + sec. 555-6110

HARVEY—2 bedrooms. Apt. newly dec. Tenants pay util. $400 + 1 mo. sec. Sect. 8 welcome. 731-2049

2 blks from Jeff Pk Terminal. 2br apt. Oak flrs. 2nd flr of quiet bldg. No pets. Nonsmokr pref. $500 + sec. 555-5167

Lrg. 4 rm., 1 BR in English Tudor bldg. Very classy, very bright. Walk-in closet & more. No pets please. Managed by owner. Avail. 5/1. 5543 N. Washington (4300W). $425. Eves. 555-3765

HAMPTON/MILWAUKEE
6 rms., clean, quiet, stv./refg., firepl. $535 mo., htd. 555-7878

NEWLY REMOD.—Near 63rd & Ashland. 5 rms., 3 bdrms., living room, large cabinet kitchen, tile bath. $450 + utilities. 644-4441

and, of course, a contact phone number. Depending on the street traffic pattern, the sign can be double- or single-faced in an appropriate size to allow easy readability from the street.

Depending on the number of units you own, a sign may be installed permanently, subject to local sign restrictions imposed by your municipality or building codes. If there are no vacancies at one particular property, the sign can serve as a referral to other locations where you may have vacancies, or it can direct prospective tenants to a waiting list.

A sign should always be fresh, clean and professional-looking. A poorly lettered, weather-beaten sign gives a poor first impression. Again, signs must conform with any codes and restrictions (size and placement) imposed by local ordinances.

EXHIBIT 5: Sample Sign

APARTMENTS

FOR RENT

In This Building

FLOOR	ROOMS	RENTAL
2nd	3½	$525.00 month

Sunny, one-bedroom, parquet floors, fully applianced kitchen, one month security deposit.

Utilities not included.

Apply to:

Mr. J. Neits
555-1616 Days
555-1212 Evenings

Buyers' Markets and Sellers' Markets

How you advertise will depend on the demand for apartments in your neighborhood. If the market is strong, meaning there are very few vacancies in your neighborhood (a sellers' market), you'll be able to rent at a good price with a minimum amount of effort. But if the market is soft, with many vacancies in the area (a buyers' market), you'll have to be more creative in your approach.

For example, in a buyers' market situation you may have to place larger ads with additional selling points about what makes your property appealing. You may want to offer a type of discount or rent concession. It might be necessary to advertise in more than one newspaper.

Selling the Product

Once you have located a prospective tenant, you must sell your product to him or her. This is a complex task. It involves preparing the apartment for showing, doing preliminary interviews to determine the prospect's needs and making a good first impression when greeting the prospect in person. You then need to present the apartment in the best possible light, handle objections diplomatically and ask for the closing.

Preparing the Apartment

Before letting prospective tenants see your building or apartments, you must first make certain that the property is clean, freshly painted and in good operating condition. First impressions are lasting ones. Do not show an apartment if it is not ready to be seen. For more information on this subject, refer to chapter 10.

Greeting the Prospective Tenant

A prospect is any person who calls or walks in to inquire about an apartment. Each prospect should be treated as a future resident who will provide the income to sustain your business.

See exhibits 6 and 7 for a detailed review of effective presentation techniques.

EXHIBIT 6: How To Greet a Prospect

When greeting a prospect:

1. *Stand up* and greet the customers as soon as they enter.
2. Introduce yourself and *ask* for their name. Shake their hand.
3. Ask them, "How may I help you?"
4. Talk to the customers and find out what they are interested in. *LISTEN.*
5. Tell them about the apartments that *meet their needs* and offer to show them the apartment.
6. Show them a *clean* apartment.
7. *Ask* them if the apartment meets their needs. *LISTEN.* Then ask what specifically they wanted. *LISTEN.*
8. *Ask* them if they would like to reserve the apartment.
   Ask them to fill out an application.
   Ask them when they would like to move in.
   Ask them to rent the apartment.
9. *Ask* for a deposit.
10. Thank them for visiting.

EXHIBIT 7: Checklist of Presentation Techniques

1. Did I introduce myself? _____
2. Did I ask their name? _____
3. Did I offer them a chair and a cold drink/coffee? _____
4. Did I ask about their family size and composition? _____
5. Did I ask when they expected to move? _____
6. Did I ask why they are moving and how long they expect to stay in their new apartment? _____
7. Did I ask what type of apartment and what facilities they are looking for? _____
8. Did I ask where they are working? _____
9. Did I point out the convenience and accessibility of this apartment complex? _____
10. Did I discuss neighborhood advantages, shopping, schools, recreational facilities? _____
11. Did I exhibit a "spic and span," completely prepared apartment that was suitable to their needs? _____
12. Did I describe apartment benefits and offer proof? (Example: "After you move into this apartment it will feel just like your own home because the rooms are unusually spacious.") _____
13. Did I build enthusiasm by eliciting "yes" (positive) responses? _____
14. Did I attempt to close the sale? _____
15. Did I offer an application to be completed? _____
16. Did I ask for a deposit? _____
17. Did I use a persuasive "close"? ("Would you prefer to leave your deposit by cash or check?") _____
18. Did I continue to sell even after they indicated uncertainty? _____
19. Did I try to close a second time after reviewing the key benefits? _____
20. Did I appear sincere and interested in their needs? _____
21. Did I discuss the number of vacant apartments available? _____

Qualifying the Prospect

Begin your qualifying of prospective tenants over the telephone when they respond to your advertising. In this preliminary interview, find out as much as you can about their lifestyle and apartment expectations. Strike up a friendly conversation. Ask a lot of questions. For example, find out what they do for a living, how many people will occupy the apartment, why are they moving, what apartment features are they looking for and so on.

The more you know about your prospects' needs and desires, the easier it will be to match them with an apartment. One way to get prospects to elaborate on what they like is to ask them what they don't like about their present living quarters. Based on their answers, you can point out the particular advantages of your apartment.

Qualifying is essentially conversation used to establish a rapport with prospects and put them at ease, and to inquire about the prospects' backgrounds and needs.

This information will help you in selling your property to the prospects. Some important questions to ask include:

- When do you need an apartment?
- Do you have a pet?
- How far do you (and other residents) commute to work?
- What features of apartment living are important: large rooms, large kitchen, balcony or patio, privacy, quiet, high or low floor in a high-rise and so on.
- What's wrong with your present apartment? Why do you want to move?
- How many people will occupy the apartment and how many bedrooms are needed?

With answers to these questions, you can determine whether to go on to subsequent steps. For instance, if you have only a one-bedroom apartment available, there is no reason to attempt to rent that apartment to prospects with large families. It is up to you to identify what the prospects need. If you don't have a suitable apartment available, you can offer to put the prospects on a waiting list.

The prospects have been qualified when the following details are worked out and/or requirements fulfilled:

- An apartment of the appropriate type and size is available.
- The prospects are of legal age to sign contracts.
- The prospects are employed or otherwise earning a qualifying income.

- The prospects have the appropriate family size for the particular unit.
- The prospects are moving out of their present accommodations legally.

All of this information can be obtained during your initial conversation.

Convincing the Prospect

Once you have qualified the prospects, you must convince them that you have the best apartment available.

Here are some techniques to convince prospects to rent:

Talk to the prospects. Show interest in them. If you are dealing with a couple, find out if one of them will not be employed outside the home. The nonworking individual will be spending a lot of time in the home, so this is the person you have to please.

People will sometimes rent an apartment that is not as perfectly suited to their needs as others they've seen because the rental agent or owner gave them a warm, welcome feeling and showed sincerity when talking to them. On the other hand, if you leave the prospects feeling cold and unwelcome or treat them indifferently, they won't rent even if the apartment is perfect and the rent is less than others. Your personal and professional image is all-important in making or breaking a potential rental.

Ask questions about the prospects' lifestyle and gear your presentation to this lifestyle. You must appeal to the emotions of your prospects because it's on that level that they will make the decision. Remember, prospects see only walls, floors and ceilings. You must create an image, allowing them to envision and desire the apartment and complex as a home. As an example, instead of making obvious statements such as "This is the living room," "This is the kitchen," let the prospects make these observations while you point out the benefits of your unit. You can say, "Doesn't this view give you a peaceful feeling?" or "The neutral color of the carpet will go well with your furniture."

Accentuate the positive. Offset negative aspects with positive comments. You will get objections and hesitations. If you have studied the marketplace you will know all about your competition, enabling you to emphasize your strong points.

If there are many vacant apartments in the area, do not point this out to the prospects. Good salespeople demonstrate that their product is in great demand, thereby creating a sense of urgency that helps close the sale. Most prospects want to be sold and only get confused if the salesperson points out dozens of other alternatives. They want you to help them make up their minds.

Show the prospects the apartment that you want to rent, but remember to customize your presentation, taking into account what the prospects have told you during the qualifying interview. If the actual apartment does not show well because it's dirty or needs decorating, you can show another unit, but you should make every effort to show the actual unit before a lease is signed.

Certain states require the actual apartment be shown to prospective tenants, but this can be accomplished after they have decided to rent. In these jurisdictions, failure to show the actual unit can result in a cancellation, possibly requiring you to return all monies collected. Quite a few apartments have been rented through showing only the model unit. Quite often the actual apartment may not have been built yet. Don't forget that lease provisions should permit access to occupied units; thus you can show an occupied apartment as a model.

Handling Objections

Prospects will often point out objections to the apartment. It might be a legitimate complaint, or they might be bickering to get a rent reduction or other concession. They do expect a response. Learn how to respond positively, avoiding anything that resembles an apology or a leaning towards agreeing to a concession. For example, if someone comments, "The kitchen is very small," your positive response could be, "Yes, it is; cleaning it will be a snap, and look at the spacious, well-lit dining room you have."

Here is a list of common objections with suggested responses:

The rent is too high.

Point out the rent is comparable to similar units in the area. The amount of rent you are asking is adjusted to the market for the type of apartment and amenities offered. You can control the rental rate, however, and may elect to lower it for other considerations (but don't be hasty).

The view is bad.

Some "bad" views are privacy views. Not everybody is looking for the spectacular scenic skyline view. The amount of rent for the unit has been adjusted accordingly. There isn't much you can do to change the view, but you can suggest a variety of window treatments to offset a poor view.

The rooms are too small.

Mention that efficient room sizes are good for energy savings. There isn't much you can do to make the rooms bigger, but you may be able to counter the objection if you have large closets or other amenities such as storage lockers, a bike room and so on.

The apartment is dirty.

A dirty apartment should *never* be shown. If you must show an occupied apartment that is dirty, explain that it will be cleaned and redecorated. This is the type of complaint you can take action on.

The closets are too small.

Point out to your prospects that smaller closets take up less square footage space allowing for more living space. It's pretty difficult to add more closet space, but you can suggest having the closets more efficiently reorganized using new shelving and rods specifically designed for this purpose.

The kitchen is too small.

Smaller kitchens are usually step-saver kitchens with less floor area and cabinetry to clean. While you usually cannot make the kitchen larger, you can point out the larger living room, bedroom or bathroom and show how the kitchen layout is very efficient. When showing the apartment, let the prospects enter the kitchen first; don't walk into it and ask them to come in after you.

We don't like the electric stove.

Electric stoves are modern and usually trouble-free. Unless all the tenants agree to switch to gas stoves it will be difficult to change just one. Everyone adapts to electric cooking after a few weeks. More benefits: Electric cooking is cleaner; less odor; cooking vapor residue does not build up; gas fumes will fade clothes, furniture, drapes and get things dirty.

An all-electric apartment is expensive.

Many all-electric heating and cooling systems allow for individually controlled thermostats located in the apartment, allowing the tenants to selectively control the temperature in each room. Electric is controlled by the tenants who pay only for what they use. Where utilities are included in the rent, the landlord must charge more to offset these costs, and the tenants then pay not only for what they use but also for what their neighbors use. You may not be able to change the system, but you can point out energy-saving tips for using the heating and air-conditioning units.

There is no door attendant.

A smaller building with 40 or fewer units will not warrant having a door attendant. A larger condominium property where you own and rent out an investment unit may benefit from having an attendant to help maintain privacy; however, providing 24-hour coverage can cost a building upwards of $100,000 and this expense is added into the assessments forcing the landlord to increase the rent. Attendants do not provide security and only serve as a convenience to the tenant. If you think having the entrance staffed is necessary, you can suggest it to the board of directors of your association.

The carpet is the wrong color.

Carpeting cannot be replaced to suit each new resident's color choice. Suggest using an area rug. Explain that once furniture is put in place there won't be much perimeter carpet showing. Carpeting can be dyed; however, a dark-colored carpet cannot be dyed a lighter color.

The carpeting is old.

Carpets are replaced due to tears or bad stains. New carpeting would increase the monthly rent if replaced unnecessarily. Suggest putting in new carpeting if the tenants agree to pay for it themselves or if you amortize the expense over a 36-month period. The tenants must agree to pay any outstanding balance should they terminate the lease sooner than three years.

The appliances are old (or the wrong color).

If the appliances are in good working condition they will be replaced only as needed. Appliances cannot be replaced to suit each new resident's color choice. Suggest that the tenants pay for new appliances or amortize them over a three-year period.

There is no parking garage.

In some cases, street parking is available. You have no control over this factor; provide information about parking garages or lots in the area. Most residents of downtown areas use public transportation and many do not own cars.

There is no balcony or patio.

Most tenants seldom use their balconies or patios, which serve only as storage areas for bicycles and miscellaneous debris. You cannot add a balcony, but you may suggest sunbathing at the pool, rooftop sundeck or nearest public facility. Tenants can barbecue in the park or nearby picnic grounds.

We don't like the layout of rooms.

You can't change the floor plan, but you can point out the advantages of your floor plan. As an example, if the bedrooms are side by side, down the hall from the living room, point out how this arrangement is suited for entertaining while allowing privacy and quiet in the sleeping areas. If the bedrooms are on opposite sides of the living room, point out how this facilitates privacy between roommates or parents and children.

We don't like hardwood floors.

Mention that they won't need a vacuum cleaner and hardwood floors don't create dust. You can carpet the floor (at a price); suggest an area rug as an option.

There's no swimming pool.

Properties with pools usually demand higher rents. Tell the prospects the locations of the nearest public pools and/or beaches.

There's no security.

The word *security* should never be used. Instead of saying *security doors* use *controlled access*; instead of saying *security guards* use *patrol* and so on. Security is a function of the residents themselves. Whatever security management does provide is for the building and building property–not the residents.

There are no storage facilities.

Properties without separate storage facilities usually have bigger apartments with larger closets. If lack of storage space is a common objection, you should provide information about the closest self-storage facility.

There aren't enough bathrooms.

This is another objection you can't change, although you might point out that previous residents lived there satisfactorily with one bath.

The apartment needs decorating.

The apartment will be decorated as far as being cleaned, painted, carpet cleaned and so on. Make the residents aware that they can decorate the apartment themselves, according to the lease or management policies.

The apartment needs repairs.

If you must show an apartment in need of repairs, explain that the owner will have all repairs completed before move-in. Sometimes you can allow the resident to do the repairs in exchange for a rent deduction. This is generally not a good practice.

There's no dishwasher.

Many people prefer washing dishes by hand because they feel they get much cleaner. A dishwasher will increase the electric bill. Depending on kitchen size and layout, there might be room to install a compact-sized dishwasher, or the tenants may want to use their own portable unit.

The building accepts pets.
(Prospect has no pet and fears smells, noise and so on.)

If one chooses to keep a pet in a rental unit, a large deposit and sometimes monthly pet rent is charged. If your property does not allow pets you will not be able to accept tenants who insist on maintaining one in their apartment.

There's no health club.

When a property offers a health club, the rents are higher and all tenants pay for it whether they use it or not. Provide information on the nearest public facility.

Remember, it is the prospects who will be paying the rent and not you, so don't let your personal opinions of the apartment influence the customers' decision. Just because you may not like some aspect of the apartment doesn't mean they will feel the same way.

Don't let prospective tenants wander around an apartment unit unattended. Always remain at a discreet distance, yet close enough to hear and observe any negative comments that may arise. Familiarize yourself with the surrounding community and be prepared to answer questions about schools, shopping, commuting, local laws and nearby services.

Closing

Many people in the property management business are excellent at greeting, qualifying and showing apartments, yet they produce very few actual rentals. The reason for this is that they fail to ask for the closing.

You should ask for a signature on the application and a security deposit while the prospects are still with you. Discourage people from saying, "We want to think about it," or, "We'll be back." It is worth being a little pushy at this point. Indicate that your units rent quickly; if the prospects hesitate, they will lose the apartment. Press to get a commitment, a deposit and a closing.

Follow Up

You will not rent the first time to every prospect. This does not mean that you have lost the prospect, or that you should give up. Keeping in touch with prospects can be productive.

Send a post card the day after the prospects visit the property. The card should be handwritten and should politely encourage further questions and visits.

Telephone the prospect 24 hours after they have seen the unit. Be prepared to give the prospects some new piece of information that was not covered previously. Be enthusiastic. Impress the prospects with your desire to see them living in your apartment property.

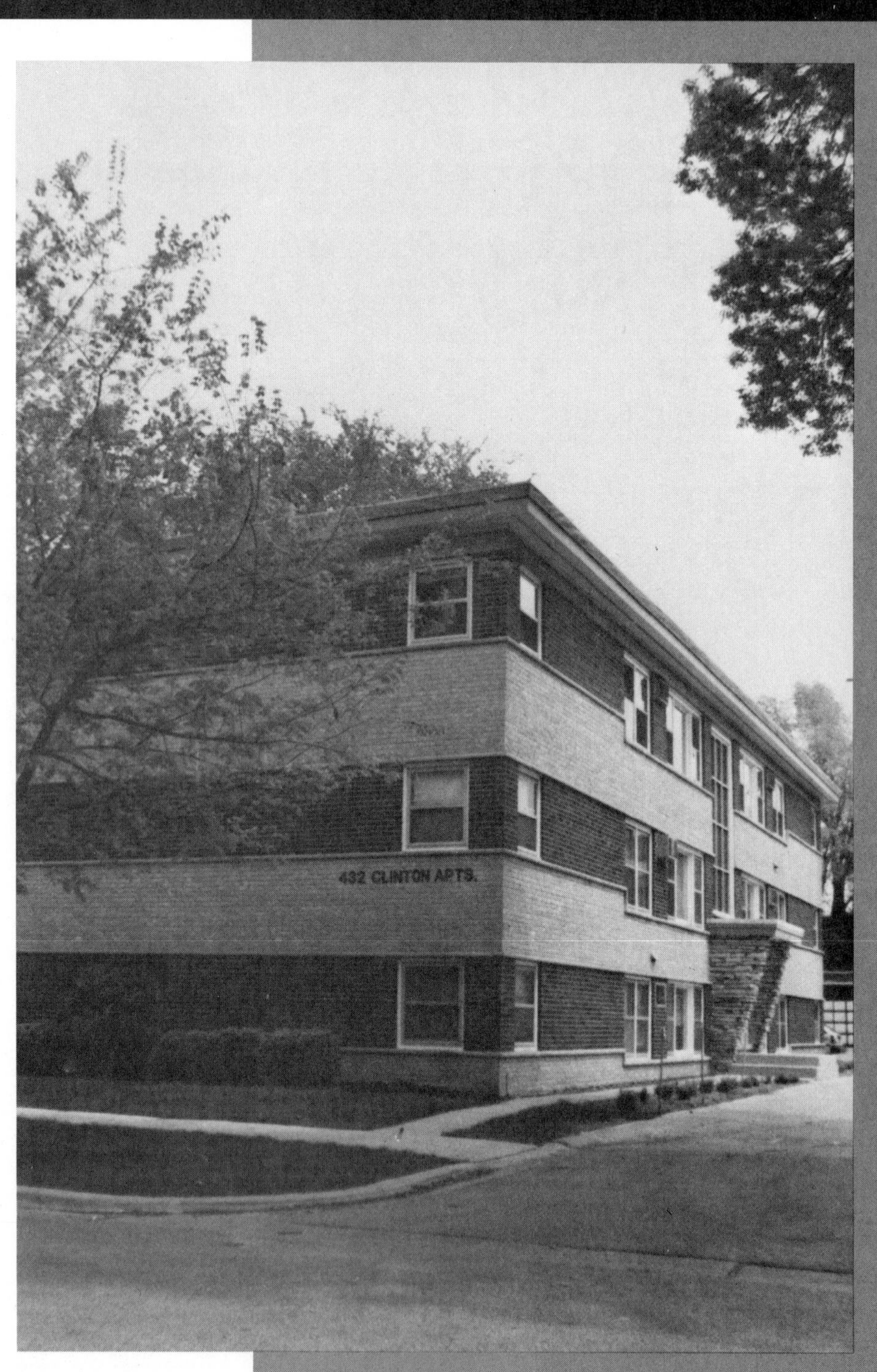
432 CLINTON APTS.

4

Applications, Leases and Rental Agreements

***Steve Holowicki** is an accountant and has been employed in the real estate industry for six years.*

"It has been my goal for about three years to own and manage income-producing real estate, but the main stumbling block that kept me from reaching that goal was a lack of time to devote to the property and my limited knowledge of maintenance. I recently overcame these limitations by forming a partnership with four friends to acquire and manage a six-flat building. We share the workload and pool our abilities.

"The most important point about leases and applications is to have a standard form and to know the terms of that form backward and forward; however, I never limit my negotiating options to the terms of the standard form. The standard lease or application is presented as an initial offer of tenancy. If the applicant takes exception to a particular clause of the lease or application, I negotiate to modify or delete that clause.

"Lease modification is usually not an issue with initial move-ins. It is most useful when dealing with tenants who want to renew their lease

EXHIBIT 8: Application for Lease

☐ NEW RENTAL:
☐ PRERENT FOR:
☐ RELET FROM:
☐ ROOMMATE WITH:

APPLICATION FOR LEASE

COMPLEX	MAIN OFFICE
S/D Pd: ______	S/D Recd: ______
C/C Pd: ______	C/C Recd: ______
Rent Pd: ______	Rent Recd: ______
Bal. Due: ______	Date: ______
Riders: ______	By: ______

APPLICANT:
SS # ______
DRIV. LIC. # ______

SPOUSE:
SS # ______
DRIV. LIC. # ______

TERMS OF LEASE:
From: ______ To: ______
Move in date: ______
Rent: ______ / Addl. Rent ______
Senior Citizen Rent: ______
Sec. Dep.: ______
Additional Sec. Dep.: ______
Pet Deposit: ______
Address: ______
City: ______ Apt. # ______
Bedrooms: 0 1 2 3 (circle one)

PLEASE DO NOT WRITE ABOVE THIS LINE

APPLICANT

NAME ______ AGE ______ DATE OF BIRTH ______
CURRENT ADDRESS ______ CITY ______ ZIP CODE ______ PHONE ______
LANDLORD NAME ______ PHONE ______ HOW LONG ______ DATE VERIFIED ______
PREVIOUS ADDRESS ______ CITY ______ PHONE ______
LANDLORD NAME ______ PHONE ______ HOW LONG? ______
CURRENT EMPLOYER ______ PERSON TO CONTACT ______
EMPLOYMENT ADDRESS ______ CITY ______ PHONE ______ DATE VERIFIED ______
POSITION ______ YEARS SERVICE ______ WEEKLY GROSS EARNINGS ______
PREVIOUS EMPLOYER ______ PERSON TO CONTACT ______
PREVIOUS EMPL. ADDRESS ______ CITY ______ PHONE ______
POSITION ______ YEARS SERVICE ______ WEEKLY GROSS EARNINGS ______
ADDITIONAL INCOME $ ______ EXPLAIN ______

SPOUSE

NAME ______ AGE ______ DATE OF BIRTH ______
CURRENT EMPLOYER ______ PERSON TO CONTACT ______
EMPLOYMENT ADDRESS ______ CITY ______ PHONE ______
POSITION ______ YEARS SERVICE ______ WEEKLY GROSS EARNINGS ______
ADDITIONAL INCOME $ ______ EXPLAIN ______

EXHIBIT 8: Application for Lease *(Continued)*

CREDIT

CREDIT ACCOUNTS 1. ________ # ________ 3. ________ # ________
2. ________ # ________ 4. ________ # ________

CHECKING ACCT. AT: ________ # ________ HOW LONG? ________

SAVINGS ACCT. AT: ________ # ________ HOW LONG? ________

MISCELLANEOUS

HOW MANY PEOPLE WILL OCCUPY THIS APARTMENT? ________ Adults? ________ Children? ________

CHILDREN: Name ________ Age ___ Sex ___ Name ________ Age ___ Sex ___

Name ________ Age ___ Sex ___ Name ________ Age ___ Sex ___

DO YOU HAVE ANY PETS? ________ Yes ________ No IF YES, TYPE ________ WEIGHT ________

IN EMERGENCY NOTIFY ________ RELATIONSHIP ________

ADDRESS ________ CITY ________ PHONE ________

CAR MAKE(S) ________ YEAR(S) ________ LICENSE NO(S) ________ FINANCED BY ________

DATE APPROVED: ________ RESIDENT NOTIFIED: ________ PERSON CONTACTED: ________ BY: ________

I represent to you that I have read this entire application and that all of the above information hereon is true and correct. I further represent that my rental and credit records are in good standing with no judgements or liens against me. If any of the above information is false, I hereby agree that my entire deposit may be forfeited to you. I also agree that if I am accepted and fail to complete this transaction by signing your lease, my entire deposit will be forfeited to you. I understand that this application is subject to your approval, and if my application is not accepted, my deposit will be returned in full. understand that my $20.00 credit check fee is nonrefundable. I also understand that this is not a lease and should my application be accepted, I agree to sign your lease form currently in use. If for any reason whatsoever you are unable to make the apartment which is the subject of this application available at the beginning of the lease term, I hereby waive any and all rights to seek to recover any damages whatsoever against you, including without limitation, actual, punitive or consequential damages. IT IS POLICY NOT TO DISCRIMINATE RENTALS ON THE BASIS OF RACE, CREED, COLOR, NATIONAL ORIGIN, RELIGION, AGE OR SEX.

________ APPLICANT ________ RECEIVED BY

________ APPLICANT ________ DATE

for a period of less than one year, or who are not certain of when they wish to move out; for example, if they are building a house and don't know when it will be ready for occupancy.

"I have a standard lease cancellation rider and modify it according to circumstances involving the tenant. Good tenant relations will, of course, reflect favorably on lease cancellation terms."

Application for Lease (Rental Agreement)

When prospects apply for an apartment, they should fill out an application for lease form (exhibit 8). Have the prospects complete the form while in your presence. Never take an application over the telephone. You should meet the prospects and discuss the lease terms in person. You want to be sure they understand and agree to the rules and regulations that pertain to the property before they sign a lease. Also, this is the time to ask for their security deposit and credit-check funds.

A married couple can fill out a joint application using only one form, but roommates or co-tenants should fill out individual applications. Check the credit and verify employment for all joint tenants, including a husband and wife if they are listed together on the lease as being jointly and severally responsible. All applicants should be asked to fill out the pertinent areas indicated and to sign the form while in your presence.

When the prospective residents have completed and signed the form, review the application for any incomplete or missing information. Question the prospects to obtain the information and record a brief explanation in any blanks where the information cannot be provided or completed.

At the time of signing the rental application, explain to the applicants that they will receive a refund of the security deposit if the application is not accepted, and that the entire deposit will be forfeited if they cancel. When an applicant submits a security deposit and is later rejected, he or she should expect to wait a few days for a refund unless the payment was in cash or a cancelled check is submitted. This time is required to ensure that the check or money order is backed by sufficient funds.

Approving the Application

Tell applicants that you will verify income and other items listed on the application, after which you will contact them as soon as possible. It is imperative that prospective residents be notified immediately of acceptance or rejection. Get a telephone number where the prospects can be reached, or where you may leave a message. If the process of verification takes too long, your apartment may become vacant or the residents may not find suitable housing.

Income Requirements

Check the applicants' income against the income requirements table (exhibit 9). The applicants should earn above the gross income listed. If the applicants earn an amount that falls within the parentheses, you may want to request a double security deposit, if permitted by law (see double deposit clause in this chapter), or ask the prospects to have a qualified cosigner fill out an application and sign the lease also.

If applicants earn less than the lowest figure within the parentheses, you can reject the prospects or demand to have the lease put in a qualified cosigner's name with the prospects listed as additional residents.

Verifying Employment and Other Sources of Income

Using the information a prospect has provided on the application, you can call his or her current employer and explain why you want to verify employment. If the employer insists you make the request in writing, ask to speak to the "person to contact" named by the prospect on the application. If you cannot get verification over the telephone, you will have to send the employer a verification request letter. Prospects should be asked to expedite a prompt response from their employers in order to speed up the approval process.

If the employer reports lower gross earnings than the applicant indicated, the income requirements chart must be rechecked to be sure the applicant still qualifies for the apartment. If the employer will not verify any information, the applicant should be asked to provide a letter, on company stationery, verifying length of employment and amount of income.

EXHIBIT 9: Income Requirements Table

	Gross Wages		Gross Wages		Gross Wages	
Rent	*Week*		*Month*		*Year*	
150	115	(104–114)	500	(450–499)	6000	(5400–5999)
155	119	(107–118)	517	(465–516)	6200	(5580–6199)
160	123	(111–122)	533	(480–532)	6400	(5760–6399)
165	127	(114–126)	550	(495–549)	6600	(5940–6599)
170	131	(118–130)	567	(510–566)	6800	(6120–6799)
175	135	(121–134)	583	(525–582)	7000	(6300–6999)
180	138	(125–137)	600	(540–599)	7200	(6480–7199)
185	142	(128–141)	617	(555–616)	7400	(6660–7399)
190	146	(132–145)	633	(570–632)	7600	(6840–7599)
195	150	(135–149)	650	(585–649)	7800	(7020–7799)
200	154	(138–153)	667	(600–666)	8000	(7200–7999)
205	158	(142–157)	683	(615–682)	8200	(7330–8199)
210	162	(145–161)	700	(630–699)	8400	(7560–8399)
215	165	(149–164)	717	(645–716)	8600	(7740–8599)
220	169	(152–168)	733	(660–732)	8800	(7920–8799)
225	173	(156–172)	750	(675–749)	9000	(8100–8999)
230	177	(159–176)	767	(690–766)	9200	(8280–9199)
235	181	(163–180)	783	(705–782)	9400	(8460–9399)
240	185	(166–184)	800	(720–799)	9600	(8640–9599)
245	188	(170–187)	817	(735–816)	9800	(8820–9799)
250	192	(173–191)	833	(750–832)	10000	(9000–9999)
255	196	(177–195)	850	(765–849)	10200	(9180–10199)
260	200	(180–199)	867	(780–866)	10400	(9360–10399)
265	204	(183–203)	833	(795–882)	10600	(9540–10599)
270	208	(187–207)	900	(810–899)	10800	(9720–10799)
275	212	(190–211)	917	(825–916)	11000	(9900–10999)
280	215	(194–214)	933	(840–932)	11200	(10080–11199)
285	219	(197–218)	950	(855–949)	11400	(10260–11399)
290	233	(201–222)	967	(870–966)	11600	(10440–11599)
295	227	(204–226)	983	(885–982)	11800	(10620–11799)
300	231	(208–230)	1000	(900–999)	12000	(10800–11999)
305	235	(211–234)	1017	(950–1060)	12200	(10980–12199)
310	238	(215–237)	1033	(930–1032)	12400	(11160–12399)
315	242	(218–241)	1050	(945–1049)	12600	(11340–12599)
320	246	(222–245)	1067	(960–1066)	12800	(11520–12799)
325	250	(225–249)	1083	(975–1082)	13000	(11700–12999)
330	254	(228–253)	1100	(990–1099)	13200	(11880–13199)
335	258	(232–257)	1117	(1005–1116)	13400	(12060–13339)
340	262	(235–261)	1133	(1020–1132)	13600	(12240–13599)
345	265	(239–264)	1150	(1035–1149)	13800	(12420–13799)
350	269	(242–268)	1167	(1050–1166)	14000	(12600–13999)
355	273	(246–272)	1183	(1065–1182)	14200	(12780–14199)
360	277	(249–276)	1200	(1080–1199)	14400	(12960–14399)
365	281	(253–280)	1217	(1095–1216)	14600	(13140–14599)
370	285	(256–284)	1233	(1110–1232)	14800	(13320–14799)
375	288	(260–287)	1250	(1125–1249)	15000	(13500–14999)
380	292	(263–291)	1267	(1140–1266)	15200	(13680–15199)
385	296	(267–295)	1283	(1155–1282)	15400	(13860–15399)
390	300	(270–299)	1300	(1170–1299)	15600	(14040–15599)
395	304	(273–303)	1317	(1185–1316)	15800	(14220–15799)

EXHIBIT 9: Income Requirements Table *(Continued)*

Rent	Gross Wages Week		Gross Wages Month		Gross Wages Year	
400	308	(277–307)	1333	(1200–1332)	16000	(14400–15999)
405	312	(280–311)	1350	(1215–1349)	16200	(14580–16199)
410	315	(284–314)	1367	(1230–1366)	16400	(14760–16399)
415	319	(287–318)	1383	(1245–1382)	16600	(14940–16599)
420	323	(291–322)	1400	(1260–1399)	16800	(15120–16799)
425	327	(294–326)	1417	(1275–1416)	17000	(15300–16999)
430	331	(298–330)	1433	(1290–1432)	17200	(15480–17199)
435	335	(301–334)	1450	(1305–1449)	17400	(15660–17399)
440	338	(305–337)	1467	(1320–1466)	17600	(15840–17599)
445	342	(308–341)	1483	(1335–1482)	17800	(16020–17799)
450	346	(312–345)	1500	(1350–1499)	18000	(16200–17999)
455	350	(315–349)	1517	(1365–1516)	18200	(16380–18199)
460	354	(318–353)	1533	(1380–1532)	18400	(16560–18399)
465	358	(322–357)	1550	(1395–1549)	18600	(16740–18599)
470	362	(325–361)	1567	(1410–1566)	18800	(16920–18799)
475	365	(329–364)	1583	(1425–1582)	19000	(17100–18999)
480	369	(332–368)	1600	(1440–1599)	19200	(17280–19199)
485	373	(336–372)	1617	(1455–1616)	19400	(17460–19399)
490	377	(339–376)	1633	(1470–1632)	19600	(17540–19599)
495	381	(343–380)	1650	(1485–1649)	19800	(17820–19799)
500	385	(346–384)	1667	(1500–1666)	20000	(18000–19999)
505	388	(350–387)	1683	(1515–1682)	20200	(18180–20199)
510	392	(353–391)	1700	(1530–1699)	20400	(18360–20399)
515	396	(357–395)	1717	(1545–1716)	20600	(18540–20599)
520	400	(360–399)	1733	(1560–1732)	20800	(18720–20799)
525	404	(363–403)	1750	(1575–1749)	21000	(18900–20999)
530	408	(367–407)	1767	(1590–1766)	21200	(19080–21199)
535	412	(370–411)	1783	(1605–1782)	21400	(19260–21399)
540	415	(374–414)	1800	(1620–1799)	21600	(19440–21599)
545	419	(377–418)	1817	(1635–1816)	21800	(19620–21799)
550	423	(381–422)	1833	(1650–1832)	22000	(19800–21999)
555	427	(384–426)	1850	(1665–1849)	22200	(19980–22199)
560	431	(388–430)	1867	(1680–1866)	22400	(20160–22399)
565	435	(391–434)	1883	(1695–1882)	22600	(20340–22599)
570	438	(395–437)	1900	(1710–1899)	22800	(20520–22799)
575	442	(398–441)	1917	(1725–1916)	23000	(20700–22999)
580	446	(402–445)	1933	(1740–1932)	23200	(20880–23199)
585	450	(405–449)	1950	(1755–1949)	23400	(21060–23399)
590	454	(408–453)	1967	(1770–1966)	23600	(21240–23599)
595	458	(412–457)	1983	(1785–1982)	23800	(21420–23799)
600	462	(415–461)	2000	(1800–1999)	24000	(21600–23999)
605	465	(419–464)	2017	(1815–2016)	24200	(21780–24199)
610	469	(422–468)	2033	(1830–2032)	24400	(21960–24399)
615	473	(426–472)	2050	(1845–2049)	24600	(22140–24599)
620	477	(429–476)	2067	(1860–2066)	24800	(22320–24799)
625	481	(433–480)	2083	(1875–2082)	25000	(22500–24999)
630	485	(436–484)	2100	(1890–2099)	25200	(22680–25199)
635	488	(440–487)	2117	(1905–2116)	25400	(22360–25399)
640	492	(443–491)	2133	(1920–2132)	25600	(23040–25599)
645	496	(447–495)	2150	(1935–2149)	25800	(23220–25799)

EXHIBIT 9: Income Requirements Table *(Continued)*

Rent	Gross Wages Week		Gross Wages Month		Gross Wages Year	
650	500	(450–499)	2167	(1950–2166)	26000	(23400–25999)
655	504	(453–503)	2183	(1965–2182)	26200	(23580–26199)
660	508	(457–507)	2200	(1980–2199)	26400	(23760–26399)
665	512	(460–511)	2217	(1995–2216)	26600	(23940–26599)
670	515	(464–514)	2233	(2010–2232)	26800	(24120–26799)
675	519	(467–518)	2250	(2025–2249)	27000	(24300–26999)
680	523	(471–522)	2267	(2040–2266)	27200	(24480–27199)
685	527	(474–526)	2283	(2055–2282)	27400	(24660–27399)
690	531	(478–530)	2300	(2070–2299)	27600	(24840–27599)
695	535	(481–534)	2317	(2085–2316)	27800	(25020–27799)
700	538	(485–537)	2333	(2100–2332)	28000	(25200–27999)
705	542	(488–541)	2350	(2115–2349)	28200	(25380–23199)
710	546	(492–545)	2367	(2130–2366)	28400	(25560–28399)
715	550	(495–549)	2383	(2145–2382)	28600	(25740–28599)
720	554	(498–553)	2400	(2160–2399)	28800	(25920–28799)
725	558	(502–557)	2417	(2175–2416)	29000	(26100–28999)
730	562	(505–561)	2433	(2190–2432)	29200	(26280–29199)
735	565	(509–564)	2450	(2205–2449)	29400	(26460–29399)
740	569	(512–568)	2467	(2220–2466)	29600	(26640–29599)
745	573	(516–572)	2483	(2235–2482)	29800	(26820–29799)
750	577	(519–576)	2500	(2250–2499)	30000	(27000–29999)
755	581	(523–580)	2517	(2265–2516)	30200	(27180–30199)
760	585	(526–584)	2533	(2280–2532)	30400	(27360–30399)
765	588	(530–587)	2550	(2295–2549)	30600	(27540–30599)
770	592	(533–591)	2567	(2310–2566)	30800	(27720–30799)
775	596	(537–595)	2583	(2325–2582)	31000	(27900–30999)
780	600	(540–599)	2600	(2340–2599)	31200	(28080–31199)
785	604	(543–603)	2617	(2355–2616)	31400	(28260–31399)
790	608	(547–607)	2633	(2370–2632)	31600	(28440–31599)
795	612	(550–611)	2650	(2385–2649)	31800	(28620–31799)
800	615	(554–614)	2667	(2400–2666)	32000	(28800–31999)
805	619	(557–618)	2683	(2415–2682)	32200	(28980–32199)
810	623	(561–622)	2700	(2430–2699)	32400	(29160–32399)
815	627	(564–626)	2717	(2445–2716)	32600	(29340–32599)
820	631	(568–630)	2733	(2460–2732)	32800	(29520–32799)
825	635	(571–634)	2750	(2475–2749)	33000	(29700–32999)
830	638	(575–637)	2767	(2490–2766)	33200	(29880–33199)
835	642	(578–641)	2783	(2505–2782)	33400	(30060–33399)
840	646	(582–645)	2800	(2520–2799)	33600	(30240–33599)
845	650	(585–649)	2817	(2435–2816)	33800	(30420–33799)
850	654	(588–653)	2833	(2550–2832)	34000	(30600–33999)
855	658	(592–657)	2850	(2565–2849)	34200	(30780–34199)
860	662	(595–661)	2867	(2580–2866)	34400	(30960–34399)
865	665	(599–664)	2883	(2595–2882)	34600	(31140–34599)
870	669	(602–668)	2900	(2610–2899)	34800	(31320–34799)
875	673	(606–672)	2917	(2625–2916)	35000	(31500–34999)
880	677	(609–676)	2933	(2640–2932)	35200	(31680–35199)
885	681	(613–680)	2950	(2655–2949)	35400	(31860–35399)
890	685	(616–684)	2967	(2670–2966)	35600	(32040–35599)
895	688	(620–687)	2983	(2685–2982)	35800	(32220–35799)

EXHIBIT 9: Income Requirements Table *(Continued)*

Rent	Gross Wages Week		Gross Wages Month		Gross Wages Year	
900	692	(623–691)	3000	(2700–2999)	36000	(32400–35999)
905	696	(627–695)	3017	(2715–3016)	36200	(32580–36199)
910	700	(630–699)	3033	(2730–3032)	36400	(32760–36399)
915	704	(633–703)	3050	(2745–3049)	36600	(32940–36599)
920	708	(637–707)	3067	(2760–3066)	36800	(33120–36799)
925	712	(640–711)	3083	(2775–3082)	37000	(33300–36999)
930	715	(644–714)	3100	(2790–3099)	37200	(33480–37199)
935	719	(647–718)	3117	(2805–3116)	37400	(33660–37399)
940	723	(651–722)	3133	(2820–3132)	37600	(33840–37599)
945	727	(654–726)	3150	(2835–3149)	37800	(34020–37799)
950	731	(658–730)	3167	(2850–3166)	38000	(34200–37999)
955	735	(661–734)	3183	(2865–3182)	38200	(34380–38199)
960	738	(665–737)	3200	(2880–3199)	38400	(34560–38399)
965	742	(668–741)	3217	(2895–3216)	38600	(34740–38599)
970	746	(672–745)	3233	(2910–3232)	38800	(34920–38799)
975	750	(675–749)	3250	(2925–3249)	39000	(35100–38999)
980	754	(678–753)	3267	(2940–3266)	39200	(35280–39199)
985	758	(682–757)	3283	(2955–3282)	39400	(35460–39399)
990	762	(685–761)	3300	(2970–3299)	39600	(35640–39599)
995	765	(689–764)	3317	(2985–3316)	39800	(35820–39799)
1000	769	(692–768)	3333	(3000–3332)	40000	(36000–39999)
1005	733	(696–772)	3350	(3015–3349)	40200	(36180–40199)
1010	777	(699–776)	3367	(3030–3366)	40400	(36360–40399)
1015	781	(703–780)	3383	(3045–3382)	40600	(36540–40599)
1020	785	(706–784)	3400	(3060–3399)	40800	(36720–40799)
1025	788	(710–787)	3417	(3075–3416)	41000	(36900–40999)
1030	792	(713–791)	3433	(3090–3432)	41200	(37080–41199)
1035	796	(717–795)	3450	(3105–3449)	41400	(37260–41399)
1040	800	(720–799)	3467	(3120–3466)	41600	(37440–41599)
1045	804	(723–803)	3483	(3135–3482)	41800	(37620–41799)
1050	808	(727–807)	3500	(3150–3499)	42000	(37800–41999)
1055	812	(730–811)	3517	(3165–3516)	42200	(37980–42199)
1060	815	(734–814)	3533	(3180–3532)	42400	(38160–42399)
1065	819	(737–818)	3550	(3195–3549)	42600	(38340–42599)
1070	823	(741–822)	3567	(3210–3566)	42800	(38520–42799)
1075	827	(744–826)	3583	(3225–3582)	43000	(38700–42999)
1080	831	(748–830)	3600	(3240–3599)	43200	(38880–43199)
1085	835	(751–834)	3617	(3255–3616)	43400	(39060–43399)
1090	838	(755–837)	3633	(3270–3632)	43600	(39240–43599)
1095	842	(758–841)	3650	(3285–3649)	43800	(39420–43799)
1100	846	(762–845)	3667	(3300–3666)	44000	(39600–43999)
1105	850	(765–849)	3683	(3315–3682)	44200	(39780–44199)
1110	854	(768–853)	3700	(3330–3699)	44400	(39960–44399)
1115	858	(772–857)	3717	(3345–3716)	44600	(40140–44599)
1120	862	(775–861)	3733	(3360–3732)	44800	(40320–44799)
1125	865	(779–864)	3750	(3375–3749)	45000	(40500–44999)
1130	869	(782–868)	3767	(3390–3766)	45200	(40680–45199)
1135	873	(786–872)	3783	(3405–3782)	45400	(40860–45399)
1140	877	(789–876)	3800	(3420–3799)	45600	(41040–45599)
1145	881	(793–880)	3817	(3435–3816)	45800	(41220–45799)

If the applicant is self-employed, you can request copies of his or her latest tax returns that would show gross earnings. In lieu of this, a prospect can provide a financial statement verified by a bank. A letter of reference or recommendation from an officer of a banking or other financial institution is a reasonable request. Although such a letter will not demonstrate an applicant's credit history, it may give you a better idea of his or her general overall credit-worthiness. Your primary goal is to ascertain that the prospect earns enough income to qualify for the apartment.

Rental Agreements and Lease Forms

The lease is the primary legal document that specifies the terms of the rental agreement binding the owner and the resident. A lease is a contract between an owner of real property and a tenant for the possession and use of lands and improvements in return for payment in rent.

Oral Leases

It is extremely important to use a written lease; oral leases are not recommended. Years ago, it was to the landlord's advantage not to give the tenant a written lease. The tenant was then at the mercy of the landlord, who could raise rents at will and give short termination notices. The problem is that oral leases run on a month-to-month basis, cannot be substantiated and may not always be enforceable. A lease is a binding contract on both parties and, if you have a written document, it is usually upheld in court.

Commercially Available Lease Forms

Many lease forms are available. Some of the best are offered through local real estate boards, the Institute of Real Estate Management and local chapters of the National Association of Apartment Managers.

If your local real estate board does not sell leases or other forms they should be able to provide the name of a business forms stationery store and recommend one or two brands. These must be reviewed carefully to see that they are up-to-date and will work for you.

In major urban areas a number of different lease forms are available through stationery stores. Several samples are included as exhibits. Apartment lease form 15 (exhibit 10), published by the Chicago Board of Realtors®, is widely used in Illinois and is more or less standard, containing most of the language necessary to serve and protect the rights of both tenant and owner.

NOTE: Most of the forms contained in the exhibits can be photocopied and adapted for your personal use. However, this is not true of the lease forms. Always purchase and use original blank leases.

A lease is a contract that defines the formal relationship between the landlord and tenant. In addition to what common sense and state laws dictate about tenant-landlord obligations, the lease spells out specific agreements that bind both parties.

Owners and residents may add to a preprinted form lease any terms and conditions that are not prohibited by state or local ordinances or other rules of law. Additions to a lease document may include: additional rent, additional terms of agreement, additional rules and regulations, lease riders and other provisions governing the rights and obligations of the parties.

Terms and Conditions of Leases

The following brief summary discusses the terms and conditions of most standard apartment rental agreements (leases). Riders to a lease and additional lease clauses will be discussed later in this chapter.

Filling out the Lease

You may be familiar with some of the basic lease language and definitions. Pay special attention to the following areas where you will be inserting the specific details concerning your property and prospective tenants. Refer to the sample leases (exhibits 10, 11, 12 and 13) as you read the text.

Lessor is you, the landlord.

Lessee is the tenant. Enter the full names of all occupants 18 years or older on the lease. If there is a cosigner, this name is added under the occupant's name and the word *cosigner* should appear.

The date the lease begins is the date the resident starts paying rent. This could be a different date than the actual move-in date. For example, you may be offering a concession such as one month's free rent (see prorated or free rent programs later in this chapter).

EXHIBIT 10: Chicago Apartment Lease

UNIVERSITY PRINTING COMPANY
CHICAGO, ILL

No. 15C-

CHICAGO APARTMENT LEASE

DATE OF LEASE	TERM OF LEASE		MONTHLY RENT	SECURITY DEPOSIT*
	BEGINNING	ENDING		

**IF NONE, WRITE "NONE." Paragraph 5 of Lease Agreements and Covenants then INAPPLICABLE.*

TENANT		LESSOR (Owner or agent authorized to manage the Apartment)	
TENANT	•	**NAME**	•
APARTMENT	•	**ADDRESS**	•
BUILDING	•	**CITY**	•
CITY	•	**PHONE**	•

In consideration of the mutual agreements and covenants set forth below and on the reverse side hereof (the same being full included as part of this Lease) Lessor hereby leases to Tenant and Tenant hereby leases from Lessor for use in accordance with paragraph 8 hereof the Apartment designated above, together with the fixtures and accessories belonging thereto, for the above Term. All parties listed above as Lessor and Tenant are herein referred to individually and collectively as Lessor and Tenant respectively.

193.1-10 Building Code Violations

Tenant is hereby notified that, during the 12 month period prior to the date of execution of this lease, the following code violations have been cited for the Apartment and or the Building (If none write "none"; if enforcement litigation is pending, state the case number):

ADDITIONAL AGREEMENTS AND COVENANTS (including DECORATING AND REPAIRS), if any.

EXHIBIT 10: Chicago Apartment Lease *(Continued)*

TENANT(S)	SIGNATURES	LESSOR(S)
______________________(SEAL)		______________________(SEAL)
______________________(SEAL)		______________________(SEAL)

LEASE AGREEMENTS AND COVENANTS

1. **RENT:** Tenant shall pay to the Lessor at the above address (or such other address as Lessor may designate in writing) the monthly rent set forth above on or before the first day of each month in advance. **The time of each and every payment of rent is of the essence of this lease. The monthly rent set forth above shall be increased $10 if paid after the 5th of the month. Rent mailed shall be deemed paid on date of postmark.**

2. **POSSESSION:** At the commencement of the Term of this Lease, Lessor shall deliver possession of the apartment to Tenant. If Lessor cannot deliver possession of the Apartment to Tenant on the date set for commencement of the Term, this Lease shall remain in full force and effect with rent abated until such time as the Apartment is available for Tenant's occupancy, unless Tenant elects to maintain an action for possession of the Apartment or, upon written notice to Lessor, elects to terminate this Lease.

3. **APPLICATION:** The application for this lease and all representations and promises contained therein are hereby made a part of this lease. Tenant warrants that the information given by Tenant in the application is true. If such information is false, Lessor may at Lessor's option terminate this Lease by giving Tenant not less than 30 days prior written notice, which shall be Lessor's sole remedy.

4. **PROMISES OF THE PARTIES:** The terms and conditions contained herein shall be conclusively deemed the agreement between Tenant and Lessor and no modification, waiver or amendment of this Lease or any of its terms, conditions or covenants shall be binding upon the parties unless made in writing and signed by the party sought to be bound.

5. **SECURITY DEPOSIT:** Tenant has deposited with Lessor the Security Deposit in the amount set forth above for the performance of each and every covenant and agreement to be performed by Tenant under this Lease. Lessor shall have the right, but not the obligation, to apply the Security Deposit in whole or in part as payment of such amounts as are reasonably necessary to remedy Tenant's defaults in the payment of rent or in the performance of the covenants or agreements contained herein. Lessor's right to possession of the Apartment for non-payment of rent or any other reason shall not be affected by the fact that Lessor holds security. Tenant's liability is not limited to the amount of the Security Deposit.

Lessor shall give Tenant written notice of the application of the Security Deposit or any part thereof within thirty (30) days of said application. If the application is on account of maintenance, repairs or replacements necessitated by Tenant, said notice shall include the estimated or actual cost of the same, attaching estimates or paid receipts. Upon receipt of said notice, Tenant shall at once pay to Lessor an amount sufficient to restore the Security Deposit in full. Upon termination of this Lease, full payment of all amounts due and performance of all Tenant's covenants and agreements (including surrender of the Apartment in accordance with Paragraph 15), the Security Deposit or any portion thereof remaining unapplied shall be returned to Tenant within 45 days of said termination.

Security Deposit shall not be deemed or construed as advance payment of rent for any month of the lease term.

6. **LESSOR TO MAINTAIN:**

A. Tenant hereby declares that Tenant has inspected the Apartment, the Building and all related areas and grounds and that Tenant is satisfied with the physical condition thereof. **Tenant agrees that no representations, warranties (expressed or implied) or covenants with respect to the condition, maintenance or improvements of the Apartment, Building, or other areas have been made to Tenant except those contained in this Lease, the application, or otherwise in writing signed by Lessor.**

B. Lessor agrees that Lessor will perform work set forth in this Lease within a reasonable time not to exceed 30 days from the commencement of the Term.

C. Lessor covenants that at all times during the Term hereof, the Lessor shall maintain the Apartment and the Building to the following minimum standards:

(1) Effective weather protection, including unbroken windows and doors;
(2) Plumbing facilities in good working order;
(3) A water supply which either under the control of the Tenant is capable of producing hot and cold running water, or under the control of the Lessor produces hot and cold running water, furnished to appropriate fixtures, and connected to a sewerage system;
(4) Heating (and, if furnished, air conditioning and ventilation) facilities in good working order which, if under the control of the Tenant, are capable of producing, or, if under the control of the Lessor, produce heat (and, if furnished, air conditioning and ventilation) in fixtures provided (and no other) within reasonable accepted tolerances and during reasonable hours. (In the case of heat, minimum tolerances shall be those established by municipal code);
(5) Gas and/or electrical appliances which are supplied by Lessor in good working order, and appropriate gas piping and electrical wiring system to the extent existing in the Building maintained in good working order and safe condition;
(6) Building, grounds and areas under the control of the Lessor in clean, sanitary and safe condition free from all accumulations of debris, filth, rubbish, garbage, rodents and vermin;
(7) Adequate and appropriate receptacle(s) for garbage and rubbish, and, if under the control of the Lessor, in clean condition and good repair;
(8) Floors, stairways, and railings and common areas in good repair;
(9) Apartment floors, wall and ceilings in good repair and safe condition; and:
(10) Elevators (if existing) in good repair and safe condition.

D. It is, however understood and agreed that buildings are physical structures subject to aging, wear, tear, abuse, inherent defects, and numerous forces causing disrepair or breakdown beyond Lessor's reasonable control, and that components and skilled workmen are not always immediately available. Lessor's costs of operation are fixed and unavoidable and to permit rent abatement or damages to Tenant would create an intolerable burden on Lessor, other tenants and surrounding neighborhood. It is, therefore, understood and agreed that breakdowns of equipment or disrepair caused by (1) conditions caused by Tenant, members of Tenant's household, guests or other persons on the premises with Tenant's consent; (2) Tenant's unreasonable refusal of or other interference with entry of Lessor or Lessor's workmen or contractors into the Apartment or Building for purposes of correcting defective conditions; (3) lack of reasonable opportunity for Lessor to correct defective conditions; (4) conditions beyond Lessor's reasonable control, including strikes or lockouts; or (5) Lessor's not having actual knowledge of such defective conditions shall be an absolute defense in any action against Lessor for breach of covenant based upon the duties of Lessor to maintain the Apartment or Building.

EXHIBIT 10: Chicago Apartment Lease *(Continued)*

E. Nothing herein contained shall in the event of fire, explosion or other casualty impose upon Lessor any obligation to make repairs which are more extensive or different from those required by the provisions of Paragraph 14 of this Lease (Fire & Casualty).

7. UTILITIES: Unless otherwise agreed in writing, if the Apartment is individually metered, payment to the utility company or authorized metering agency of the applicable charges for gas, electricity or water consumed by the Tenant in the Apartment, including, if applicable, current used for electric heating, ventilation, air conditioning, hot water, etc., shall be Tenant's sole responsibility.

8. TENANT'S USE OF APARTMENT: The Apartment shall be occupied solely for residential purposes by Tenant, those other persons specifically listed in the Application for this Lease, and any children which may be born to or legally adopted by Tenant during the Term. Unless otherwise agreed in writing, guests of Tenant may occupy the Apartment in reasonable numbers for no more than three weeks each during each year of the Term hereof. Neither Tenant nor any of these persons shall perform nor permit any practice that may damage the reputation of or otherwise be injurious to the Building or neighborhood, or be disturbing to other tenants, be illegal, or increase the rate of insurance on the Building.

9. TENANT'S UPKEEP: Tenant covenants to perform the following obligations during the term hereof: (A) maintain the Apartment and appurtenances in a clean, sanitary and safe condition; (B) dispose all rubbish, garbage and other waste in a clean, sanitary and timely manner from the Apartment into the refuse receptacles provided; (C) properly use and operate all appliances, electrical, gas and plumbing fixtures; (D) not place in the Apartment or Building any furniture, plants, animals, or any other things which harbor insects, rodents, or other pests; (E) keep out of the Apartment or Building materials which cause a fire hazard or safety hazard and comply with reasonable requirements of Lessor's fire insurance carrier; (F) not destroy, deface, damage, impair, nor remove any part of the Building or Apartment or facilities, equipment or appurtenances thereto, and (G) prevent any person in the Apartment or Building with Tenant's permission from violating any of the foregoing Tenant obligations. Tenant shall not suffer or commit any waste in or about the Apartment or Building and shall at Tenant's expense keep the Apartment in good order and repair. On termination of this Lease, Tenant shall return the Apartment to Lessor in like condition, reasonable wear excepted.

10. ALTERATIONS, ADDITIONS, FIXTURES, APPLIANCES, PERSONAL PROPERTY: Tenant shall make no alterations or additions nor install, attach, connect, or maintain in the Apartment or any part of the Building, interior or exterior, major appliances or devices of any kind without in each and every case the written consent of the Lessor and then, if granted, only upon the terms and conditions specified in such written consent.

11. ACCESS: At Lessor's discretion, Lessor shall be provided with and may retain and use any keys necessary for access to the Apartment. Lessor reserves the right in accordance herewith to enter Apartment in order to inspect same, make necessary or agreed repairs, decorations, alterations, improvements, supply necessary or agreed services, exhibit the Apartment to prospective or actual purchasers, mortgagees, tenants (within 60 days or less prior to the expiration of this Lease), workman, or contractors, or as is otherwise necessary in the operation and/or protection of the Building, its components or persons therein. In the event repairs or maintenance elsewhere in the Building unexpectedly require access and in any case of apparent or actual emergency, Lessor may enter the Apartment at any time without notice, except that Lessor shall give Tenant notice within two days after such entry. In all other cases, entry by Lessor shall be in accordance with agreement with Tenant or, if same is impractical or refused after two days notice and at reasonable times. Entry between 8:00 a.m. and 8:00 p.m., or at any other time expressly requested by Tenant shall be presumed reasonable. Notice for the purpose hereof may be by regular mail, telephone, personal delivery or other means designed in good faith to provide notice to Tenant.

12. SUBLETTING AND RELETTING:

A. In the event it becomes necessary for Tenant to vacate the Apartment prior to the end of the Lease Term, Lessor shall make a good faith effort to relet or sublet the Apartment at a fair market rental, which shall be the rent charged for a comparable apartment in the Building or in the same neighborhood. Tenant shall, upon demand, pay in advance, (i) the deficiency, if the aggregate rent from the reletting or subletting for the balance of the Term hereof is less than the aggregate rent then remaining to be paid under this Lease and (ii) all expenses of reletting or subletting (if any) including, but not limited to, decorating, repairs, replacements, commissions, advertising and/or an administrative fee for performing the details attendant to such transaction. Lessor, at its option, may determine whether said transaction shall be in the form of a subletting, assignment or reletting.

B. Lessor may at any time and for any reason reject any prospective new tenant provided, however, that if Lessor shall do so without cause Tenant shall be liable to Lessor only for the deficiency described in Subparagraph A(i) above which would have been due from Tenant if the prospective new tenant had been accepted. Cause shall be deemed to be the failure, based on information and data made available to Lessor, of such prospective new tenant to meet the criteria customarily employed by Lessor to evaluate the acceptability of prospects for comparable apartments in the Building. During the last three months of the Term, Lessor shall be obligated to accept an otherwise qualified prospective new tenant only if said prospective new tenant enters into a lease for a term for which leases are customarily offered for comparable apartments in the Building.

C. Leasing other vacancies in the Building prior to reletting or subletting the Apartment shall not be deemed to be failure on the part of Lessor to make a good faith effort to relet or sublet the Apartment.

D. Tenant shall neither sublet the Apartment nor any part thereof, nor assign this Lease, nor permit by any act or default of himself or any other person any transfer of Tenant's interest by operation of law nor offer the Apartment or any part thereof for lease or sublease except in accordance herewith. Unless Lessor enters into a new lease with respect to the Apartment with a new tenant, nothing herein contained shall be construed as relieving Tenant of Tenant's obligations under this Lease or applicable law.

(3) If Lessor fails to notify Tenant within 45 days of said termination date of Lessor's election under either (1) or (2), Tenant's continued occupancy shall be for a month-to-month term.

(4) No action or non-action by Lessor except as herein provided shall operate as a waiver of Lessor's right to terminate this Lease or Tenant's right of possession nor operate to extend the term hereof.

16. EMINENT DOMAIN (CONDEMNATION): If the whole or any subsequent part of the Building is taken or condemned by any competent authority for any public use or purpose, or if any adjacent property or street shall be so condemned or improved in such a manner as to require the use of any part of the Building, the term of this Lease shall at the option of the Lessor or the condemning authority be terminated upon, and not before, the date when possession of the part so taken be required for such use or purpose and Lessor shall be entitled to receive the entire award without appointment with Tenant. Rent shall be apportioned as of the date of Tenant's vacating as the result of said termination.

17. LESSOR'S MORTGAGE: This Lease is not to be recorded and is and shall, hereafter, be deemed to be subordinated to any present or future mortgages on the real estate (or any part of it) upon which the Building is situated and to all advances upon the security of such mortgages.

18. LEASE BINDING ON HEIRS, ETC: All the covenants and agreements of this Lease shall be binding and inure to the benefit of heirs, executors, administrators, successors, and assigns of Lessor and Tenant, subject to the restrictions set forth in Paragraph 12 hereof, except that where there are only one or two persons named or remaining as Tenants herein, then, in the event of the death of one or both Tenant(s), the surviving Tenant and/or the heirs or legal representatives of the deceased Tenant may terminate this Lease at the end of any calendar month within 120 days of said occurence by giving Lessor not less than 45 days prior written notice.

19. NOTICES: Except as herein provided, any demand to be made or notice to be served, including those provided by statute, shall be construed to mean notice in writing signed by or on behalf of the party giving same, and served upon the other party (A) in person, or (B) by certified or registered mail, return receipt requested, postage prepaid, at the address herein set forth or at such other address as either party may designate by written notice to the other. Notice by mail shall be deemed given, served and effective at the time deposited into the United States Mail, regardless of when received. Notice served in person on Tenant may be served if left with some person residing in or in possession of the Apartment above the age of 12 years, and in the event of an apparent abandonment, notice may be served by posting same on the door of the Apartment in addition to service by mail in accordance herewith. Notices served in person on Lessor may be served on any office employee of Lessor, or, if Lessor receives rent at his home, in the same manner as on Tenant.

20. RULES AND REGULATIONS: The rules and regulations at the end of this Lease shall be a part of this Lease. Tenant covenants and agrees to keep and observe these rules and regulations as may later be promulgated by Lessor or Lessor's agent for the necessary, proper and orderly care of the Building, (provided such later rules do not materially change the terms contained in the body of this Lease).

21. TENANT TO INSURE POSSESSIONS: Lessor is not an insurer of Tenant's person or possessions. Tenant agrees that all of Tenant's person and property in the Apartment or elsewhere in the Building shall be at the risk of Tenant only, and that Tenant will carry such insurance as Tenant deems necessary therefore.

22. REMEDIES CUMULATIVE, NON-WAIVER:

A. All rights and remedies given to Tenant or to Lessor shall be distinct, separate, and cumulative, and the use of one or more thereof shall not exclude or waive any other right or remedy allowed by law;

B. No waiver of any breach or default of either party hereunder shall be implied from any omission by the party to take any action on account of a similar or different breach or default;

C. No express waiver shall affect any breach other than the breach specified in the express waiver and such express waiver shall be effective only for the time and to the extent therein stated.

23. TENANT'S WAIVER. Tenant's covenant to pay rent is and shall be independent of each and every other covenant of this Lease.

24. LESSOR'S REMEDIES:

A. If Tenant:

(1) defaults in the payment of any single installment of rent or in the payment of any other sum required to be paid under this Lease or under the terms of any other agreement between Tenant and Lessor and such default is not cured within five days of written notice: or

(2) defaults in the performance of any other covenant or agreement hereof, and such default is not cured by Tenant within 10 days after written notice to Tenant from Lessor (unless the default involves a hazardous condition which shall be cured forthwith);

Lessor may treat such event as a breach of this Lease and Lessor may exercise all rights and remedies provided at law or in equity including, if applicable, the termination of this Lease and the term created hereby, in which event Lessor may forthwith repossess the Apartment in accordance with Paragraph 15(**A**) hereof.

B. If Tenant is the subject of an involuntary proceeding under any section of any bankruptcy act and any court or tribunal shall adjudge Tenant insolvent or unable to pay Tenant's debts and such order is not vacated within 30 days after its entry, or if Tenant files any voluntary petition or similar proceedings under any section of any bankruptcy act in any court or tribunal to delay or reduce or modify Tenant's debts or obligations, or if Tenant is declared insolvent according to law, or if any assignment of Tenant's debts or obligations, or if Tenant is declared insolvent according to law, or if any assignment of Tenant's property shall be made for the benefit of creditors, or if any receiver or trustee is appointed for Tenant or his property, this Lease shall automatically terminate without need of an election by Lessor and Lessor's remedy shall be as set forth in Subparagraph **A** above.

EXHIBIT 10: Chicago Apartment Lease *(Continued)*

13. **ABANDONMENT:** Tenant shall be deemed to have abandoned the Apartment when (a) Tenant has provided Lessor with actual notice indicating Tenant's intent not to return to the Apartment; (b) Tenant has been absent from the Apartment for 21 days, has removed his personal property from the Apartment and has failed to pay rent for that period; (c) Tenant has been absent from the Apartment for 32 days and has failed to pay rent for that period; or (d) Tenant has not removed his personal property from the Apartment after termination of the Lease by lapse of time or otherwise. In the event Tenant has been deemed to have abandoned the Apartment, Lessor shall attempt to sublease the Apartment in accordance with Paragraph 12.

If Tenant abandons the Apartment, Tenant shall be deemed, conclusively, to have abandoned any personal property remaining in the Apartment. Lessor may remove any personal property from the Apartment and store the same for a period of 7 days after which period the personal property may be disposed of. However, Lessor may, at any time after the abandonment, dispose of property subject to spoilage or property that Lessor reasonably believes to be valueless or of such little value that the cost of storage of such property would exceed that amount realized from sale thereof.

Nothing in this Paragraph shall affect the remedies provided to Lessor under Paragraphs 15 and 24 of this Lease.

14. **FIRE AND CASUALTY:** If the Apartment is damaged or destroyed by fire or casualty and:
   A. the Apartment is only partially damaged and is inhabitable and Lessor makes full repairs within 60 days, this Lease shall continue with apportionment of rent.
   B. If the Apartment is rendered (1) uninhabitable, or (2) continued occupancy would be illegal, Tenant may immediately vacate the Apartment and notify Lessor in writing within 14 days thereafter of his intent to terminate, in which case this Lease shall terminate as of the date of the fire or casualty and all prepaid rent and unapplied Security Deposit shall be returned to Tenant.

15. **TERMINATION AND RETURN OF POSSESSION:**
   A. Upon the termination of this Lease, whether by lapse of time or otherwise, or upon termination of Tenant's right of possession without termination of this Lease, Tenant shall yield up immediate possession to Lessor and deliver all keys to Lessor at the place where rent is payable, or as otherwise directed by Lessor. The mere retention of possession thereafter shall constitute a forcible detainer. Lessor shall have the right and license with process of law (and if Tenant abandons the Apartment, Tenant grants Lessor and Lessor shall have such right and license without process of law) to enter into the Apartment, to have the Apartment returned to Lessor as Lessor's estate, to take possession of the Apartment and to expel and remove Tenant, and any others who may be occupying or within the Apartment, and any and all property from the Apartment, without relinquishing Lessor's right to rent or any other right given to Lessor hereunder or by operation of law.
   B. Tenant agrees that in the event Tenant fails to vacate the Apartment upon termination of this Lease or Tenant's right of possession that:
      (1) Tenant shall pay as liquidated damages for the entire time that possession is withheld a sum equal to three times the amount of rent herein reserved, pro rated per day of such withholding, or Lessor's actual damages if same are ascertainable; or
      (2) Lessor, at its sole option, may, upon giving Tenant written notice, extend the term of this Lease for a like period of time not to exceed one year at such rent as Lessor has stated prior to said termination date; or

   C. Tenant shall pay Lessor all Lessor's costs, expenses and attorney's fees in and about the enforcement of the covenants and agreements of this Lease, unless otherwise prohibited by law.

25. **RECEIPT OF REQUIRED DOCUMENTS:** By execution of this Lease, Tenant confirms and acknowledges that Tenant has received the following documents from Lessor:
   A. A summary of the City of Chicago Residential Landlord and Tenant Ordinance (Chicago, IL Municipal Code Ch. 193.1) and,
   B. A receipt for the Security Deposit, if any, as required by said Ordinance.

26. **OTHER AGREEMENTS:**
   A. The headings or captions of paragraphs are for identification purposes only and do not limit or construe the contents of the paragraphs.
   B. "Lessor" as used herein shall refer to the person, partnership, corporation or trust hereinabove set forth in that capacity. If such person be designated an agent Lessor shall also refer to and include the principal. Obligations and duties to be performed by Lessor may be performed by Lessor, its agents, employees or independent contractors. Only Lessor or its designated agent may amend or modify this Lease or Lessor's obligations thereunder.
   C. All rights and remedies of Lessor under this Lease, or that may be provided by law, may be exercised by Lessor in Lessor's own name individually, or in Lessor's name by Lessor's agent, and all legal proceedings for the enforcement of any such rights or remedies, including distress for rent, forcible detainer, and any other legal or equitable proceedings, may be commenced and prosecuted to final judgment and execution by Lessor in Lessor's own name individually, or by agent of any Lessor who is a principal.
   D. Tenant agrees that Lessor may at any time and as often as desired assign or re-assign all of its rights as Lessor under this Lease.
   E. The words "Lessor" and "Tenant" as used herein shall be construed to mean plural where necessary and the necessary grammatical changes required to make the provisions hereof apply to corporations or persons, women or men, shall in all cases be assumed as though in each case fully expressed.
   F. The obligations of two or more persons designated Tenant in this Lease shall be joint and several. If there be more than one party named as Tenant, other than children in a family, all must execute this Lease and any modification or amendment hereto.
   G. "Apartment" used herein shall refer to the dwelling unit leased to Tenant.
   H. Tenant's occupancy of any storeroom, storage area or garage space in or about Building shall be as licensee only. Tenant understands that due to the construction, location and use of storeroom, storage area or garage spaces, Lessor cannot and shall not be liable for any loss or damage of or to any property placed therein. **Do not store valuable items in such areas.** The termination of this Lease for any reason shall also serve to terminate Tenant's right to use such storeroom, storage area, or garage space.
   I. "Building" as used herein shall include the entire physical structure located at and about the address hereinabove stated, including machinery, equipment and appurtenances which are a part thereof, grounds, recreational areas and facilities, garages and out-buildings, and other apartment buildings which form a complex owned an operated as a single entity.
   J. The invalidity or unenforceability of any provision hereof shall not affect or impact any other provision.

RULES AND REGULATIONS

These rules are for the mutual benefit of all tenants. Please cooperate. Violations may cause termination of your Lease.

1. No pets or animals without written consent of Lessor or Lessor's agent (which may be revoked on (10) ten days notice at any time). No animals without leash in any public area of the Building.
2. Passages, public halls, stairways, landings, elevators and elevator vestibules shall not be obstructed or be used for child's play or for any other purpose than for ingress to and egress from the Building or apartments, nor shall children be permitted to congregate or play in or around the common interior areas of the Building. All personal possessions must be kept in the Apartment or in other storage areas if provided.
3. All furniture, supplies, goods and packages of every kind shall be delivered through the rear or service entrance, stair way or elevator.
4. Carriages, velocipedes, bicycles, sleds and the like shall not be allowed in the lobbies, public halls, passageways, courts or elevators of the Building and are to be stored only in places designated for their storage by the Lessor.
5. Laundry and drying apparatus shall be used in such a manner and at such times as the Lessor may clearly post in such area. Clothes washers and dryers, and dishwashers, unless installed by Lessor, cannot be kept in the Apartment.
6. The use of garbage receptacles or incinerators shall be in accordance with posted signs and only garbage and refuse wrapped in small, tight parcels, may be placed in garbage receptacles or incinerator hoppers. Aerosol cans or inflammable materials shall be placed in garbage receptacles or dropped into the incinerator only if so posted. They are highly explosive.
7. No sign, signal, illumination, advertisement, notice or any other lettering, or equipment shall be exhibited, inscribed, painted, affixed or exposed on or at any window or on any part of the outside or inside of Apartment or Building without the prior written consent of the Lessor.
8. No awnings or other projections including air conditioners, television or radio antennas or wiring shall be attached to or extend from or beyond the outside walls of the Building.
9. The Tenant shall not alter any lock or install a new lock or a knocker or other attachment on any door of the Apartment without the written consent of the Lessor.
10. No waste receptacles, supplies, footwear, umbrellas or other articles shall be placed in the halls, on the staircase landings, nor shall anything be hung or shaken from the windows or balconies or placed upon the outside window sills.
11. No noise, music or other sounds shall be permitted at any time in such manner as to disturb or annoy other occupants of the Building.
12. The water closets, basins and other plumbing fixtures shall not be used for any purpose other than for those for which they were designed; no sweepings, rubbish, rags or any other improper articles shall be thrown into them. Any damage resulting from misuse of such facilities shall be paid for by the Tenant.
13. There shall be no cooking or baking done in or about the apartment except in the kitchen. **Cooking on a barbeque or other similar equipment on a porch, terrace, or balcony is expressly forbidden.**
14. If Lessor provides television master antenna hookup, only Lessor's authorized agent shall install Tenant's television set to master antenna and Tenant agrees to pay installation cost and annual maintenance fee. Tenant shall permit access to disconnect hookup for nonpayment. Tenant agrees to pay $50.00 liquidated damage to Lessor's authorized agent for each illegal hookup in Tenant's Apartment.
15. No furniture filled with a liquid or semi-liquid shall be brought in or used in the Apartment.

Guarantee

On this ________________________, 19_____ in consideration of Ten Dollars ($10.00) and other good and valuable consideration, the receipt and sufficiency of which is hereby acknowledged, the undersigned Guarantor hereby guarantees the payment of rent and performance by Tenant, Tenant's heirs, executors, administrators, successors or assigns of all covenants and agreements of the above Lease.

________________________________ (SEAL)   ________________________________ (SEAL)

EXHIBIT 11: Apartment Lease

APARTMENT LEASE

RAMCO FORM 30

Apartment Lease

THIS LEASE, made this..........................day of..A. D., 19........, by and between ...., owner and proprietor of the..or.. his duly authorized agent, both of.., hereinafter called the Lessor, and ....of.. hereinafter called the Lessee..................

WITNESSETH, That in consideration of the sum of..Dollars paid by the Lessee............, which said sum is hereby acknowledged to have been received as part payment of rents accruing under this Lease, and in the further consideration of the covenants, agreements and conditions herein contained, on the part of the Lessee.......... to be kept, done and performed, the said Lessor does hereby lease to the Lessee.........Apartment No.......... ....on the..floor in the.. ...., situated..., with the full understanding that.............................family consists of..........................adults and...........................child..............................and no more.

TO HAVE AND TO HOLD THE SAME for the full term of..from the ....day of.......................................A. D., 19........, to the................day of............................., 19........, the said Lessee........ yielding and paying to the Lessor therefor the total rent of...Dollars.

And the said Lessee.........covenant..........with the Lessor to pay said rent in advance in..payments, the first payment of......................................Dollars on the......................day of.....................................A. D., 19............., which said sum has been paid and acknowledged herein, and the remaining payments as follows, namely:

....

....

....

....

....

AND THE SAID LESSEE..............................further covenant..................and agree...................not to use nor permit to be used the premises leased for any illegal, immoral or improper purposes; not to make nor permit any disturbance, noise or annoyance whatsoever detrimental to the premises or to the comfort and peace of any of the inhabitants of said building or its neighbors, and particularly, said Lessee.......................... agree................that under no circumstances will...allow or permit their child or children to play in the halls, lobby, porches or stair-cases of said building or in any other way to annoy the tenants of other Apartments, and the Lessor does hereby reserve the right to terminate this lease at any time this condition is permitted to exist; not to assign this lease nor sub-let any part of the premises here leased, except with the written consent of the owner and only at a price which shall be an amount not less than the proportional rate for the full term; not to use said premises for any other purpose than as a private dwelling for the members of ....family; to pay the cost of repairing all damage to the apartment occasioned by the Lessee........or any of............................... family; and especially the cost of removing foreign substances from toilets and sinks.

EXHIBIT 11: Apartment Lease *(Continued)*

AND THE LESSEE..........hereby covenant.........and agree...........that if default is made in the payment of rent as above set forth or any part thereof, or if said Lessee........or.................................family shall violate any of the covenants, agreements and conditions of this lease, then the Lessee........shall become a tenant at sufferance, and the entire rent for the rental period next ensuing shall at once be due and payable and the Lessee will at the end of h........term without demand quietly and peaceably deliver up the possession of said premises in as good condition as they now are (ordinary wear and the decay and damage by fire or the elements only excepted).

SAID LESSEE........hereby acknowledges receipt of the articles enumerated on the reverse side of this lease and by agreement made a part hereof and further covenants and agrees to assume full responsibility for said articles and to make good any damage or deficiency therein at the expiration of this lease; to return all linens clean and pay for cleaning of same upon termination of lease.

....

....

....

And the Lessor, upon performance of the said covenants, agreements and conditions by said Lessee........hereby covenants that the said Lessee........shall have the quiet and peaceable enjoyment of said premises, herein reserving the right to inspect said premises so often as shall be deemed necessary and to show the apartment at reasonable hours to prospective tenants during the thirty days next prior to the expiration of this lease.

Witness our hands and seals this.........................day of..A. D., 19........

Signed and sealed in the presence of:

....(Seal)
Lessor.

....(Seal)
Agent for Lessor.

....(Seal)
Lessee.

....(Seal)
Lessee.

EXHIBIT 11: Apartment Lease *(Continued)*

LIVING ROOM

- Table
- Desk
- Mirror
- Chairs
- Smoking stand
- Lamps
- Settee
- Ash trays
- End tables
- Rugs
- Drapes
- Shades
- Waste Baskets
- Pictures
- Vases
- Table scarfs
- Curtains
- Venetian Blinds
- Statues

BED ROOM

1 2

- Bed, springs, Mattress
- " Pads
- " Spreads
- Rugs
- Lamp
- Table
- Dresser
- Chest
- Vanity
- Blankets
- Chair
- Pillows
- Dresser scarfs
- Shades
- Curtains
- Night Stand

DISHES

- Dinner plates
- Bread and butter plates
- Soup plates
- Pie plates
- Cups
- Saucers
- Sauce dishes
- Cereal "
- Vegetable dishes
- platters

DINING ROOM

- Dining table
- Dining chairs
- Buffet
- Rugs
- Pictures
- Drapes
- Shades
- Scarfs
- Curtains
- Venetian Blinds

LINEN

- Sheets
- Pillow slips
- Face towels
- Bath towels
- Table cloths
- Napkins
- Kitchen towels
- Bath mats
- Shower curtains
- Blankets
- Bed spreads

SILVER

- Knives
- Forks
- Small spoons
- Soup spoons
- Sugar shell
- Salad forks
- Butter knives
- Sugar spoon

- Sugar bowl
- Cream pitcher
- Salt shaker
- Pepper shaker
- Water glasses
- Ice tea glasses
- Water pitcher
- Glass dishes

KITCHEN

- Carpet sweeper
- Shades
- Broom
- Oil mop
- Wet mop
- Dust pan
- Ironing board
- Waste baskets
- Garbage can
- Water bucket
- Refrigerator
- Range
- Chair
- Towel rack
- Pc Canister set
- Frying pans
- Grater
- 6-cup muffin pan
- Roaster
- Cake pans
- Pie pans
- Bread pans
- Tea pot
- Coffee pot
- Tea kettle
- Stew kettle and cover
- Sauce pans
- Egg-beater
- Fruit squeezer
- Pancake turner
- Dish pan
- Double boiler
- Mixing bowl
- Drip pan
- Dipper
- Colander
- Flour sifter
- Sink strainer
- Strainers
- Potato masher
- Bread box
- Bread board
- Rolling pin
- Can opener
- Large spoon
- " fork
- Carving knife
- Paring "
- Bread "
- Bulbs
- Stool
- Venetian blinds

RAMCO'S FORM 30

Apartment Lease

FROM

To

on the following property:

Commencing................, 19....

Expires................, 19....

EXHIBIT 12: Residence Lease

RESIDENCE LEASE
(REPLACES OLD FORMS 14 AND 14B)

No. 14
FEBRUARY, 1986

GEORGE E. COLE®
LEGAL FORMS

RESIDENCE LEASE

CAUTION: Consult a lawyer before using or acting under this form. Neither the publisher nor the seller of this form makes any warranty with respect thereto, including any warranty of merchantability or fitness for a particular purpose.

DATE OF LEASE	TERM OF LEASE		RENT	SECURITY DEPOSIT*
	BEGINNING	ENDING		

IF NONE, WRITE "NONE"; Paragraph 2 of this Lease then INAPPLICABLE.

LESSEE		LESSOR	
NAME	•	NAME	•
ADDRESS OF	•	ADDRESS	•
PREMISES	•	CITY	•
CITY	•		

In consideration of the mutual covenants and agreements herein stated, Lessor hereby leases to Lessee and Lessee hereby leases from Lessor for a private dwelling the house designated above (the "Premises"), together with the appurtenances thereto, for the above term.

RENT

1. Lessee shall pay Lessor as rent for the Premises the sum stated above, monthly in advance, until termination of this lease, at Lessor's address stated above or such other address as Lessor may designate in writing. Time of each such payment is of the essence of this agreement.

SECURITY DEPOSIT

2. Lessee has deposited with Lessor the Security Deposit stated above as security for the performance of all covenants and agreements of Lessee hereunder. Lessor may at any time or times apply all or any portion thereof in payment of any amounts due Lessor from Lessee. Upon termination of the lease and full performance of all of Lessee's obligations hereunder, so much of the Security Deposit as remains unapplied shall be returned to Lessee. The Security Deposit shall not bear interest unless and except as required by Illinois statute.

CONDITION OF PREMISES

3. Lessee acknowledges that the Premises are in good repair, except as herein otherwise specified, and that no representations as to the condition or repair thereof have been made by the Lessor, or Lessor's agent, prior to or at the execution of this lease, that are not herein expressed.

REPAIR

4. The Lessee covenants and agrees with Lessor to take good care of and keep in clean and healthy condition the Premises and their fixtures, and to commit or suffer no waste therein; that no changes or alterations of the Premises shall be made or partitions erected, nor walls papered without the consent in writing of Lessor; that Lessee will make all repairs required to the walls, windows, glass, ceilings, paint, plastering, plumbing work, pipes, and fixtures belonging to the Premises, whenever damage or injury to the same shall have resulted from misuse or neglect; and Lessee agrees to pay for any and all repairs that shall be necessary to put the Premises in the same condition as when he entered therein, reasonable wear and loss by fire excepted, and the expense of such repairs shall be included within the terms of this lease and any judgment by confession entered therefor.

LIMITATION OF LIABILITY

5. Except as required by Illinois statute, the Lessor shall not be liable for any damage occasioned by failure to keep the Premises in repair, and shall not be liable for any damage done or occasioned by or from plumbing, gas, water, steam, or other pipes, sewerage, or the bursting, leaking or running from any cistern, tank, washstand, water closet or waste pipe in, above, upon or about the Premises, nor for damage occasioned by water, snow or ice, being upon or coming through the roof, skylight, trap door or otherwise, nor for any damage arising from acts or neglect of any owners or occupants of adjacent or contiguous property.

USE; SUBLET; ASSIGNMENT

6. Lessee will not allow the Premises to be used for any purpose that will increase the rate of insurance thereon, nor for any purpose other than that hereinbefore specified, nor to be occupied, in whole or in part, by any other person, and will not sublet the same, or any part thereof, nor assign this lease, without in each case the Lessor's written consent had, and will not permit and transfer, by operation of law, of the interest in the Premises acquired through this lease; and will not permit the Premises to be used for unlawful purpose or purposes that will injure the reputation of the same or of the neighborhood; will keep no dogs, cats or other animals or pets in or about the Premises; will not permit the Premises to remain vacant or unoccupied for more than ten consecutive days; and will not permit any alteration of or upon any part of the Premises, nor allow any signs or placards posted or placed thereon, except by written consent of the Lessor; all alterations and additions to the Premises shall remain for the benefit of the Lessor unless otherwise provided in said consent.

RIGHT TO RELET

7. If Lessee shall abandon or vacate the Premises, the same shall be re-let by the Lessor for such rent, and upon such terms as Lessor may see fit; and if a sufficient sum shall not be thus realized, after paying the expenses of such re-letting and collecting, to satisfy the rent hereby reserved, the Lessee agrees to satisfy and pay all deficiency.

HOLDING OVER

8. If the Lessee retains possession of the Premises or any part thereof after the termination of the term by lapse of time or otherwise, then the Lessor may at Lessor's option within thirty days after the termination of the term serve written notice upon Lessee that such holding over constitutes either (a) renewal of this lease for one year, and from year to year thereafter, at double the rental specified under Section 1 for such period, or (b) creation of a month to month tenancy, upon the terms of this lease except at double the monthly rental specified under Section 1, or (c) creation of a tenancy at sufferance, at a rental of

__________ dollars per day for the time Lessee remains in possession. If no such written notice is served then a tenancy at sufferance with rental as stated at (c) shall have been created. Lessee shall also pay to Lessor all damages sustained by Lessor resulting from retention of possession by Lessee.

FLAMMABLES

9. Naphtha, benzine, benzole, gasoline, benzine-varnish, gunpowder, fireworks, nitroglycerine, phosphorus, saltpeter, nitrate of soda, camphene, spirit-gas, or any flammable fluid or oil, shall not be allowed or used on the Premises without the written permission of the Lessor.

TAXES AND UTILITIES

10. Lessee shall pay (in addition to the rent above specified) all water taxes and all gas, electricity and power bills, levied or charged on or in respect of the Premises, for and during the term of this lease,

and in case no water taxes are levied specifically on or in respect of the Premises, to pay the__________ part of all water taxes levied or charged on orin respect of the building of which the Premises constitutes a part; and in case said water taxes and gas, electricity and power bills shall not be paid when due, Lessor shall have the right to pay the same, which amount so paid, together with any sums paid by Lessor to keep the Premises and their appurtenances in good condition as hereinbefore specified, shall be due and payable with the next installment of rent due thereafter under this lease.

EXHIBIT 12: Residence Lease *(Continued)*

SIGNS 11. Lessor reserves the right to put up a "To Rent" sign sixty days prior to the expiration of this lease and a "For Sale" sign at any time during the term of this lease.

COMPLIANCE 12. Lessee will in every respect comply with the ordinances of the municipality aforesaid, with the rules and orders of the health officers thereof, with the orders and requirements of the police department, with the requirements of any underwriters' association so as not to increase the rates of insurance upon the building and contents thereof, and with the rules and orders of the fire department in respect to any matters coming within their jurisdiction.

DEFAULT 13. If default be made in the payment of the above rent, or any part thereof, or in any of the covenants herein contained to be kept by Lessee, it shall be lawful for Lessor at any time, at his election, without notice, to declare said term ended and to re-enter the Premises, or any part thereof, with or without process of law, and to remove Lessee or any persons occupying the same, without prejudice to any remedies which might otherwise be used for arrears of rent, and Lessor shall have at all times the right to distrain for rent due and shall have a valid and first lien upon all personal property which Lessee owns or may hereafter acquire or have an interest in, whether exempt by law or not, as security for payment of the rent herein reserved.

CONFESSION 14. The Lessee hereby irrevocably constitutes any attorney of any court of record in this state, attorney for Lessee in Lessee's name, on default by Lessee of any of the covenants herein, and upon complaint made by Lessor, his agent or assigns, and filed in any such court to enter Lessee's appearance in any such court of record, waive process and service thereof, and confess judgment, from time to time, for any rent which may be due to Lessor, or the Lessor's assignees, by the terms of this lease, with costs and a reasonable sum for attorney's fees, and to waive all errors and all right of appeal from said judgment, and to consent in writing that a writ of execution may be issued immediately.

RENT AFTER NOTICE OR SUIT 15. After the service of notice, or the commencement of a suit, or after final judgment for possession of the Premises, the Lessor may receive and collect any rent due, and the payment of said rent shall not waive or affect said notice, said suit, or said judgment.

FIRE AND CASUALTY 16. In case the Premises shall be rendered untenantable by fire or other casualty, Lessor may at his option terminate this lease, or repair the Premises within thirty days, and failing so to do, or upon the destruction of the Premises by fire, the term hereby created shall cease and determine.

PAYMENT OF COSTS 17. The Lessee further covenants and agrees to pay and discharge all reasonable costs, attorney's fees and expenses that shall be made and incurred by Lessor in enforcing the covenants and agreements of this lease.

PLURALS; SUCCESSORS 18. The words "Lessor" and "Lessee" wherever herein occurring and used shall be construed to mean "Lessors" and "Lessees" in case more than one person constitutes either party to this lease, and all such persons shall be jointly and severally liable hereon; and all the covenants and agreements herein contained shall be binding upon, and inure to, their respective successors, heirs, executors, administrators and assigns and be exercised by his or their attorney or agent.

SEVERABILITY 19. If any clause, phrase, provision or portion of this lease or the application thereof to any person or circumstance shall be invalid, or unenforceable under applicable law, such event shall not affect, impair or render invalid or unenforceable the remainder of this lease nor any other clause, phrase, provision or portion hereof, nor shall it affect the application of any clause, phrase, provision or portion hereof to other persons or circumstances.

WITNESS the hands and seals of the parties hereto, as of the Date of Lease stated above.

__________________________(SEAL)

__________________________(SEAL)

GUARANTEE

For value received__________hereby guarantee the payment of the rent and the performance of the covenants by the Lessee in the within lease covenanted and agreed, in manner and form as in said lease provided.

WITNESS__________hand__and seal__this________day of______________, 19____.

__________________________(SEAL)

__________________________(SEAL)

ASSIGNMENT BY LESSOR

In consideration of One Dollar, to the Lessor in hand paid, the Lessor hereby transfers, assigns and sets over to__________

__________________________and________

Successors and assigns Lessor's interest in the within lease, and the rent thereby secured______________

____

WITNESS__________hand and seal this________day of______________, 19____.

__________________________(SEAL)

__________________________(SEAL)

NOTE: Use Form Number 12-1 for assignment by Tenant.

EXHIBIT 13: Apartment Lease Unfurnished

APARTMENT LEASE — UNFURNISHED
(For Use In Illinois)

GEORGE E. COLE®
LEGAL FORMS

NO. L-17
FEBRUARY 1986

CAUTION: Consult a lawyer before using or acting under this form. Neither the publisher nor the seller of this form makes any warranty with respect thereto, including any warranty of merchantability or fitness for a particular purpose.

IF UNHEATED, CHECK HERE: _____
(SEE PARAGRAPH 11)

APARTMENT LEASE

UNFURNISHED

DATE OF LEASE	TERM OF LEASE		MONTHLY RENT	SECURITY DEPOSIT*
	BEGINNING	ENDING		

* *IF NONE, WRITE "NONE". Paragraph 2 of this Lease then INAPPLICABLE.*

LESSEE		LESSOR	
NAME	•	NAME	•
APT. NO.	•	BUSINESS ADDRESS	•
ADDRESS OF PREMISES	•		

In consideration of the mutual covenants and agreements herein stated, Lessor hereby leases to Lessee and Lessee hereby leases from Lessor for a private dwelling the apartment designated above (the "Premises"), together with the appurtenances thereto, for the above Term.

ADDITIONAL COVENANTS AND AGREEMENTS *(if any)*

LEASE COVENANTS AND AGREEMENTS

RENT

1. Lessee shall pay Lessor or Lessor's agent as rent for the Premises the sum stated above, monthly in advance, until termination of this lease, at Lessor's address stated above or such other address as Lessor may designate in writing.

SECURITY DEPOSIT

2. Lessee has deposited with Lessor the Security Deposit stated above for the performance of all covenants and agreements of Lessee hereunder. Lessor may apply all or any portion thereof in payment of any amounts due Lessor from Lessee, and upon Lessor's demand Lessee shall in such case during the term of the lease promptly deposit with Lessor such additional amounts as may then be required to bring the Security Deposit up to the full amount stated above. Upon termination of the lease and full performance of all matters and payment of all amounts due by Lessee, so much of the Security Deposit as remains unapplied shall be returned to Lessee. This deposit does not bear interest unless and except as required by law. Where all or a portion of the Security Deposit is applied by Lessor as compensation for property damage, Lessor when and as required by law shall provide to Lessee an itemized statement of such damage and of the estimated or actual cost of repairing same. If the building in which Premises are located (the "Building") is sold or otherwise transferred, Lessor may transfer or assign the Security Deposit to the purchaser or transferee of the Building, who shall thereupon be liable to Lessee for all of Lessor's obligations hereunder, and Lessee shall look thereafter solely to such purchaser or transferee for return of the Security Deposit and for other matters (including any interest or accounting) relating thereto.

CONDITION OF PREMISES; REDELIVERY TO LESSOR

3. Lessee has examined and knows the condition of Premises and has received the same in good order and repair except as herein otherwise specified, and no representations as to the condition or repair thereof have been made by Lessor or his agent prior to, or at the execution of this lease, that are not herein expressed or endorsed hereon; and upon the termination of this lease in any way, Lessee will immediately yield up Premises to Lessor in as good condition as when the same were entered upon by Lessee, ordinary wear and tear only excepted, and shall then return all keys to Lessor.

LIMITATION OF LIABILITY

4. Except as provided by Illinois statute, Lessor shall not be liable for any damage occasioned by failure to keep Premises in repair, and shall not be liable for any damage done or occasioned by or from plumbing, gas, water, steam or other pipes, or sewerage, or the bursting, leaking or running of any cistern, tank, wash-stand, water-closet, or waste-pipe, in, above, upon or about the Building or Premises, nor for damage occasioned by water, snow or ice being upon or coming through the roof, skylight, trap-door or otherwise, nor for damages to Lessee or others claiming through Lessee for any loss or damage of or to property wherever located in or about the Building or Premises, nor for any damage arising from acts or neglect of co-tenants or other occupants of the Building, or of any owners or occupants of adjacent or contiguous property.

USE; SUBLET; ASSIGNMENT

5. Lessee will not allow Premises to be used for any purpose that will increase the rate of insurance thereon, nor for any purpose other than that hereinbefore specified, nor to be occupied in whole or in part by any other persons, and will not sublet the same, nor any part thereof, nor assign this lease, without in each case the written consent of the Lessor first had, and will not permit any transfer, by operation of law, of the interest in Premises acquired through this lease, and will not permit Premises to be used for any unlawful purpose or purpose that will injure the reputation of the same or of the Building or disturb the tenants of the Building or the neighborhood.

USE AND REPAIR

6. Lessee will take good care of the apartment demised and the fixtures therein, and will commit and suffer no waste therein; no changes or alterations of the Premises shall be made, nor partitions erected, nor walls papered, nor locks on doors installed or changed, without the consent in writing of Lessor; Lessee will make all repairs required to the walls, ceilings, paint, plastering, plumbing work, pipes and fixtures belonging to Premises, whenever damage or injury to the same shall have resulted from misuse or neglect; no furniture filled or to be filled wholly or partially with liquids shall be placed in the Premises without the consent in writing of Lessor; the Premises shall not be used as a "boarding" or "lodging" house, nor for a school, nor to give instructions in music, dancing or singing, and none of the rooms shall be offered for lease by placing notices on any door, window or wall of the Building, nor by advertising the same directly or indirectly, in any newspaper or otherwise, nor shall any signs be exhibited on or at any windows or exterior portions of the Premises or of the Building without the consent in writing of Lessor; there shall be no lounging, sitting upon, or unnecessary tarrying in or upon the front steps, the sidewalk, railing, stairways, halls, landing or other public places of the Building by Lessee, members of the family or others persons connected with the occupancy of Premises; no provisions, milk, ice, marketing, groceries, furniture, packages or merchandise shall be taken into the Premises through the front door of the Building except where there is no rear or service entrance; cooking shall be done only in the kitchen and in no event on porches or other exterior appurtenances; Lessee, and those occupying under Lessee, shall not interfere with the heating apparatus, or with the lights, electricity, gas, water or other utilities of the Building which are not within the apartment hereby demised, nor with the control of any of the public portions of the Building; use of any master television antenna hookup shall be strictly in accordance with regulations of Lessor or Lessor's agent; Lessee and those occupying under Lessee shall comply with and conform to all reasonable rules and regulations that Lessor or Lessor's agent may make for the protection of the Building or the general welfare and the comfort of the occupants thereof, and shall also comply with and conform to all applicable laws and governmental rules and regulations affecting the Premises and the use and occupancy thereof.

ACCESS

7. Lessee will allow Lessor free access to the Premises at all reasonable hours for the purpose of examining or exhibiting the same or to make any needful repairs which Lessor may deem fit to make for the benefit of or related to any part of the Building; also Lessee will allow Lessor to have placed upon the Premises, at all times, notice of "For Sale" and "To Rent," and will not interfere with the same.

EXHIBIT 13: Apartment Lease Unfurnished *(Continued)*

RIGHT TO RELET

8. If Lessee shall abandon or vacate the Premises, the same may be re-let by Lessor for such rent and upon such terms as Lessor may see fit, subject to Illinois statute, and if a sufficient sum shall not thus be realized, after paying the expenses of such reletting and collecting, to satisfy the rent hereby reserved, Lessee agrees to satisfy and pay all deficiency.

HOLDING OVER

9. If the Lessee retains possession of the Premises or any part thereof after the termination of the term by lapse of time or otherwise, then the Lessor may at Lessor's option within thirty days after the termination of the term serve written notice upon Lessee that such holding over constitutes either (a) renewal of this lease for one year, and from year to year thereafter, at double the rental specified under Section 1 for such period, or (b) creation of a month to month tenancy, upon the terms of this lease except at double the monthly rental specified under Section 1, or (c) creation of a tenancy at sufferance, at a rental of __________ dollars per day for the time Lessee remains in possession. If no such written notice is served then a tenancy at sufferance with rental as stated at (c) shall have been created, and in such case if specific per diem rental shall not have been inserted herein at (c),such per diem rental shall be one-fifteenth of the monthly rental specified under Section 1 of this lease. Lessee shall also pay to Lessor all damages sustained by Lessor resulting from retention of possession by Lessee.

RESTRICTIONS ON USE

10. Lessee will not permit anything to be thrown out of the windows, or down the courts or light shafts in the Building; nothing shall be hung from the outside of the windows or placed on the outside window sills of any window in the Building; no parrot, dog or other animal shall be kept within or about the Premises; the front halls and stairways and the back porches shall not be used for the storage of carriages, furniture or other articles.

WATER AND HEAT

11. The provisions of subsection (a) only hereof shall be applicable and shall form a part of this lease unless this lease is made on an unheated basis and that fact is so indicated on the first page of this lease, in which case the provisions of subsection (b) only hereof shall be applicable and form a part of this lease.

(a) Lessor will supply hot and cold water to the Premises for the use of Lessee at all faucets and fixtures provided by Lessor therefor. Lessor will also supply heat, by means of the heating system and fixtures provided by Lessor, in reasonable amounts and at reasonable hours, when necessary, from October 1 to April 30, or otherwise as required by applicable municipal ordinance. Lessor shall not be liable or responsible to Lessee for failure to furnish water or heat when such failure shall result from causes beyond Lessor's control, nor during periods when the water and heating systems in the Building or any portion thereof are under repair.

(b) Lessor will supply cold water to the Premises for the use of Lessee at all faucets and fixtures provided by Lessor therefor. Lessor shall not be liable or responsible to Lessee for failure to furnish water when such failure shall result from causes beyond Lessor's control, nor during periods when the water system in the Building or any portion thereof is under repair. All water heating and all heating of the Premises shall be at the sole expense of Lessee. Any equipment provided by Lessee therefor shall comply with applicable municipal ordinances.

STORE ROOM

12. Lessor shall not be liable for any loss or damage of or to any property placed in any store room or any storage place in the Building, such store room or storage place being furnished gratuitously and not as part of the obligations of this lease.

DEFAULT BY LESSEE

13. If default be made in the payment of the above rent, or any part thereof, or in any of the covenants herein contained to be kept by the Lessee, Lessor may at any time thereafter at his election declare said term ended and reenter the Premises or any part thereof, with or (to the extent permitted by law) without notice or process of law, and remove Lessee or any persons occupying the same, without prejudice to any remedies which might otherwise be used for arrears of rent, and Lessor shall have at all times the right to distrain for rent due, and shall have a valid and first lien upon all personal property which Lessee now owns, or may hereafter acquire or have an interest in, which is by law subject to such distraint, as security for payment of the rent herein reserved.

NO RENT DEDUCTION OR SET OFF

14. Lessee's covenant to pay rent is and shall be independent of each and every other covenant of this lease. Lessee agrees that any claim by Lessee against Lessor shall not be deducted from rent nor set off against any claim for rent in any action.

RENT AFTER NOTICE OR SUIT

15. It is further agreed, by the parties hereto, that after the service of notice or the commencement of a suit or after final judgment for possession of the Premises, Lessor may receive and collect any rent due, and the payment of said rent shall not waive or affect said notice, said suit, or said judgment.

PAYMENT OF COSTS

16. Lessee will pay and discharge all reasonable costs, attorney's fees and expenses that shall be made and incurred by Lessor in enforcing the covenants and agreements of this lease.

RIGHTS CUMULATIVE

17. The rights and remedies of Lessor under this lease are cumulative. The exercise or use of any one or more thereof shall not bar Lessor from exercise or use of any other right or remedy provided herein or otherwise provided by law, nor shall exercise nor use of any right or remedy by Lessor waive any other right or remedy.

FIRE AND CASUALTY

18. In case the Premises shall be rendered untenantable during the term of this lease by fire or other casualty, Lessor at his option may terminate the lease or repair the Premises within 60 days thereafter. If Lessor elects to repair, this lease shall remain in effect provided such repairs are completed within said time. If Lessor shall not have repaired the Premises within said time, then at the end of such time the term hereby created shall terminate. If this lease is terminated by reason of fire or casualty as herein specified, rent shall be apportioned and paid to the day of such fire or other casualty.

SUBORDINATION

19. This lease is subordinate to all mortgages which may now or hereafter affect the real property of which Premises form a part.

PLURALS; SUCCESSORS

20. The words "Lessor" and "Lessee" wherever herein occurring and used shall be construed to mean "Lessors" and "Lessees" in case more than one person constitutes either party to this lease; and all the covenants and agreements herein contained shall be binding upon, and inure to, their respective successors, heirs, executors, administrators and assigns and be exercised by his or their attorney or agent.

SEVERABILITY

21. Wherever possible each provision of this lease shall be interpreted in such manner as to be effective and valid under applicable law, but if any provision of this lease shall be prohibited by or invalid under applicable law, such provision shall be ineffective to the extent of such prohibition or invalidity, without invalidating the remainder of such provision or the remaining provisions of this lease.

WITNESS the hands and seals of the parties hereto, as of the Date of Lease stated above.

LESSEE: LESSOR:

____________________ (seal) ____________________ (seal)

____________________ (seal) ____________________ (seal)

ASSIGNMENT BY LESSOR

On this ____________________, 19____, for value received, Lessor hereby transfers, assigns and sets over to ____________________ all right, title and interest in and to the above lease and the rent thereby reserved, except rent due and payable prior to ____________________, 19____.

____________________ (seal)

GUARANTEE

____________________ (seal)

On this ____________________, 19____, in consideration of Ten Dollars ($10.00) and other good and valuable consideration, the receipt and sufficiency of which is hereby acknowledged, the undersigned Guarantor hereby guarantees the payment of rent and performance by Lessee, Lessee's heirs, executors, administrators, successors or assigns of all covenants and agrements of the above lease.

____________________ (seal)

____________________ (seal)

The date the lease ends should be the last day of a month.

Unless the rental agreement fixes a definite term, the tenancy is week-to-week in the case of a roomer who pays weekly rent and, in all other cases, month-to-month.

Monthly rent is the dollar amount the resident will pay for rent each month. Extra payments such as garage rent should not be included in this amount.

Other required rent may be additional monthly rent for a parking space, garage, pet, furniture rental or other applicable charges at your property. These amounts can be reflected on the appropriate lease clause or rider.

The *security deposit* is normally less than or equal to one or two months' rent; this can vary from state to state. Many landlords request a flat fee ranging from $100 to $200. In soft rental markets a smaller security deposit might serve as an added inducement to a potential renter. There is no legal requirement to charge a security deposit.

Other required deposits are additional deposits for pets, furniture rental or other extraordinary security deposit fees.

Premises is the complete address of the apartment being leased.

The special provisions section of the lease is for documentation of any additional riders to the lease such as pet, garage and furniture riders and so on or of any special provisions that require additional security deposits.

Prohibited Provisions in Rental Agreements

Many states have restrictions on the language and agreements in leases. For example, in Illinois the following provisions would be prohibited:

- an agreement to waive or to forgo any rights or remedies granted by law
- a provision that authorizes any person to confess judgment on a claim arising out of the rental agreement
- an agreement to exculpate or limit any liability of the other party arising as a result of the other party's willful misconduct or negligence; or to indemnify the other party for that liability or the cost connected therewith
- an agreement to waive attorney's fees as provided by state or local ordinance, or to pay the attorney's fees of the other party except as may be required by law
- a provision that the rental agreement shall be terminated if there are, or shall be, any children under the age of 14 years in resident's family

If any of the above provisions are included in a rental agreement, the provision would be unenforceable; however, generally the rest of the lease would remain valid provided there is a clause that states this provision.

If a party is injured by a prohibited provision in a rental agreement initiated by the other party and such injury results in damages, the injured party may bring suit to recover actual damages and reasonable attorney's fees. If the inclusion was deliberate and with knowledge, an additional monetary amount may be awarded.

Security Deposits

An owner may, pursuant to a written rental agreement, require a security deposit from the resident, in an amount or value that generally should not be in excess of two months' rent. However, nothing prevents an owner from requiring prepaid rent in any amount.

If the resident does prepay rent, the money cannot be applied as security, but only to the payment of rent as it becomes due. A security deposit shall not be used nor applied as rent except as provided by law.

Applicants should pay you the full required security deposit upon signing the lease and always prior to moving into the property. Avoid taking a partial payment. Apartments should not be taken off the market unless the full security deposit has been paid.

Most form-lease provisions pertaining to security deposits provide that the lessor has the right, but not the obligation, to apply the security deposit in payment of any unpaid delinquent rent or other monies due from the tenant. Some leases also provide that the lessor's right to possession of the apartment for nonpayment of rent or any other reason is not affected by the fact that the lessor holds a security deposit.

In some states, if you apply a security deposit to the payment of unpaid rent due, or to compensate for damages caused by the resident's noncompliance with the rental agreement, you must notify the resident within a reasonable time period–ten to 30 days–after such application. In the case of compensation for damages, include an itemized statement of the damage allegedly caused to the dwelling unit or the premises and the estimated or actual cost for repairing or replacing each item on that statement, with estimates or paid invoices or copies attached.

If estimated costs are given on this statement, owners should furnish the resident with copies of paid invoices within 30 days from the date of the statement.

Tenants have a specified time limit, normally 15 days, after receiving notice that the security deposit has been applied to rent or damages, to pay the owner an amount sufficient to restore the security deposit in full.

Security deposit laws in most states dictate that within a certain amount of time of termination of the tenancy (usually 14 to 45 days), owners must refund the security deposit or any portion thereof remaining unapplied. Each state differs on the exact number of days; check with your local real estate board to find out how much time you have. Failure to return a security deposit within the legal time limit may result in additional monetary fines.

Owners should not withhold any portion of the security deposit because of the resident's failure to give the owner advance notice of vacating the dwelling unit, unless the requirement of advance notice is stated on the face of the rental agreement and the resident fails to give such notice, the dwelling unit is vacant for a subsequent period and local laws permit the same.

In the event of a sale, lease or other transfer of the property, owners have to transfer or assign any security deposit funds to the new owner (purchaser, lessee, assignee, mortgagee). When the owner notifies each resident affected by a transfer, the new owner assumes the obligations with respect to security deposits and is bound by law to perform. If a new owner comes into possession of a premises and has not in fact received the security deposit monies, he or she would not be liable to the residents for the return of the security deposits unless otherwise agreed to in advance.

States have different rules governing the handling of security deposit funds. In Illinois, for example, security deposits for residential properties containing 25 or more units must be deposited in a bank or savings and loan association chartered by the state or a federal agency. Deposits are not subject to claims of creditors of the owner. Interest paid on the account is paid to the owner. This number of units may be reduced in future legislation; other states have no exemption.

Even if your state does not require it, you should deposit and keep the security deposit money in a separate interest-bearing bank account instead of mingling it with your personal funds. Many states now require landlords to pay semiannual interest to the tenant on the security deposit amount (see chapter 12).

If owners fail to comply with a security deposit provision of their state statutes, residents can sue to recover the property or money due them, and in some cases can be awarded punitive damages and reasonable attorney's fees.

Restrictions on Use

Many leases contain specific rules and regulations that limit the use of a dwelling unit and the common areas of the apartment building. Common restrictions include prohibiting pets, water beds and cooking with a barbecue; they often govern the use of air conditioners and the replacement of locks. These restrictions are legal in most cases; however, if there is an ambiguity in the meaning of the restriction, the language would be construed in favor of the tenant against the landlord.

Owners can adopt new rules or regulations concerning the resident's use and occupancy of the premises, but such new rules are generally enforceable against the resident only if they meet the following criteria:

- Their purpose must be to promote the convenience, safety or welfare of all the residents on the premises; preserve the owner's property from abusive use; or make a fair distribution of services and facilities offered to residents in general.
- They must be reasonable in relation to the purpose for which they are adopted.
- They must apply to all residents on the premises in a fair manner.
- They must be sufficiently explicit in their prohibition, direction or limitation to fairly inform the resident of what the resident must or must not do to comply.
- They are not for the purpose of evading the obligations of the owner.
- The resident must be notified of the rules and regulations at the time the resident enters into the rental agreement.

A rule or regulation incorporated after the resident enters into the rental agreement is enforceable against the resident only if reasonable notice of its adoption is given to the resident and it does not bring about a substantial reduction of the resident's value in renting the apartment.

For example, if someone rented an apartment in your property because you allowed them to keep a pet and you subsequently adopted a new rule outlawing pets, or if someone rented because your property had a swimming pool that was free and open until 10 P.M. and then you decided to charge a fee or reduce the hours the pool was open, these would be reductions in value to the tenant.

Riders and Additions to the Lease

The standard apartment rental agreement covers most but not all aspects of the landlord-tenant relationship. You may want to add clauses and riders to the document to cover such matters as garage rent, pets, agreements to extend or cut short the term of the lease, furniture rental and so on. Clauses are typed onto the lease; riders are separate sheets that are attached to the lease.

The following are some commonly used riders and clauses.

Security Deposit Agreement

This form (exhibit 14) specifies the conditions under which a security deposit will be returned and it should be signed by all parties signing the lease and attached to the lease form. The second page lists charges for various repairs. You can modify the schedule and prices to suit your specific situation. The amount of the required security deposit should correspond with the amount indicated on the lease.

Garage and Vehicle Riders

If your property has carports or garages available for rent and your resident elects to lease a space, you should execute a garage rider form (exhibit 15). The form spells out the terms and conditions under which a space is rented.

Indicate the rental amount and deposit in the spaces marked "other required rent" and "other required deposit" on the lease. If your lease does not contain this blank space, write the information on the top of the form. On the rider, indicate the deposit and the monthly rental amount.

The resident should also complete a vehicle information form (exhibit 16), listing all pertinent information concerning the vehicles that will use the facility.

If you want the garage rental term to coincide with the apartment lease, be sure the resident understands that the garage rental agreement applies to every month covered by the lease.

EXHIBIT 14: Security Deposit Agreement

SECURITY DEPOSIT AGREEMENT

Due from________________________________$____________________
LESSEE

____**Dollars**

as Security Deposit for____
ADDRESS

Apartment #__________in_______________________,____________________
CITY/VILLAGE STATE

RELEASE OF SECURITY DEPOSIT IS SUBJECT TO THE FOLLOWING PROVISIONS

1. Full term of lease has expired and all provisions herein complied with.
2. Should lessee desire to RERENT (sublet or assign) under the provisions of the lease, a 'one half month's rent' service charge will be assessed.
   a. Approval must be obtained from lessor prior to initiating a rerent or sublet.
   b. Notice in writing must be given to management by certified mail prior to initiating a rerent or sublet.
3. For company transfers, comply with No. 2 above, with notice given on Company letterhead.
4. Entire apartment including range, oven, refrigerator, bathroom, closets, cabinets, windows, carpet, balcony, etc., cleaned.
5. No damage to apartment beyond normal wear and tear.
6. No unpaid late charges or delinquent rents.
7. Forwarding address left with management.
8. No indentations or scratches in wood or resilent floor caused by furniture or other means. Floor must be restored to the original condition if tack down or wall-to-wall carpeting was installed by lessee.
9. No wallcoverings, stickers, scratches, or large holes on walls.
10. All keys including those from mailboxes must be returned.
11. All debris, rubbish, and discards to be placed in proper rubbish containers in designated area.
12. All building-owned carpeting must be professionally cleaned.

IF THE PREREQUISITE CONDITIONS ARE NOT COMPLIED WITH, LESSEE WILL BE CHARGED THE CURRENT RATES LESSOR IS PAYING TO HAVE ITEMS REPAIRED AND/OR CLEANED.

The cost of labor and materials for cleaning, repairs, removals and replacements, where applicable, or rent loss due to necessary repair time, and numerous other charges based on actual damages will be deducted from the security deposit. See reverse side for charges.

EXHIBIT 14: Security Deposit Agreement *(Continued)*

Lessor agrees that subject to the conditions listed above, this Security Deposit will be refunded in full.

Lessee agrees that this Security Deposit may NOT be applied as rent and is fully aware of the provision set forth on this agreement. Lessee further agrees that he will be present for final inspection of apartment.

BY: ______________________

DATE: ______________________

____
LESSEE

____
LESSEE

____
LESSEE

4306 REV.

EXHIBIT 14: Security Deposit Agreement *(Continued)*

MINIMUM CHARGES

Cleaning

1.	Trash removal	10.00 per hour	
2.	Kitchen:		
	Stove		$25.00
	Refrigerator		15.00
	Cabinets & Countertops		15.00
	Floor		15.00
3.	Bathrooms (each)		
	Toilet		$ 5.00
	Shower & Tub		20.00
	Medicine Cabinet		5.00
	Vanity		5.00
	Floor		5.00
4.	Closets		10.00
5.	Windows		5.00
6.	Floors		
	Vacuum		$ 5.00
	Tile Cleaning	1 Bedroom	40.00

EXHIBIT 14: Security Deposit Agreement *(Continued)*

		2 Bedroom	50.00
	Carpet Cleaning	1 Bedroom	35.00
		2 Bedroom	45.00
7.	Excessive Cleaning $10.00 per hour		

Decorating

1.	Patching Holes: ½″ to 2″	$10.00 each
2.	Double Coating	10.00 each wall
3.	Removal of wall coverings	16.00 per hour

Maintenance

1.	Materials plus labor at	$16.00 per hour
2.	Light bulb replacement	1.50 each

EXHIBIT 15: Garage Rider

GARAGE RIDER

THIS RIDER is hereby made a part of and incorporated as part of a certain lease agreement ("Lease") dated ______________________, 19 ____, for an apartment located at ______________________ in ______________________________________, Illinois ("Premises"), by and between ______________________________________("Lessor") and ______________________ ____ ____ ("Lessee").

TO THE EXTENT OF ANY CONFLICT IN TERMS, THE TERMS AND CONDITIONS OF THIS RIDER SHALL GOVERN OVER THE TERMS AND CONDITIONS OF THE AFORESAID LEASE.

In consideration of the deposit of the sum of ______________________________________ ($ ______________) DOLLARS to be paid by Lessee to Lessor upon the execution hereof, the parties hereto agree to the following:

1. Lessor shall permit Lessee to use ________ parking space(s) designated as space number(s) __________ at the Premises for the term of the Lease.

2. Lessee agrees to maintain the space(s) in a clean and sanitary condition at all times.

3. Lessee agrees to utilize the space(s) only for the purpose of parking the assigned vehicle(s).

4. Lessee agrees to remove any vehicle deemed unsightly or in non-working condition by Lessor within five (5) days of notification.

5. Lessee agrees that in the event of any violation of the terms and conditions set forth above, the Lessor shall have the right to make a demand for immediate possession of said space(s). Any refusal by Lessee to comply with such demand by Lessor to return said space(s) shall be material breach of the Lease, and Lessor shall be entitled to retain aforementioned deposit as well as be entitled to any and all other remedies provided by law or equity. However, if Lessee returns said space(s) upon such demand, the deposit shall be returned less damages, if any, caused by violation hereof and said Lease shall continue in effect, except that this rider shall be deemed null and void.

IN WITNESS WHEREOF, the Lessor and Lessee have executed this document on the ______________ day of ______________, 19 _____.

LESSOR

By: ______________________________

____
LESSEE

____
LESSEE

$ __________ is required deposit for each garage transmitter.

$ __________ is the required monthly rental amount.

EXHIBIT 17: Condominium Apartment Lease Rider

RIDER TO

CONDOMINIUM APARTMENT LEASE

THIS RIDER is made this__________day of__________, 19____, and is incorporated into and shall be deemed to amend and supplement that certain Condominium Apartment Lease dated of even date herewith ("Lease") between__________

__________("Lessor") and__________

__________("Lessee"),

demising the condominium apartment described as Unit No.__________at__________

__________("Premises").

CONDOMINIUM COVENANTS: In addition to the covenants, conditions and agreements made in the Lease, Lessor and Lessee further covenant and agree as follows:

Lessee shall abide by all covenants and restrictions (excepting the requirement to pay monthly condominium common expense assessments) running with the title to the Premises contained in the declaration of condominium for the Condominium ("Declaration"), and the by-laws ("By-Laws") thereto, as amended, together with all rules and regulations promulgated from time to time by the unit owners' association ("Association") responsible for the overall administration of the Condominium property of which the Premises are a part.

In addition to all the rights and remedies contained in the Lease, Lessee shall be subject to all of the rights and remedies of the Association for breach of any covenants or restrictions contained in the Declaration, By-Laws, or rules and regulations of the Association from time to time, and Lessee agrees to indemnify and hold Lessor harmless from any damages, costs, expenses or attorney's fees incurred by Lessor, or any fines, penalties, or assessments levied against the Premises by the Association in connection with Lessee's use of the same, any such amount being payable by Lessee upon demand by Lessor as additional rent under the Lease. Failure to abide by any covenant or restriction contained in the Declaration, by any By-Law, or rules or regulations of the Association shall constitute a material breach of the Lease, and such default shall entitle Lessor to exercise any and all remedies as set forth in the Lease.

Lessee agrees to park in only such parking space or spaces as are designated in the Lease, if any, and that the use of the same shall be subject to the terms and provisions of the Declaration, By-Laws and rules and regulations of the Association from time to time.

In the event the Declaration and/or By-Laws contain any "right of first refusal" or "right of first option" providing that the Association shall have the first right or option to lease the Premises under the same terms and provisions contained in the Lease (notwithstanding Lessee's execution of the same), then Lessee agrees that (i) the terms and provisions of the Lease shall be subject to the Association's "right of first refusal" or "right of first option", (ii) that Lessor shall be under no obligation to cause the termination or waiver of such "right of first refusal" or "right of first option", and (iii) in the event that the Association elects to exercise any such "right of first refusal" or "right of first option", Lessor shall not be responsible for any costs, damages or expenses to Lessee, whether direct or indirect, resulting therefrom.

Lessee acknowledges that, under the Declaration, the responsibility for the maintenance and repair of certain portions of the Condominium and for the provision of certain services Lessee may expect to enjoy is the responsibility of the Association and not of Lessor. Accordingly, Lessor shall have no obligation to provide, maintain, or repair those facilities and services under the control of and the responsibility for which lies with the Association.

Lessee shall promptly forward to Lessor any notice received by Lessee from the Association or relating to Association meetings or business or complaints about Lessee's or Lessor's actions or omissions.

__________ (Lessee) LESSOR

__________ (Lessee) By:__________

__________ (Lessee)

DATE:__________, 19____ DATE:__________, 19____

4311

EXHIBIT 18: Condominium Unit Apartment Lease

UNIT LEASE

1. **PARTIES**
LANDLORD ("I") ______________________________

____

Tel: ______________________________

TENANT ("YOU") ______________________________

____

____

2. **AGREEMENT TO LEASE: PROPERTY DESCRIPTION**
I, as Landlord, lease to you, ______________________, as Tenant, Unit No. ________ and Garage Unit No. ________ in [PROJ], [Town], [State] (called the "Unit"). The building and the land on which the building is located known as [PROJ] will be called the "Common Interest Community." The portion outside the Unit including sidewalks, entrances, and passages will be called the "Common Elements." You are also being leased the ownership interest of the Unit in the Common Elements. This lease includes responsibilities toward [ASSN], the association of Unit Owners of [PROJ] ("Association").

3. **TERM OF LEASE**
The term of this Lease is ______________________. The term begins on ______________________ and ends at 12:00 noon on ______________________.

4. **RENT**
You agree to pay me the total rent of __________. Rent is due in advance in monthly installments of __________, on the first day of each month, starting ______________________. The first month's rent is paid upon signing this lease. I will not have to make a demand or send you a bill for payment of rent. If I elect to send rent bills, they will be for convenience only and not a condition of your payment. Payments must be sent to ______________________________ unless I notify you otherwise in writing. You will directly pay to the Association as additional rent, any increase in monthly Common Expense Assessments assessed by the Association against the Unit, above the monthly Common Expense Assessments presently assessed, mending all times late charges. Attorney fees and costs and charges attributed to your tenancy or your default in your obligations under this lease. Also, if this lease, or any options to extend this lease, are for over a year, you will pay as increased monthly rent, one-twelfth of the increase in taxes, insurance and interest payment on my mortgage attributable to the Unit, over those expenses which are currently paid by the Landlord. You will also pay one fifth of any special assessment for capital improvements levied by the association for budget shortfalls or expense items. You will also pay, as additional rent, the cost of electricity billed to the unit, when such bill is sent to you.

5. **SECURITY DEPOSIT**
You agree to pay me a security deposit of __________ on or before ______________________. The security deposit will be held in escrow. It will be returned to you, with interest as required by law, if you fully perform your promises in this Lease. If you breach this Lease, I may apply the security deposit to offset all or part of my damages. The security deposit is not a payment of rent. If I spend some or all of the security deposit for any legal purpose attributable to your tenancy during the term of this Lease, then you will restore it to the full amount on demand.

If I sell the Unit to a new owner, I may assign your security deposit to the new owner. If the security deposit is assigned, I will have no further liability to you with respect to the security deposit.

6. **UTILITIES, SERVICES AND FURNISHINGS**
I will provide the following through the Association:

(a) Hot and cold water in reasonable quantities;

(b) Heat at reasonable hours during cold seasons of the year;

(c) Elevator service;

(d) Electricity in reasonable quantities; and

(e) Air conditioning during warm seasons of the year by through-the-window air conditioner.

The Unit includes a master television antenna and window shades. Either carpeting or hardwood flooring also will be furnished. I will not be required to provide utilities and services during any period when you are in default in payment of rent.

7. **ABUSE OF UTILITIES AND SERVICES**
You agree not to abuse the use of utilities and services provided by the Common Interest Community. If I or the Association believe you are abusing the utilities and/or services, then I may separately meter such utilities and services and charge you for excess use. The charge will be based on your excess use over the average consumed by all units in the Common Interest Community. The Association will compute any such charge.

8. **YOUR RIGHT TO TERMINATE THIS LEASE IF TRANSFERRED OR DRAFTED**
You may terminate this Lease if you are involuntarily activated into the armed forces or if your employer transfers you to a site more than 50 miles away. In order to terminate, you must do the following:

(a) Give me written notice of intent to terminate and of the date of termination, which will be not fewer than 2 months after the next rent payment is due following receipt of the notice;

(b) Give me written proof of transfer or involuntary activation; and

(c) Pay rent in full to the date of termination.

9. **INSURANCE**
If my cost for insurance coverage on the Unit, or the Association's coverage is increased as a result of your occupancy of the Unit and I receive an assessment for such increase, then I may do either of the following:

(a) I may terminate this lease by giving you 30 days' written notice; or

(b) I may charge my increased cost to you as additional rent.

You will pay such charge on demand.

You will be responsible for obtaining your own insurance coverage, including insurance against the risks described in Section 15.

10. **BREACH OF THIS LEASE BY YOU**
If you vacate the Unit or do not pay any installment of rent within 10 days after it is due, then I may take any of the following actions:

(a) I may sue you for damages; and/or

(b) I may terminate the lease immediately by giving you written notice of termination; and/or

(c) I may take any other action against you that I may legally take. Such action can include bringing a summary process lawsuit against you to have you evicted.

If you do not perform any other agreement in this Lease, then I may give you a written notice describing how you have breached the Lease and giving you 21 days from the date when you receive the notice during which you must cure the breach. If you do not cure the breach within 21 days, then I may take any of the following actions:

(a) I may sue you for damages; and/or

(b) If the notice so states, I may terminate this Lease 30 days after your receipt of the notice; and/or

(c) I may take any other action against you that I may legally take. Such action can include bringing a summary process lawsuit to have you evicted.

Nothing in this Section will limit my statutory remedies for breach of this Lease.

11. **COMMON INTEREST COMMUNITY PROVISIONS**
I assign to you my rights, and privileges associated with my ownership of a Unit. You assume, and agree to undertake, the duties and obligations of a Unit Owner. These are described in the Declaration Bylaws, Rules and associated documents for the Common Interest Community ("Common Interest Community Instruments").

However, I exclusively retain the right to vote, to affect my ownership interest, to hold office and receive insurance and other awards and proceeds.

You must communicate with the Association through me, and you must notify me whenever you receive any communication from the Association.

You will hold me harmless for any of your acts or omissions of any kind that adversely affect me under the Common Interest Community Instruments.

Default of any requirement under the Common Interest Community Instruments is a default of this Lease.

You acknowledge receipt of a copy of the Common Interest Community Instruments, which you have examined to the extent you desire—in particular, the Rules attached as an Exhibit to the Public Offering Statement. You also understand that the Association can take enforcement action directly against you for the breach of the Common Interest Community Instruments (as if it were the landlord) and that it may levy fines and other penalties.

12. **COSTS; ATTORNEY'S FEES**
You promise to pay all of my costs of correcting any breach of this Lease by you. If I sue you to enforce my rights under this Lease, then you will pay all of my costs of suit, including attorney's fees to the extent permitted by law.

EXHIBIT 18: Condominium Unit Apartment Lease *(Continued)*

13. OCCUPANCY
This Lease is contingent on the Unit being ready for occupancy by you on the starting date of the term. If it is not ready and I do not give you possession on that date, then the following will result:

(a) The starting date of the term of this Lease will be postponed until possession can be given; and

(b) I will not be liable for any damage incurred by you as a result of such delay; and

(c) The ending date of the term of this Lease will not be extended; and

(d) Your liability for rent will start on the date when I notify you that the Unit is ready for occupancy; and

(e) If occupancy is delayed more than 60 days, you will have the option to cancel this Lease by giving written notice to me.

If you do not take possession of the Unit when possession is offered, or if you vacate or abandon the Unit during the term of this Lease, then I may do the following:

(a) I may enter the Unit as your agent, without a court order and without liability to you;

(b) I may lease the Unit to another tenant, for any term, as your agent; and

(c) I may collect the rent and apply it to your rent and other sums due under this lease.

In such a case, you will be liable for any damages suffered by me. The Unit will be deemed abandoned when you vacate, regardless of whether keys are delivered to me.

14. COMMON ELEMENTS
The Common Elements are provided to accommodate you and the other occupants of the Common Interest Community. To the extent permitted by law, you use those areas solely at your risk. To the extent permitted by law, neither I nor the Association will be liable for any damage, injury or loss of property occurring in the Common Elements, unless caused by our gross negligence.

15. INJURY OR DAMAGE
To the extent permitted by law, neither I nor the Association will be liable for injury or damage to persons or property resulting from risks against which you can insure under an all-risk, extended coverage, comprehensive property insurance policy, including sprinkler leakage insurance.

To the extent permitted by law, neither I nor the Association will be liable for injury or damage resulting from falling plaster or from steam, gas, electricity, water, rain, ice or snow that may leak or flow from or into the Common Interest Community or Unit. To the extent permitted by law, neither I nor the Association will be liable for injury or damage resulting from breakage, leakage, obstruction, or other defects in the pipes, wiring, appliances, plumbing or lighting fixtures in the Common Interest Community, nor resulting from any other cause, unless due to our gross negligence.

You promise to give me and the Association prompt notice of any accident to or defects in the water pipes, gas pipes, heating apparatus, or other equipment or appliances in the Unit.

To the extent permitted by law, neither I nor the Association will be liable for any latent defect in the Common Interest Community, any package left with any of the Association's employees, or any loss by theft or otherwise. Neither I nor the Association will be liable for the acts of the other occupants or for the acts of our employees during the course of work contracted for by you with such employees.

16. RIGHT TO ENTER THE UNIT
I and the Association may enter the Unit without your consent in case of emergency.

We may enter the Unit with your consent at reasonable times after giving you reasonable oral or written notice. Such entries may be made to inspect the Unit, to make necessary or agreed-to repairs, alterations, or improvements, to supply necessary or agreed-to services. I may also enter to show the Unit to interested people. "Interested people" include prospective or actual purchasers, mortgage lenders, tenants, workmen or contractors. You will not unreasonably withhold your consent to such entries.

I and the Association will have all other rights to enter the Unit as may be provided by law.

We will not be responsible for any damage from such entries, except damage caused by our own negligence.

17. REDUCTION OR ABATEMENT OF RENT; INTERRUPTION OF SERVICES
You also will not be entitled to any reduction or abatement of rent or other compensation when services or utilities are interrupted by causes beyond my control or by repairs, alterations or improvements to the Common Interest Community. Such interruptions will not be considered constructive evictions.

18. DAMAGE CAUSED BY YOU
You are liable to me and the Association for any damage sustained by us, or the Unit Owners and caused by you or your guests, family, agents, or employees. I will charge such damage to you as additional rent, which will be due on demand.

19. TERMINATION OF LEASE
You will vacate and surrender the Unit promptly at the end of the term or on the earlier termination of this Lease. You will leave the Unit in good condition, broom clean, reasonable wear and tear expected. You will repair any damages caused by you, restoring the Unit to its condition at the starting date of this Lease. You will clean, scrub, and polish all fixtures, appliances, and apartment surfaces prior to surrender. If you delay in surrendering the Unit, you will indemnify me against any damages resulting from such daily delay. Such damages may include claims by a succeeding tenant against me based on delay in delivering possession.

20. DAMAGE TO COMMON INTEREST COMMUNITY
If the Common Interest Community is damaged by fire or other cause, where applicable, the Association will repair the Common Elements, and that portion of the Unit that it must insure, to the extent of insurance, pursuant to the Common Interest Community Instruments. I will repair the damage on that portion of the Unit that I must insure as quickly as is reasonably possible after receipt of notice of the damage. You will notify both me and the Association of any such damage. The time for making repairs will be extended by any time lost due to adjustment of insurance claims, labor disputes, or causes beyond control.

If the damage is so extensive as to render the Unit untenantable, then you will not be required to pay rent from the time of the damage until the Unit has been restored to a tenantable condition.

If the Common Interest Community suffers substantially total destruction, or if the damage cannot be repaired within 90 days, or if the Association decides to remodel or reconstruct the Common Interest Community, then this Lease will terminate as of the date of the destruction. You will have no duty to pay rent after such destruction. Any rent paid for a period after the destruction will be refunded. In such event, you will promptly vacate the Unit. You will remain liable for any damage caused by you or by your family, guests, agents, or employees.

21. EMINENT DOMAIN
If any part of the Common Interest Community is taken by eminent domain, then I will have the option of terminating this Lease. In order to terminate, I must give you 10 days' written notice of termination. If I elect to terminate this Lease, you will be liable for rent up to the time of termination.

You will have no claim to any awards for or taking by eminent domain. You hereby assign all such awards to me.

22. ASSIGNMENT, SUBLET
You will not assign this Lease, sublet, or permit occupancy of any portion of the Unit by anyone other than you, without my prior written consent, which I may withhold in my absolute discretion.

23. RENT COLLECTION
If I accept a partial payment of rent, it will not constitute a waiver of my right to full payment. No endorsement on a check or letter accompanying a partial payment of rent will be a waiver of my right to full payment or will be an accord and satisfaction.

If rent is not paid or postmarked by the 5th day of the month, a late charge of $15.00 per month will be added. You will pay such late charge promptly, without my having to make a demand.

If this Lease is assigned or sublet, or if the Unit is occupied by anyone other than you, I may collect rent from such other occupant. Acceptance of rent will not be a waiver of your promise not to assign, sublet, or permit occupancy. Nor will acceptance of rent be acceptance of the other occupant as tenant. You will remain personally liable for all promises in this Lease, regardless of any assignment, sublease, or other occupancy.

24. TRANSFER BY LANDLORD
Whenever any third party succeeds to my rights under this Lease, I will be released from my obligations under this Lease. Your only remedy for any subsequent violation of my promises in this Lease will be against the third party. The terms of this Section will apply whether or not the third party has assumed my duties under this Lease.

25. SUBORDINATION
This Lease is subordinate to all existing mortgages, of the Unit and the Common Interest Community and to any mortgages of the Unit or the Common Interest Community in the future. You will not have to sign any documents to make this Lease subordinate to those mortgages. However, if any of my mortgage landers so request, you will sign such a document. You hereby irrevocably appoint me your attorney-in-fact to sign and deliver any such documents.

26. CONTINUING POSSESSION
If you do not vacate the Unit when this Lease expires and if you remain in possession with my consent or acquiescence, then your occupancy will be a two-month-to-two-month tenancy under the terms of this Lease.

I may notify you at least 45 days before this Lease expires that I intend to extend this lease for an additional period of time equal to the original term of this Lease. Any such extension must be on the same terms as this Lease, except that I may increase the rent.

If you receive such a notice and *do not want* to extend this Lease under those terms, you may give me notice of your intent to leave. You must deliver that notice to me at least 30 days before the expiration of this Lease. You also must vacate the Unit by the time when the Lease expires. This Lease will be extended automatically if you do not give the required notice and vacate.

If you receive such a notice, and you *want* to stay in the Unit under those terms you do not have to take any action. This Lease will be extended automatically.

27. WAIVER
If either party does not insist on strict performance of the promises in this Lease, it is not a waiver. Either party may insist on strict performance if the Lease is breached in the same manner again.

EXHIBIT 18: Condominium Unit Apartment Lease *(Continued)*

28. MODIFICATIONS
Any modifications of this Lease must be in writing, signed by me and by you.

29. ENTIRE AGREEMENT
This Lease is the entire agreement between me and you. It supersedes all previous discussions or agreements, whether written or oral, execpt as described in Section 30.

30. LEASE APPLICATION
Your lease application is made a part of this Lease. If your application contains any material misrepresentations, it will be a breach of this Lease by you.

31. NOTICES
Notices must be in writing and must be mailed or hand delivered to me or to you at the addresses shown in Section 1 and to you at your Unit.

32. ALTERATIONS
You will make no alterations, additions or improvements to the Unit without my prior, written approval. If such alterations are those requiring approval, you must also receive that approval, which must be requested through me. If approved, you will use only contractors or mechanics acceptable to me. I and the Association must also approve the time and manner of performing the work. You will keep the Unit free of mechanics' liens resulting from the work. You will promptly remove any such liens that attach to the Unit.

Any alterations or improvements that are attached to the building or grounds so that they cannot be removed without injury to the building or grounds will be my property.

33. SEVERABILITY
If any portion of this Lease is found to be void, unenforceable, or against public policy, the remaining portions of this Lease will not be affected.

34. RULES
You will comply with the following rules and the rules of the Association. These rules may be modified or supplemented by me or the Association from time to time. Any new or modified rules will not substantially alter the terms of this Lease. You will be notified in writing of any changes in the rules.

(a) You will not post any sign of any kind on the Unit.

(b) No sign indicating commercial uses may be displayed outside a Unit.

(c) You will not attach any awnings or other projections to the outside of the Unit. You will not install any blinds, shades, screens, or drapes, except drapes having a beige lining, without my prior written consent.

(d) You will receive two keys to the Unit. Additional keys will be furnished at a charge of $2.00 each.

(e) I, the Executive Board, and the Manager or its designated agent may retain a pass key to the Unit for immediate entry in emergency situations and entry for general repair purposes on 12 hour notice. No new locks may be installed and no locks may be altered without my consent. If consent is given, you will provide me, the Executive Board, and the Manager or its designated agent with all keys necessary to gain access to the Unit.

(f) If you require the loan of a duplicate key from the Association, there may be a charge. The charge is payable to the employee giving you entrance.

(g) No lessee will alter any lock or install a new lock on any door of any premises without immediately providing the Executive Board and the Manager or its agent, with a key therefor.

(h) Employees of the Association will not be sent on errands off the property by a tenant, at any time, for any purpose.

(i) Nothing will be allowed to fall from windows or doors. Nothing will be swept or thrown into the Common Elements, ventilators or other areas.

(j) Nothing will be hung from windows or doors.

(k) No air conditioning or appliance installation, telephone extension, or exterior radio or television antenna installation will be made without my prior, written consent. Any attachment to the outside of the building without the Association's consent may be removed by me or the Association. When consent is granted, you will pay the cost of installation.

(l) You and your visitors, agents, employees, and family members may park only in the area, if any, assigned to your Unit. You will abide by the Parking Rules established by the Association.

(m) Each Unit is restricted to residential use as a single-family residence including home professional pursuits not requiring regular visits from the public or unreasonable levels of mail, shipping, trash or storage requirements. A single-family residence is defined as a single housekeeping Unit, operating between its occupants on a nonprofit, noncommercial basis, cooking and eating with a common kitchen and dining area, with not more regular overnight occupants than two per bedroom as designated on the plans on file with the building official of [Town] or by local ordinance.

(n) Roomers and boarders paying consideration for their tenancy are prohibited.

(o) Rent will be paid at the address above, by mail or in person. Checks will be payable to me.

(p) The garbage disposal will be used only for food waste.

(q) Any changes in your family size or composition must be reported to me.

(r) I will provide light bulbs at the start of the Lease. You will replace all light bulbs that burn out during the term of this Lease.

(s) Any packages, keys, money, or other property left by you with any employee of the Association are left at your risk.

(t) Nothing will be fastened to any part of the Unit or the Common Elements. No holes will be drilled or nails or screws inserted in any structure, and no interior surfaces will be decorated or covered, without my prior, written consent.

(u) You will not run any exposed wires for electrical appliances or fixtures.

(v) Toilets, sinks, faucets, and other water equipment will be used only for the purposes for which they are intended. No improper articles may be thrown into them. No faucets will be left open. Damage caused by the misuse of water equipment will be borne by you, if it is caused by you or occurs in the Unit.

(w) Carpeting will be cared for in accordance with my instructions.

(x) All noises, including music, television and radio, will be held to reasonable levels. During the time from 11:00 p.m. to 7:00 a.m., no noises will be audible outside of the Unit.

(y) You must not place doormats or other obstructions at the Unit entrance.

(z) All exterior Unit doors must be kept closed. Sliding windows and glass doors will be kept closed when the Unit is unoccupied.

(aa) You must exercise diligence to conserve heat, air conditioning, electricity, and water.

(bb) You must comply with all government laws and regulations, whether federal, state, or municipal, and the Association rules, that impose on you the duty of compliance. You will indemnify me against any damage or fines resulting from your violation of any such laws and regulations.

(cc) Nothing may be done or kept in any Unit which will increase the rate of insurance of the buildings or the contents thereof beyond the rates applicable for residential apartments without prior written consent of the Executive Board. No Unit owner may permit anything to be done or kept in his Unit which will result in the cancellation of insurance on any of the buildings or the contents thereof or which would be in violation of any law. You will comply with the rules and regulations contained in any fire insurance policy, Association or landlord policy affecting the Unit.

(dd) No electrical appliances may be used in the Unit except those that may be connected or disconnected by a standard floor or wall plug. No washers or dryers may be installed or used in the Unit, except where outlets and vents are located.

(ee) No dogs, cats or other pets will be kept in the Unit without my prior, written consent, and the consent of the Association. Seeing eye dogs will be permitted for those persons holding certificates of blindness and necessity (20/200 in the better with correction).

(ff) Pets may not be kept, bred or maintained for any commercial purposes.

(gg) Any pet causing or creating a nuisance or unreasonable disturbance or noise will be permanently removed from the Property upon three (3) days' written Notice and Hearing from the Executive Board.

(hh) No knockers may be installed on any doors.

(ii) No noxious of offensive activities may be carried on in any Unit nor may anything be done therein either willfully or negligently which may be or become an annoyance or nuisance to the other Unit Owners or occupants or which interferes with the peaceful possession and proper use of the property by its residents. All valid laws, zoning ordinances and regulations of all governmental bodies having jurisdiction thereof will be observed. Each Lessee will be obligated to maintain his/her own Unit and keep it in good order and repair.

(jj) Each Unit may have closets, safes or vaults not exceeding 50 cubic feet in capacity which may be locked and to which the Executive Board may not have access.

(kk) No sprinkler head will be tampered with, painted, blocked, enclosed or otherwise interfered with so as to hinder its efficiency or purpose, nor may anything be hung from it.

(ll) Weathertight integrity of windows and doors will be maintained by the Unit Owner and/or Lessee.

(mm) Lessees will not cause or permit anything to be hung or displayed on the windows or placed on the outside walls of any of the buildings and no sign, awning, canopy, shutter or radio or television antenna will be affixed to or placed upon the exterior walls or roofs without the prior consent of the Executive Board, nor will they cause or permit anything to be hung or displayed on the inside of windows intended to be seen from the outside except for the standard blinds and draperies described below, as follows, including without limiting the foregoing, "For Sale" or "For Lease" signs and the like.

(nn) A smoke detector must be installed, and operative, in every Unit.

(oo) In the event any sales or service tax is imposed upon a Unit which is not owner-occupied or which is otherwise not imposed equally on all Unit Owners, the landlord or other Unit Owner will pay such tax through the Association as an additional Common Expense assessment. The Association may require certificates of status from Unit Owners in order to enforce and determine applicability of such impositions.

(pp) The use of Common Elements is subject to the Bylaws and the Rules of the Association.

(qq) Heat must be maintained in each Unit to at least ________°F at all times so as to maintain the integrity of the sprinkler system and to prevent freezing of lines or components.

EXHIBIT 18: Condominium Unit Apartment Lease *(Continued)*

(rr) Unit Owners or Lessees are advised to clean the air filters of their air conditioning and heat pump system at least 4 times per year to minimize operating costs and reduce risk of equipment failure.

(ss) No lease may be for a period of less than 60 days.

(tt) Utility charges through separate meters, community antenna T.V. and telephone charges will be paid directly by the Unit Owner and/or Lessee to the utility providing such service.

(uu) Washer hookups are provided in the Unit. Dryer connections and vents are provided; however, some dryer vent stacks may be long and require adequate fan pressure to get rid of the exhaust. Vents and stacks will have to be cleaned by the Lessee contributing to the lint build-up.

(vv) Trash removal is by dumpster at various locations in the premises. Each Lessee is responsible for removal of trash to the dumpster location. In the future, trash may have to be separated and segregated by type. This will be the occupant's responsibility.

(ww) Heat is by heat pump, with roof compressors maintained by the Unit Owner or Lessee and normal maintenance, major repairs or component replacement is at the cost of the appurtenant Unit Owner. Heat pumps are efficient down to air temperature in the twenties F°, at which point resistance heat is used to supplement the heat pump. Resistance heat is very expensive, and occupants should be judicious in maintaining high inside temperatures, open windows or other heat leaks or the cost may go up significantly. The Unit Owner is responsible for his or her own maintenance fees.

(xx) Except pursuant to Article ____________ of the Declaration, nothing may be done to any Unit which will impair the structural integrity of the building or buildings or which will structurally change them. No Lessee may do any work which may jeopardize the soundness or safety of the property, reduce the value thereof or impair any easements, right of purchase or any interest constituting a Common Element.

35. SPECIAL TERMS
Special terms of this Lease, if any, are as follows:

____

____

____

____

____

____

36. BINDING EFFECT
This Lease is binding on you and me and on our respective heirs, successors, executors, and administrators.

This Lease will be placed on file with the Association at its office or agent's office located ______________________________.

Dated, this __________ day of ______________________________, 19________.

WITNESS: LANDLORD:

______________________________ By: ______________________________
Its

____

TENANT:

______________________________ ______________________________

______________________________ ______________________________

I hereby acknowledge receipt of, and acceptance of compliance with, the Declaration, survey and plans recorded and filed pursuant to the provisions of the Common Interest Ownership Act, Bylaws, and Rules of the Common Interest Community, and to attorn to the Association as Landlord, granting it severally with the Unit Owner, the right following notice to the Unit Owner of a hearing and an opportunity to cure, to evict a tenant for violation of these documents in the name of, and as attorney-in-fact for the Unit Owner.

BY:

____
Lessee

____
Date

YOUR STATEMENT AS TO PHYSICAL CONDITION AND REPAIR

You agree that you have examined the Unit and the Common Interest Community, and that you are satisfied with their condition. You agree that you have received them in good order and repair except as otherwise stated in this Lease. You agree that neither I nor the Association have made any representation as to condition or repair and no promise to decorate, alter, repair or improve the Unit except as otherwise stated in this Lease.

TENANT:

Date: ______________________________ ______________________________

____

Lease Extension Agreement

When renewing a lease you can do one of two things. One option is to present the resident with a brand-new lease, typed on a regular lease form. If you decide to use a new lease, you should type the words *First Renewal, Second Renewal* and so on on the top of the form. This will remind you that your tenant has been in occupancy for longer than one year when it comes time to renew the following year.

Another option is to use a lease extension agreement (exhibit 19) that can be used instead of a regular lease form or for lease renewals that are for periods less than a full year. Indicate the existence of this rider by making a notation on the original lease.

Refer to chapter 6 for further information on the procedures to follow and the forms to use in obtaining renewals.

EXHIBIT 19: Lease Extension Agreement

THIS AGREEMENT made this ________ day of ____________ 19 ____ by and between ____ (LESSOR) and ____ (LESSEE[S]).

WITNESSETH

WHEREAS, LESSOR and LESSEE have entered into a certain lease agreement dated ______________ 19 ____ for the rental of a certain apartment, number ______ located at ____

____

WHEREAS, LESSOR and LESSEE desire to extend the duration of said Lease;

NOW THEREFORE, for value received, receipt of which is hereby acknowledged by LESSOR, the parties agree as follows:

1. The termination date of said Lease is hereby extended from ____________ __________ 19____ to and including ______________________ 19____
2. The monthly rental amount during the aforesaid extension period will be $______
3. Except as modified hereby, the terms and conditions of aforesaid Lease are hereby confirmed and ratified and made a part of this agreement and said Lease shall remain in full force and effect.

IN WITNESS WHEREOF, this agreement has been duly executed by the parties hereto on the day and year first above written.

______________________	______________________
LESSEE	LESSOR
______________________	______________________
LESSEE	DATE

Lease Cancellation Rider

A lease cancellation rider (exhibit 20) is a useful form that can be offered to new or renewal residents who are not able to fully complete their lease term. For complete details on terminating or cancelling a lease, see chapter 7. Some acceptable reasons for agreeing to this rider: The resident has an upcoming job transfer or is in the market to purchase a home. It is not intended for use when the tenant requests to break a lease during the middle of a lease term. If tenants want to cancel their leases in mid-term, a different form can be used (exhibit 21).

Prospective tenants may ask to have a transfer clause written into the lease that would suit the same purpose of breaking a lease term early, but it is better to use the cancellation rider instead because it clearly spells out the conditions and procedures a tenant must follow to invoke it, i.e., tenants must give 60 days' notice, must not be in default of the lease, must be current in their rent and must pay a cancellation fee (the usual amount is one to two months' rent). The fee is payable in advance at the time the residents decide to exercise their right to cancel.

As with all riders, it should be signed, and you should make a notation on the original lease that a cancellation rider exists.

Furniture Rental Rider

If you rent your units as furnished apartments, you can attach a furniture rental rider (exhibit 22) to your lease forms. This document spells out the terms and conditions under which a tenant accepts the apartment as a furnished unit.

Any additional rents and/or security deposit monies should be indicated on the original lease in the space provided. On the rider, you would indicate the quantity of each item listed along with any additional items not printed on the form.

Before the tenant moves in, you, together with the tenant, should inspect the furnishings and create a written record of damaged items (a camera can be used to document the condition of your property). Repeat this process when the resident moves out, noting any new damage or missing pieces. The resident can be charged for any damages other than ordinary wear and tear, such as broken items, cuts or burns in upholstery and so on. Pay particular attention to carpet stains if a pet will be in the unit.

Furnished apartment leases, available at stationery or office supply stores, can be used for the same purpose.

EXHIBIT 20: Lease Cancellation Rider

LEASE CANCELLATION RIDER

THIS RIDER is hereby made a part of and incorporated as part of a certain lease agreement dated____________________(ie: starting date of current lease), for an apartment ("the Premises") located at____________________in____________________, Illinois, by and between ("Lessor") and ____________________ ____________________("Lessee").

THE TERMS AND CONDITIONS OF THIS RIDER SHALL GOVERN OVER THE TERMS AND CONDITIONS OF THE ATTACHED LEASE AGREEMENT.

The Lessee shall have the right to terminate this Lease on the last day of any calendar month during the Lease term by giving the Lessor **not less than sixty (60) days prior written notice** of the Lessee's intention to terminate Lease.

The Lessee's right to terminate shall only be effective under the following conditions:

1.) Not less than sixty (60) days prior written notice to the intended lease expiration.
2.) Lessee is not in default of the Lease terms and conditions.
3.) Lessee shall remit to Lessor the sum of $300.00 (three hundred dollars) as compensation for the cancellation.
4.) Fee is to be paid at the time the written notice is given.
5.) Cancellatior fee shall not be deducted from any security monies on deposit.
6.) All rents and late charges are paid in full up to the time of the intended Lease expiration.

LESSOR:

BY:____________________ ____________________
LESSEE

DATE:____________________ ____________________
LESSEE

EXHIBIT 21: Agreement to Cancel Lease

AGREEMENT TO CANCEL LEASE

FOR AND IN CONSIDERATION of ______________________________ ______________, LESSOR, allowing the undersigned to cancel prior to its expiration, that certain Lease ("Lease") dated__________________, 19________between LESSOR and____for an apartment located at ________________________________in________________Illinois, I hereby agree to the following:

1. To pay a sum equal to two months' of Lease rent prior to moving from and vacating the apartment;
2. To promptly return the apartment keys to LESSOR prior to moving from and vacating the apartment;
3. To provide my forwarding address to LESSOR prior to moving from and vacating the apartment;
4. To leave the apartment in a clean condition and free of any and all damages;
5. To move from and vacate the apartment on or before________________, 19,__ which shall be the cancellation date of the Lease.

It is further understood that my security deposit is fully refundable, provided that I have complied with the aforesaid and further provided that there are no unpaid charges of any kind on my account as of the date the Lease is cancelled.

In the event the undersigned is in default under the aforesaid Lease as determined by LESSOR then LESSOR shall have the right to keep and apply the aforesaid cancellation fee toward any damages arising as a result of such default.

The undersigned, as additional consideration for this Agreement, does hereby forever release any claim, cause or causes of action which it may have or which shall arise in the future against LESSOR its officers, directors, employees or agents arising out of the aforesaid Lease.

This agreement shall be null and void if not strictly complied with.

DATED:__________________________

______________________________	______________________________
Resident Signature	LESSOR

____
Resident Signature

EXHIBIT 22: Furniture Rental Rider

FURNITURE RIDER

This Rider is hereby made a part of and incorporated as part of a certain lease agreement ("Lease") dated__________, 19___ for an apartment located at__________ __________in__________ Illinois ("Premises"); by and between__________ ("Lessor") and__________ __________ __________("Lessee").

To the extent of any conflict in terms, the terms and conditions of this Rider shall govern over the terms and conditions of the aforesaid Lease.

In consideration of the furniture rental deposit of the sum of__________ ($__________) Dollars upon execution hereof and Lessee's covenant, hereby made, to pay to Lessor a monthly furniture rental fee in the sum of__________ ($__________) Dollars on the first day of each month commencing__________, 19___, the parties agree to the following:

1. Lessor shall permit Lessee to use the articles of personal property listed on Schedule I ("Furniture") solely in the Premises for the term of the Lease. For all purposes of the Lease not inconsistent with this Rider, the Furniture shall be considered part of the Premises, and the above rental fee shall be deemed rent under the Lease. Title to the Furniture shall at all times be in Lessor, and Lessee shall not remove from the Premises, dispose of nor cause any lien to be placed upon any of the Furniture.
2. Lessee has examined the Furniture before signing this Rider and is satisfied with its physical condition; and Lessee's execution of this Rider shall be conclusive evidence of Lessee's acknowledgement that the Furniture is in good condition and repair, except as may be indicated on this Rider and initialed by Lessor. Lessee shall at all times maintain the Furniture in good condition and repair, without alterations, and upon termination of the Lease for any reason, the Furniture shall be returned to Lessor in substantially the same condition as when received by Lessee. Lessee shall be liable to Lessor for any loss or destruction of, or damage to the furniture, from whatever cause, occurring during the term of the Lease, ordinary wear and tear excepted.
3. The Furniture is not subject to any express nor implied warranties from either the manufacturer thereof or Lessor. Specifically, but without limitation, THERE ARE NO IMPLIED WARRANTIES OF MERCHANTABILITY OR FITNESS FOR A PARTICULAR PURPOSE. Lessee shall indemnify and hold Lessor totally harmless from and against each and every claim for personal injury and/or property damage occurring in connection with any of the Furniture being on the Premises and/or its use by any person during the term hereof.
4. Lessee agrees that in the event of any violation of the terms and conditions of the Lease and/or of this Rider, in addition to all of its rights upon default under the Lease, Lessor shall have the right to make a demand for immediate possession of the Furniture. Any refusal by Lessee to comply with such demand shall entitle Lessor to retain the aforementioned deposit as well as to enforce any and all other remedies provided by law or equity. However, if Lessee returns the Furniture upon such demand, the deposit shall be returned less damages, if any, caused by violation hereof.

SCHEDULE I

Qty.	Item	Qty.	Item	Qty.	Item	Qty.	Item
	Chest Bed 1		3/3 Head Board		Chair		
	Dresser		4/6 Mattress		Ottoman		
	Mirror		4/6 Box Spring		Chair		
	Nite Table		3/3 Mattress		End Table		
	Lamp		3/3 Box Spring		Stick Lamp		
	Chest Bed 2		Frame		Cocktail Table		
	Dresser		Corner Unit		Table Lamp		
	Mirror		Corner Table		Dining Room Table		
	Nite Table		Sofa		Dining Room Chair		
	Lamp		Love Seat		Etagere		
	4/6 Head Board		Hida Bed		Bookcase		
	Bar		Bar Stool		TV		
	TV Stand		Res Desk		Res Desk Chair		
	Drapes		Picture				

IN WITNESS WHEREOF, the Lessor and Lessee have executed this document on the__________ day of__________, 19_____.

By:__________ __________
LESSEE

____
LESSEE

4314 REV. 7-1-84

Double Deposit Clause

This is not a separate rider, but a clause that is typed on the face of the lease document. The intent of this provision is to allow residents to build their credit with you.

If an otherwise desirable prospective resident has a salary that does not satisfy the minimum required to qualify for the apartment, or if the prospect is new to the area or has recently graduated college and has not yet established a credit history, you can elect to charge an additional security deposit.

Type the following clause in the special provisions section of the lease:

> $________ of security deposit may be used for *(month/year)* rent provided all prior rents have been paid on the first of the month.

We suggest using the seventh month of the lease in the clause. The resident will demonstrate financial stability by paying rent on time for six months. You then apply the extra security deposit to pay the seventh months' rent.

The extra security deposit should also be listed on the top of the lease under "other required deposit."

Appliance Clause

If residents want to use their own appliances and you, as the landlord, allow it, you can type the following statement(s) on the front of the lease: "Lessee owns refrigerator," or "Lessee owns stove," or "Lessee owns air conditioner." Record the brand name and model number of the appliance(s) on a separate sheet of paper attached to the lease or in the tenant file. This procedure can be used for new or existing leases.

The resident should be required to pay for disconnecting, moving, storing and reconnecting your appliances.

Prorated or Free-Rent Programs

For a variety of reasons, tenants often do not or cannot move in on the first day of the month. Your property may not allow moving in on the weekends, or the first day of the month may fall on a weekday and the tenant may not be able to take the day off to move. Lease start dates almost always begin on the first, and if tenants cannot move in that day, they may request a rent adjustment because of moving in late, or you may allow them to move in early.

For example, suppose you have a vacant apartment that was rented for October 1 and the tenants want to move in on Saturday, September 27, three days before the lease actually begins. You could either waive the proration and allow them the three days for free, or you could charge the tenants for three days' rent.

On the other hand, if that same Saturday fell on October 4 or 5, and that day was the first opportunity the tenants had to move, you could rebate a couple of days' rent, if requested, or elect not to make an adjustment. If your rules prevented a tenant from moving in on the first, then you should probably prorate the rent for that month. If the tenant was in possession of the keys and could have moved on October 1 you would not allow a proration.

Rent can be also prorated for middle-of-the-month leases. For example, if tenants want to move in on the fifteenth, you can charge a half month's rent. A good idea is to require tenants to pay the half month plus the first full month before moving in. The lease date would begin on the fifteenth, but end on the last day of the month one year later.

If you are in a soft rental market with a potential vacancy coming up and have decided to offer free rent as a concession (see chapter 3), the gratuity should be taken before the year's lease goes into effect. If a resident is going to move into an apartment on September 1, taking advantage of the free rent, you have two options. The first option is to give the residents a one-month lease at no rent for September and then a separate 12-month lease starting October 1.

The second option is to start the lease on September 1 and end it on September 30 of the following year, indicating on the form that the rent begins October 1. This option has one disadvantage: The lease shows that there was a rent concession. You might want to avoid revealing this in case the building is offered for sale. In both cases, the residents occupy the apartment for 13 months but pay rent for only 12 and the residents have not been allowed to move into the building without signing a lease.

Security deposit monies and the rent for October should be collected before turning over possession to the residents.

Delivering the Lease

Residents should not be permitted to move in until the lease is signed and all deposits are paid. Deposits should be paid before the lease is signed, to allow time for checks to clear. While some owners may elect to allow partial payments or other special deals, this is not a good policy.

Preparing the Lease

When initiating a new lease, the letter *N* can be typed on the top left-hand corner signifying that it is a new lease. For a renewal lease, type *R$* (indicating a renewal) and the previous rental amount: for example *R$350.*

A replacement lease can be prepared whenever there is any change in the original lease; for example, if a resident takes a roommate or a resident moves from one apartment to another in the same building. The word *Replacement* can be typed in the top left-hand corner, and a note can be stapled to the front indicating the type of change.

For replacement leases, the starting date should be the date the change takes effect and the termination date should be the same as the termination date of the original lease. A replacement lease should not be used when an original resident vacates and someone else moves in.

Type the name(s) of the resident(s) under the lessee signature lines. You will then be able to see at a glance whether you are lacking signatures on move-in day. If there is a cosigner, both names should appear and the word *cosigner* should be typed after the name. Each copy of the lease and any lease riders should carry an original signature. Separate the copies for ease of signing.

If any changes or corrections are made on the lease or lease riders after typing, each change must be initialed by both the lessor and lessee(s).

Signing the Lease

Documents in the lease package (see chapter 5) should be signed on, or preferably before, the actual day of move-in. When new residents arrive, ask them to take a few moments and read the lease package documents before signing them. If the residents seem reluctant to take the time, or are in a hurry, make sure they read at least the bold print at the top of the lease, the rules and regulations on the back of the lease and the attached riders.

Explain that these documents detail such things as the charge for late payment of rent and the penalty for using a security deposit to pay rent and that residents should be aware of these rules. If you have not already done so, explain the basic policies for residency now, so the residents can not claim ignorance of these policies later on.

All occupants 18 years old or older should sign all copies of the lease, the security deposit rider and all other riders and forms. The dates the lessee and lessor signed the lease should be noted under the signatures. If one of the occupants is not present at the time of move-in (and therefore cannot sign the lease documents), the move-in can and probably should be postponed to a later date.

Keys to the apartment should be given out only after the lease has been signed by all lessees.

The Lease Package

After the lease and other documents have been signed by both parties, the documents are ready to be sorted and placed in the lease package to be given to the resident.

Keep the originals, including all original copies of applicable riders. Staple the lease on top of all other papers. If a resident has paid any monies, for example, the first month's rent on a new lease or a security deposit upgrade on a renewal lease, a receipt, if issued, can be stapled in front of the lease.

The second copy of the lease and all riders are placed in the lease package for the resident.

Unsigned or Undelivered Lease

If a previously agreed-to rental agreement that was signed by a resident is not countersigned by the owner and the owner turns over possession of the apartment and accepts rent, the rental agreement will, in most states, still be in effect, as if it had been signed by the owner and delivered to the resident.

The same things hold true if an owner signs and delivers a previously agreed-upon lease to a tenant and the tenant does not countersign it. If the tenant takes possession of the apartment and pays rent, it will be as if the lease was actually signed.

Generally, if an unsigned or undelivered lease provided for a term longer than one year, it is effective only for one year under the Statute of Frauds in most states and, in effect, it becomes an oral lease. As an example, tenant Brown agrees to and signs a written lease covering a term of two years for a rental of $500 a month. Landlord Smith agrees to the terms of the lease but does not countersign or deliver the document. Since it is oral, the lease term is effectively reduced to a period of one year.

Resident Files

You should maintain an active alphabetical file, using legal-size manila folders, containing vital information on each resident. Keep copies of the following items in the file for each resident: lease, application, lease riders, credit information, repair bills for the apartment, letters or other correspondence, rent receipts and other receipts.

As a safeguard against possible discrimination claims, you should probably save all rejected applications for at least two years.

5900

5

Moving New Tenants In . . .

David Audino *negotiates, purchases and finances major investment–quality real estate properties for Inland Real Estate Corporation. He also owns and manages multiresidential income properties.*

"With the major impact of HR3838, the Tax Reform Act, that has stunned the real estate investor, it is now more important than ever to take a hard look at what the government will and will not allow with regard to tax shelters.

"In today's real estate environment, a concentrated effort must be demonstrated in order to play the game, especially with the type of sophisticated players out there. Remember, you must obtain a return on all three of the ingredients of a successful project: return for your time, a return for your skill and a return for your money.

"Move-in day is a critical event in the landlord-tenant relationship. It's important to make a detailed list of the apartment's condition prior to move-in. The list will be compared to a later list completed when the tenant moves out. Another important item is to make sure tenants have called the utility companies to have their services connected and the accounts placed in their names.

"Coordinating moving a new tenant in with an old tenant moving out can be tricky. Once I had a tenant ready to move in on the first, but the old tenant had not yet moved out. Luckily for me, I had a special clause in the lease stating that the lease would not take effect until delivery of the apartment and actual occupancy.

"Even so, this situation was a potential problem, but I solved it when the existing tenant vacated several days later. I prorated the rent for the new tenant and charged the old tenant $50.00 a day as hold-over rent (according to the lease). Fifty dollars per day is a financial disincentive to anyone thinking of staying on after the lease has expired. The money was deducted from the security deposit."

Make Moving Day Go Smoothly

The move-in process is important in setting the stage for the business relationship between you and the residents. Moving is an emotional and stressful experience and if the new residents are dissatisfied with their move-in, this feeling will last for months and may even permeate their entire term of residency.

Some factors adversely affecting a move are out of your control. There can be problems with the movers, delays in leaving the old residence and complications in unloading in the new apartment. If tenants are moving out of an elevator building on a busy day and cannot get an elevator reserved for their exclusive use, a relatively simple two-hour move could take all day.

You can't ease the move-in, but you can coordinate details to make the process of moving in as trouble-free and pleasurable as possible for the new residents. Make sure the keys are in order. Schedule the freight elevator for their exclusive use. Check to see that the utilities have been turned on in the new tenants' names. Give instructions on where they can store extra items. Show them the laundry room facilities. Be on hand to handle any complaints.

This is a time to keep in close communication with the tenants, being ready to assist in any way possible to ease tensions and help expedite the moving process. If at all possible, you should be on the premises during the move-in. Your physical presence can serve to reassure tenants that you care about them and share their desire to make this difficult day go as smoothly as possible.

Pre-Inspecting the Apartment

Inspecting the Apartment with the Residents

You should inspect the apartment with the new residents after they sign the lease. Items that are damaged, but not to an extent to warrant replacement (minor burns in carpeting, chips in a sink, scratches on the appliances), should be indicated on the pre-inspection form (exhibit 23). Wallpaper that is in good condition left by a previous resident and so on should be noted. If the damaged item, such as a missing closet roller or dripping faucet, is scheduled for repair, it should not be listed.

By signing this form, the residents indicate that the premises are in satisfactory physical condition at the time of move-in, and promise that the premises will be left in the same condition at the end of the tenancy.

Last-Minute Check

A few days before the residents arrive for move-in, inspect the apartment again. Fill out the property inspection form (exhibit 24). Check for cleanliness and a good paint job; see that plumbing, lights, appliances and utilities are operating properly; make sure the doors and locks open and close easily; check to ensure you have sufficient keys that properly work on all locks. This inspection should be done several days prior to move-in to allow sufficient time to make any necessary repairs. Then a follow-up inspection should be conducted when all deficiencies have been corrected.

Common Complaints at Move-In

Careful planning and scheduling and the physical inspections and hands-on testing of everything in the apartment should eliminate most potential problems. Even so, problems can arise. Here are some common complaints at move-in time, with suggested responses.

EXHIBIT 23: Pre-Inspection Form

DATE ISSUED TO RESIDENT ____________, 19 ____

RESIDENT MUST RETURN THIS FORM TO THE LESSOR WITHIN 7 DAYS

PRE-INSPECTION

Resident ______________________ Bldg. ______________ Apt. ______________

Lease Date ______________ No. of Children ________ Ages ________ Pets ________

	MGR.'S INITIALS	RESIDENT COMMENTS		MGR.'S INITIALS	RESIDENT COMMENTS
KITCHEN			**LIVING ROOM (cont'd)**		
Stove Top			Burns		
Burners			**Intercom Working**		
Light Works			**T.V. Antenna Plate In**		
Clock Works			**Air Conditioner**		
Hood			Clean		
Exhaust Fan			Working		
Light Works			Filter Inside		
Oven			**HALLWAY**		
Two Racks			**Guest Closet**		
Clean			Bi-fold Doors		
Broiler			Shelf & Rod In		
One Pan			Doors Clean		
One Grill			Handles On		
Clean			**Linen Closet**		
Refrigerator			Bi-fold Doors		
Freezer Clean			Clean		
Two Ice Trays			Shelves In		
Door Shelf Bars			Handles On		
Refrig. Clean			**BATHROOM**		
Three Shelves			**Toilet**		
Crisper Glass			Clean		
Crisper Drawer			Working		
Light Works			**Sink**		
Egg Bin			Clean		
Disposal			Faucets Okay		
Working			**Medicine Cabinet**		
Removed			Clean		
Lights			Mirrors Intact		
Over Sink			Knobs on Mirrors		
Ceiling			**Bathtub**		
Dining Area			Clean		
Door			Faucet		

EXHIBIT 23: Pre-Inspection Form *(Continued)*

Item			Item		
Deadbolt Lock			Shower Works		
No Deadbolt			Shower Rod In		
Chain Lock			**Two Towel Racks**		
Floor			**Exhaust Fan Works**		
Clean			**Light Bulbs In**		
Damage			**BEDROOMS**		
Cabinets Interior			**Tile/Carpet Intact**		
Shelves Intact			**Color**		
Clean			**Type**		
Cabinets Exterior			**Doors Clean**		
Clean			**Closet Rod & Shelf In**		
Damage			**GENERAL**		
LIVING ROOM			**Bulbs In**		
Sliding Door			**Windows Clean**		
Clean			**Screens In**		
Lock Bar			**Screen Damage**		
Lock Works			**Air Conditioner**		
Door			**MISCELLANEOUS**		
Deadbolt Lock					
No Deadbolt					
Chain Lock					
Carpet					
Color					
Clean					
Type					
Stains					

I have examined the said premises and am satisfied with the physical condition thereof. The said premises are in good order and repair except as otherwise specified hereon. I understand that I must leave the premises clean and undamaged, other than normal wear and tear.

LESSOR ______________________ Lessee ______________________ Home Phone __________

Date ______________________ Lessee ______________________ Home Phone __________

Keys Issued ______ Deadbolt ______ Door ______ Chain ______ Mail ______ Other ______________

4402

EXHIBIT 24: Property Inspection Form

PROPERTY INSPECTION

Property Name ____________ Building Address ____________

Inspected By ____________ Date ____________

Area	Condition			Maintenance Required
	Good	Fair	Poor	
EXTERIOR				
Signs				
Grounds				
Landscaping				
Parking Areas				
Sidewalks				
Trash Area				
Light Fixtures				
ENTRANCE/FOYER				
Door				
Windows				
Mailboxes/Nameplates				
Light Fixtures				
Floors				
Walls				
HALLWAYS				
Doors				
Floors				
Walls				
Light Fixtures				
Stairwells				
Ashtrays				

EXHIBIT 24: Property Inspection Form *(Continued)*

LAUNDRY ROOMS					
Floors					
Walls					
Machines					
Light Fixtures					
MISCELLANEOUS					
Elevators					
Storage Area					
Trash Chutes					
Boiler Room					

Exterior Light Timer Setting: On __________ Off __________

Comments: ______________________________

The apartment is dirty

Clean the apartment thoroughly several weeks before move-in–hire professional cleaners, if necessary. Then, on the day before move-in, vacuum or buff the floors, dust the windowsills and countertops and so on. This should meet inspection of the most meticulous tenant.

The apartment is poorly painted

This complaint can be about the color of the paint, or poor quality of work. Always paint walls white or off-white, or allow the tenants to choose the colors. Hire professional painters and make sure they clean up paint spills and spatters on appliances, floors, countertops and hardware, or do it yourself. Check the paint job as part of your pre-inspection and correct any problems before the tenants move in.

The dishwasher (stove, refrigerator or other appliance) doesn't work

Appliances should be checked at pre-inspection; even so, problems may arise. Arrange to have them fixed as soon as possible, and tell the tenants exactly when to expect service.

We saw a cockroach

If your building has an insect problem, arrange early on for an adequate extermination program. If in spite of your best efforts new tenants see a cockroach roaming around, act immediately to reassure the tenants that this is an isolated incident. Call your exterminator to make an emergency treatment of the apartment and schedule a follow-up call in a week or two.

The plumbing leaks

This should have been checked; however, like appliances, plumbing has a way of acting up on move-in day. Ascertain if it is a minor problem (dripping faucet) that can be fixed in a few days, or a major disaster (overflowing toilet) that needs immediate action, and act accordingly.

You gave us the wrong keys

If the locks and keys are checked during inspection this problem can be avoided. Have an extra set of keys on hand in case of inadvertent mixups.

Turning Over Possession

After all papers are signed and the rent and security deposit funds received (and any former tenants have vacated the apartment), the tenants are then entitled to take possession of their new leased space. From a general legal standpoint, an owner has to give possession of habitable premises to the resident in compliance with the rental agreement; habitable means that the apartment is clean and all equipment, appliances, plumbing and hardware are in good working condition.

Turning over possession includes providing the new residents with the keys that are necessary to enter the space, including the common area lobbies and parking facility if parking is provided in the lease.

If old tenants do not vacate an apartment at the end of their lease, or have prohibited possession in some other manner, you will have to take legal action to rectify the situation. Either an owner or a resident may file a law suit to gain possession and recover damages as provided by law. An owner may bring such action on behalf of the new residents even though the residents are the ones entitled to possession.

Giving Tenants Instructions (Lease Package and Move-in Kit)

To help facilitate the move-in process and make the new residents feel at home in their new apartment, you can provide information about the building and surrounding community. You might include some or all of the following documents in a move-in kit:

- Copies of the lease, security deposit agreement, applicable riders and an "as is" letter when processing a relet (chapter 7).
- Completed utility and telephone service hook-up forms. The electric and gas companies may require completed forms prior to move-in. If tenants pay for utilities, these services will have to be put in their names. Tenants should make arrangements as soon as they sign the lease to have their services connected on or before move-in day.
- A set of keys or access cards to the apartment, mailbox and building entrance and common areas such as laundry rooms, storage rooms and so on. Always keep a set of spare apartment keys in your possession.

- Change-of-address cards.
- Maps of the area.
- A list of often-called telephone numbers: police, fire, hospitals, schools, stores, restaurants, cab companies, chamber of commerce.
- Operating instructions for appliances, laundry equipment and so on.

These materials can be placed in one folder or envelope marked with the new residents' names, apartment number, new address and move-in date.

Some Final Details

Moving day is made up of many details, large and small. You will have to coordinate your new tenants move-in schedule with the former tenants' move-out schedule. Other details to consider are elevator problems, mailbox and doorbell name tags, utility hookups, disposal of packing debris and perhaps a welcome gift for the new tenants.

Reserving Elevators

Some buildings, including most high-rises, require tenants to schedule their move-in/move-out with the management office in order to reserve the elevator. Quite often, elevator buildings won't allow a move-in or move-out on weekends because most residents are home then and the elevators are busier.

Condominium associations normally require tenants to schedule a move with the management office and will sometimes ask for a deposit or charge a fee for use of the elevator. The deposit is returned after an inspection of the elevator and common areas shows no damages. A one-time fee is not returned.

Name Tags

New tenants must have their names on the mailbox and doorbell. To maintain neat and uniform appearance of doorbells and mailboxes, it is better for you to order or make the name tags rather than have tenants make their own. Some owners charge a fee for this, and larger buildings usually have the management office handle this function, but unless the property is a high-rise, a name tag fee is not a common practice.

Key Control

New tenants will usually want their locks changed as a safeguard against old tenants handing out keys to strangers. When locks are changed, be sure to get spare keys. If you own more than one unit, keep spare keys to all the apartments and buildings in a locked key cabinet. This serves two purposes: First, you can keep the keys organized and tagged, thus making it easier to locate keys in an emergency; second, a locked key cabinet is better than a peg board in keeping the keys safe from possible theft, thus helping maintain security at your properties.

Utilities

Make sure your new tenants notify the utility companies to put the utilities in their names. If they don't, you may end up paying some of their electric or gas bills. Some owners contact these services themselves to ensure that the meters are put in tenants' names. The electric or gas service will have to be re-activated if previous tenants had them disconnected. Pilot lights must be relit. If your tenants are from out of town you may want to make these arrangements for them.

Empty Packing Cartons

New tenants usually have dozens of empty boxes and lots of waste paper to dispose of. Make sure you tell them how to dispose of this type of bulk rubbish. Otherwise your corridors or common areas may be filled with debris.

Welcome Gifts

As a gesture of good will, some owners give new tenants a welcome gift such as a plant, flowers or a basket of fruit. These items are relatively inexpensive and can help maintain a positive feeling during this stressful time. Residents will appreciate your thoughtfulness and will remember gestures of this nature throughout their lease term.

405

6

Renewing Leases

Katherine Martinez *holds undergraduate degrees in commercial interior design and business administration. She works as a regional sales manager for a large health insurance firm and, on a part-time/free-lance basis, pursues her interests in interior design and residential real estate.*

"My experience in real estate over the past six years has been as an investor in residential properties. During this period, I have owned three condominiums on the near north side of the city, and three three-flat buildings on the southwest and north sides.

"As sole owner and manager of these properties, I collect rents, coordinate day-to-day maintenance, arrange for property improvements to comply with building codes, coordinate needed renovations for resale and assume all building maintenance and improvement costs.

"Even though my primary objective is to rent the property, improve it and sell quickly at a profit, there are times when I have to retain ownership for several years. Because of this, once I develop good relationships with tenants who consistently pay their rent on time, I strongly encourage them to renew their leases.

"I value having someone renew even if it means not getting as much rent as I could from a new tenant. The costs of redecorating far outweigh the additional rental increase.

"I contact the tenant by phone 90 days before the lease expires. I want to know their intentions on renewing and at that time I tell them what the new rent will be. Most of the time, I will try to get a ten percent increase; if they are desirable tenants, I will negotiate this amount down to five percent."

Financial Benefits of Lease Renewals

Obtaining lease renewals can be an owner's most productive activity. Resident turnover, which is estimated by the Institute of Real Estate Management to be 55.1 percent nationwide, carries many hidden costs. Common areas may be damaged during the move. The apartment will need cleaning and may need a new carpet or other redecorating. Time, energy and money must be spent on finding a new tenant and showing the apartment. You may not find a suitable tenant right away and the apartment may stand empty for a month or more. Even without lost income, it can easily cost three to four hundred dollars each time a tenant moves out and a new tenant moves in.

Renewing a lease, on the other hand, can afford a substantial savings. Advertising costs are lessened. Maintenance, decorating and administrative expenses are substantially reduced. The risk of damaging the halls, stairwells, doors and elevators is eliminated. Thus, it is important that every effort be made to renew leases of desirable residents.

Of course, not all residents are good candidates for renewal. Do not renew residents who are slow rent-payers, who have many late charges, who have unauthorized pets or have created noise or nuisance problems. Procedures for not renewing a tenant are listed at the end of the chapter.

Note: The current market condition will influence how strictly you will adhere to the general policies and procedures discussed in this chapter. For example, if the market is soft and you have a large number of vacancies, you might decide to renew a resident who has been slow in paying rent, but has otherwise been a good resident.

Start on Day One

The process of renewing a lease begins the day a resident moves in. The possibility of obtaining a lease renewal is tested daily by your attitude, your professionalism and your approach to dealing with residents. There is no substitute for dealing fairly with all residents.

Conscientious owners work on renewals all year long through positive interactions with residents. These landlords know their residents well enough to identify three and four months ahead of time individuals who should and should not be renewed.

Reinspecting the Apartment

All apartments should be reinspected approximately three months before the expiration of the current lease. Use the renewal inspection notice letter (exhibit 25) to notify the residents in writing of the forthcoming inspection. Give them at least one week's notice prior to the scheduled date. The details of the inspection are recorded on the renewal inspection form (exhibit 26).

EXHIBIT 25: Renewal Inspection Notice

Date: ______________________________

Dear ______________________________:

As part of our preventive maintenance program, your apartment will be inspected June 15 at approximately 10 A.M. At that time we will enter your apartment. You need not be present at this inspection.

If this time is inconvenient, please call me at ______________________________ to arrange a time that will be convenient for both of us.

We appreciate your cooperation.

Yours very truly,

EXHIBIT 26: Renewal Inspection Form

RENEWAL INSPECTION

NAME__________ UNIT CODE__________
ADDRESS__________ LEASE EXP. DATE__________
PHONE__________
NUMBER OF OCCUPANTS__________
PETS: NO_____ YES_____ TYPE: DOG/CAT/OTHER__________
CARPETS: NO_____ YES_____ COLOR_____ CONDITION__________
APPLIANCE COLORS: STOVE_____ REFRIGERATOR_____ D/WASHER_____
COMMENTS:__________

I. ENTRY AREA__________
- A. Front Door__________
  - 1.) Locks Mastered__________ Keys__________
- B. Flooring__________ Condition__________
- C. Entry Closet Doors__________

II. LIVING ROOM__________
- A. Walls__________
- B. Floor Covering__________
- C. Windows/Screens__________
- D. Heating System__________

III. KITCHEN__________
- A. Stove__________
  - 1.) Operation__________
  - 2.) Burners__________
  - 3.) Oven__________
  - 4.) Broiler__________
  - 5.) Handles__________
- B. Refrigerator__________
  - 1.) Operation__________
- C. Exhaust Fan__________
- D. Dishwasher__________
- E. Cabinets/Drawers__________
  - 1.) Counter Top__________
  - 2.) Caulk__________
- F. Floor/Condition__________
- G. Sink__________
  - 1.) Faucet__________
  - 2.) Spout__________

IV. BATHROOMS__________
- A. Vanity__________
- B. Sink__________
- C. Plumbing__________
- D. Toilet__________
  - 1.) Seat__________
  - 2.) Base__________
- E. Shower__________
  - 1.) Tile Grout/Caulk__________
  - 2.) Plumbing__________

EXHIBIT 26: Renewal Inspection Form *(Continued)*

V BEDROOMS________
- A. Floor/Covering________
- B. Door________
- C. Closet________

VI. GENERAL________
- A. Door Stops________
- B. Air Conditioner________
  - 1.) Filter________
  - 2.) Caulk________
  - 3.) Tip________
- C. Heating Unit________
- D. Balcony________
  - 1.) Railings________
  - 2.) Caulk________
  - 3.) Doors________

4507

A renewal inspection serves three purposes: First, it allows you to make an annual assessment of the physical condition of your apartments, enabling you to observe unreported problems such as dripping faucets, damaged bathroom wall tiles, broken windows and screens, drywall damage and so on.

Second, it gives you the opportunity to make sure the resident is not in violation of the lease. (Check for evidence of a pet with no pet rider, overoccupancy, poor housekeeping and so on.)

And third, it allows residents to point out any defects or deficiencies in the apartment they want corrected.

Residents whose apartments are found in an unsanitary or damaged condition should not be renewed until a follow-up inspection indicates that the problems have been corrected and the resident has paid in full for the work performed.

Redecorating

Lease-renewal time is a pivotal point in the landlord-tenant relationship. This is when tenants request redecorating, carpet cleaning, new appliances and other improvements.

During the first and second years, renewals will probably not warrant any improvements, but it is a good policy to repaint the apartment and clean the carpet every two or three years. This is not just to please the tenants, but also to prevent any serious maintenance problems through general neglect.

If the apartment is well maintained by the resident and doesn't need decorating or carpet cleaning, you might give the resident a rent rebate in an amount slightly less than what it would cost you for these expenses. This gesture on your part can also act as an incentive for the resident to renew.

If you agree to replace or repair an item as a condition of a resident agreeing to renew a lease, it is a good policy to honor that commitment as soon as possible.

Raising the Rent

It doesn't make much sense to own and operate rental property if you can't generate a positive return on your investment. Investment properties can show a negative cash flow occasionally, and for short periods, but if such a situation continues you will have to sell the property or see it placed in default.

Operating real estate is like any other business–to improve cash flow you must either reduce expenses or increase income. Chapter 10 presents ideas and suggestions that can work toward expense reductions. Increasing income is easier to accomplish, but unless the residents are on month-to-month leases, the only times you can increase rents is when year-long leases terminate, assuming the market will permit an increase.

Even professionals find it difficult to decide what percent increase to charge renewal tenants. Rent increases in the seven to ten percent range are somewhat common, but it's not unusual to see hikes as low as three percent or as high as 30 percent.

The problem is complicated by several considerations. If you hike the rent too much, the resident may not renew–leaving you with a potential vacancy and decorating costs. If you increase the rent too little, the resident may stay, but you might not have enough additional income to offset inflationary increases in operating expenses.

Some professionals use the 20 percent resistance theory: After a renewal increase has been selected and the tenants notified, if more than 20 percent of the tenants resist, the increase was too high. If fewer than 20 percent resist, the increase was too low. This theory can be applied only to properties with multiple units and even then, it acts only as an indicator to consider the next time an increase is due.

Determining an Increase

In the long run, the renewal rent is a result of successful negotiations between you and the resident. In order to begin the negotiation process, you need a starting point.

Know Market Rent

The first step in determining a renewal increase is to ascertain the current market rent for vacant comparable apartments in your area. This can be accomplished by looking at the classified ads in your local newspaper or by checking with other owners and managers in your community (see chapter 3).

Find out what similar properties are instituting as an increase. Local newspapers periodically print articles on projected rent increases for their region. Try to acquire this information before you determine your own increases.

Figure Tenants' Moving Expenses

Another consideration, in addition to how much it will cost you, is how much it may also cost your tenants to move and redecorate a new apartment. Total moving expenses, including new utility service hook-up charges, can be $500 to $1,000 depending on how much furniture they own and whether or not they use professional movers. You might set a rent increase that is slightly less than what it would cost the tenants to move. If tenants object to the rent increase, remind them of how much it would cost them to move.

Criteria for a Successful Rent Increase

Weigh all the facts you've gathered from your investigations to select a rental increase that meets the following criteria:

The increase should offset increases in expenses, including the fixed expenses that have increased due to inflation, and capital or decorating improvements.

The increase, expressed on an annual basis, should not be much more than the cost of moving expenses for the tenant, unless you own properties that are in the high-rent district with rents in the over-$800-a-month range.

The increase should not be substantially higher than what comparable properties are charging. A comparable property is one that closely resembles your apartments in size, age, location and amenities.

The increased rent should be slightly higher than what vacant comparable apartments are commanding.

Having decided on an increase, your task now is to convince the tenants to accept it and renew their lease. This is normally the time tenants start their negotiations and you should be prepared to justify the rent hike.

Expect Some Turnover

Despite your best efforts, some tenants will choose to move anyway. The national average for small investors is 45 percent retention, so if you have two apartments and one resident renews, you're doing slightly better than average.

Often tenants will leave because they have an opportunity to rent an apartment in a brand-new building. Professional managers in large urban communities having constant new construction consider a 60 percent retention of tenants to be exceptionally good. This means that even professional managers have to cope with one out of three of their residents moving out each year.

The Renewal Process

As indicated earlier, the renewal process begins on the day the tenant moves in, but the actual procedure of administratively obtaining a renewal should be initiated approximately four months before the expiration of the lease.

Note: A resident is not considered renewed until all the lease documents are signed and delivered by the appropriate parties.

When the renewal process is completed, update all resident files and the security deposit records.

Form Letters

You may use a series of form letters to assist in obtaining renewals, but letters and notices are not substitutes for information-gathering through personal contact.

90 Days Before the Lease Ends

If, in your judgment, an individual is a desirable resident, send the 90-day notice (first renewal letter) (exhibit 27). Enclose the proposed lease and security deposit agreement. This packet should be sent 90 days prior to the date the current lease expires. As an added incentive to reply promptly, you can offer a one-time rebate of $25–$30 for signing the renewal lease 60 or more days before the lease ends.

If a resident has accrued unpaid late charges or other fees and you have still decided to seek renewal, send copies of the documents with a letter requesting that these charges be brought up-to-date. Advise residents that they cannot be renewed until their account balances are paid in full.

Approximately one week after sending out the renewal packet, call the residents to make certain the materials were received and to encourage prompt responses.

EXHIBIT 27: 90-Day Notice (First Renewal Letter)

Date ______________________________

Dear ______________________________:

I am writing to offer to renew your lease, which is due to expire soon.

I am enclosing your proposed lease agreement. You will note that there is an increase in rent. This increase is necessary because of increases in taxes, utilities, labor and overhead and other operational expenses.

We have kept the rent increase to a minimum, and, in fact, this rental rate is available only if you sign your renewal ninety days prior to expiration of your present lease. If you sign later, the rent will be _______ more per month, to allow for further increases in costs.

I have also enclosed your security deposit agreement. Since your security deposit must equal your monthly rental, you are asked to increase your deposit by _______ to cover the increase in rent.

Please sign and return the lease agreement and security deposit agreement, along with your payment of _______ (to cover additional security deposit) before ____________ . After that date, if you want to renew, I will issue another lease, at the higher rate.

Please feel free to call me if you have any questions.

Very truly yours,

encl: Lease Agreement
Security Deposit Agreement

60 Days Before the Lease Ends

If you have not received a reply from the residents within 30 days of sending the packet, send a follow-up, the 60-day notice letter (exhibit 28).

EXHIBIT 28: 60-Day Notice (Second Renewal Letter)

Date ______________________________

Dear ______________________________:

According to our records your current lease expires ____________________ and you have not yet signed and delivered the renewal lease we sent you on ____________________.

We need to know as soon as possible whether or not you intend to stay in the apartment, so we can begin showing it for re-rental.

Note also that ____________________ is the last date that the renewal rent of $__________ is valid. After that date, the renewal rent will be $__________.

We would appreciate your prompt attention to this matter. Please contact us if you have any questions.

Very truly yours,

45 Days Before the Lease Ends

If the residents have not returned the lease documents 45 days prior to the lease expiration date, send a second follow-up, the 45-day notice letter (exhibit 29). This letter informs the residents that they must contact you within 24 hours if they choose to renew. Otherwise, the apartment will be considered available for showing to prospective residents.

EXHIBIT 29: 45-Day Notice (Third Renewal Letter)

Date ______________________

Dear ______________________:

We have not yet received your signed lease document for the coming term. Since your lease expires on ______________ it is extremely important that you contact us within 24 hours to let us know your plans.

If we do not hear from you by ______________ we will start showing the apartment to prospective residents on ______________.

If you are not planning to renew your lease, please complete the bottom part of this letter, detach and return to us immediately.

Thank you for your cooperation,

- -

Date ______________________

We will vacate our apartment on (date) ______________________

New address: ______________________

Signature: ______________________

30 Days Before the Lease Ends

For residents who have not responded or have indicated in writing that they will not be renewing, send a notice to vacate letter (exhibit 30) specifying the condition in which the apartment is to be left when vacated. This letter is sent 30 days prior to the lease expiration date.

EXHIBIT 30: Notice to Vacate

Date ____________________

Dear Resident:

This letter acknowledges receipt of your notice to vacate your apartment on or before ____________________.

On that day, and before we return your security deposit, we will inspect your apartment to be sure it is left clean and in good repair. Please pay particular attention to the following:

- Remove all papers and packing materials from the apartment.
- Remove all picture hooks from the walls.
- Clean stove, dishwasher and kitchen cabinets inside and out.
- Defrost refrigerator and clean it inside and out. Leave it turned on number 1 position.
- Clean and sweep out closets; remove all hangers and debris.
- Clean bathroom(s) thoroughly: toilet, tub, sink, medicine cabinet, vanity, wall and floor tile.
- Make sure all light bulbs work. Clean light fixtures and covers.
- Wash and de-wax tile floors.
- Have carpets professionally cleaned.
- Clean all windows; leave them closed and locked.
- Empty and clean storage bin.
- Leave premises undamaged, beyond normal wear and tear.
- Deliver all apartment keys and your forwarding address to ____________________.
  ____

We thank you for your cooperation and trust your stay with us has been a pleasant one. If you have any further questions regarding your move, please contact us.

Very truly yours,

Not Renewing a Tenant

Occasionally you will not want to renew a tenant. Your decision not to renew might be based on any number of reasons: collection problems, poor housekeeping, overoccupancy, problem residents who continually disturb other residents and so on. Give such a resident a 30-days notice (exhibit 31) as a courtesy.

EXHIBIT 31: 30-Day Notice

Date ______________________

Dear ______________________:

This letter will serve as notification that we have decided not to renew your lease. Please turn in your keys at our office no later than ______________. Also supply us with your forwarding address and new telephone number at that time.

Your security deposit is fully refundable provided your apartment is left in a clean, orderly and undamaged condition as detailed in the enclosed notice to vacate. Also refer to the pre-inspection form, which details the condition of the apartment when you moved in.

If you have any questions regarding this matter, please feel free to contact me.

Very truly yours,

encl: notice to vacate
pre-inspection form

In some states you may be obligated to tell the tenants why you aren't renewing the lease. You currently are not required to renew a lease; however, pending legislation in at least one state proposes just that.

As always, stay current on landlord-tenant legislation and keep in touch with your attorney.

ADAMS ST

7

When Tenants Move Out

Gerry Lynch *is the production director of a major publishing company. Ten years ago, she purchased a town house with a garden apartment that she rents to a tenant. Five years ago, she also invested in a small building in a nearby suburb.*

"I learned the hard way not to rent to friends or to become too friendly with my tenants. I once rented to friends who, when they moved out, left behind a roach-infested apartment. I learned about the roaches while showing the unit to a prospective tenant. The whole building had to be thoroughly exterminated, costing hundreds of dollars. Fortunately I was able to deduct the expense from the security deposit.

"Renting has taught me two things: inspect the apartment periodically while the tenant is living there and inspect the vacant apartment thoroughly before showing it to a prospective tenant.

"On another occasion, the tenants asked me if they could vacate the apartment and stop paying rent before the lease ended. When I said no, they became almost hostile and threatened to damage the apartment. Ultimately they moved out, changing the locks in the process to prevent me from protecting the apartment. I had to hire an attorney and a locksmith; I eventually recovered the expenses because I had a valid, enforceable signed lease."

Ending a Lease on Time

It would be nice if all good tenants stayed in their apartments year after year, paying the rent on time and never creating any problems. But of course there comes a time when tenants move out.

If they're leaving simply because the lease has expired and they want to move on, the event should not be too stressful. But if the tenants are being evicted, or you decided not to renew the lease, or the tenants want to terminate the lease early, there could be a good deal of tension until the moving day is at hand and the tenants have physically vacated the unit.

If tenants inform you that they will move out at the end of the lease, there are several steps to follow.

Notice to Vacate

Send the tenants a notice to vacate (exhibit 30, Chapter 6) about 30 days before the end of the lease. This notice reminds the tenants that you will inspect the apartment before returning the security deposit, and lists the particular areas of the apartment that will be checked for cleaning and damage.

The notice also states the date the apartment must be vacated, asks for a forwarding address and tells the tenants where to return keys.

Move-Out Inspection

The move-out inspection can be conducted on the day that the tenants vacate the apartment, or a few days before. The purpose of this inspection is to document the condition of the apartment and to ascertain what needs fixing or replacing. Based on this inspection, you will compute the amount of security deposit to return to the tenants.

To conduct the inspection, use a copy of the pre-inspection form (exhibit 23, Chapter 5) that was completed when the tenants moved in. Review this form along with any completed apartment work orders to verify deficiencies accepted by the residents and defects corrected through work orders.

Refer also to the notice to vacate form, which requires the tenants to leave the apartment clean and free of debris.

If possible, conduct the move-out inspection together with the tenants to avoid disputes about the condition of the apartment and appropriate charges for repairs and cleaning. If time permits, you might allow the residents to correct minor deficiencies such as paint touch-ups, oven cleaning and so on.

Regain Possession

Ascertain the exact day the tenants will be leaving and be on hand to receive the keys and regain possession of the apartment.

Ending a Lease Early

When tenants want to move out before the lease is over, you have several options.

If you want to enforce the lease, you have a legal right to hold tenants to the signed agreement to pay for a complete year. A lease is a contract; both parties mutually agreed to uphold their obligations in compliance with the stated terms and conditions. However, it may not be wise to take such a hard line.

There are ways in which each party can mutually agree to terminate a lease early. You can elect to cancel the lease completely. Or you might allow the tenants to sublet the apartment or assign (relet) the lease to substitute tenants.

If you let your tenants know that you are willing to negotiate an early termination of the lease, they will be less likely to move out without giving notice. In such a case, the landlord can initiate a legal suit, but it is a good idea to avoid such costly and stressful legal battles.

Subletting

Subletting occurs when a tenant enters into a separate agreement with a third party (subtenant) to use the apartment on a temporary or permanent basis. The two parties are responsible to each other for performing whatever obligations they have agreed on. The landlord often is not involved with the transaction.

As an example of a temporary sublet, tenant Smith gets a business assignment out of town for three months and decides to sublet his apartment to a friend for the period he will be gone. The friend, subtenant Jones, agrees to pay Smith an amount of rent for use of the premises. Smith, in turn, continues to pay rent to the landlord and when the three months have expired, Smith returns and Jones moves out. If everything went well, the landlord might not even know about the transaction.

Smith could also decide to permanently move out of his apartment before the lease expired, and sublet the apartment for the balance of the lease. He would collect rent from the subtenant and pay rent to the landlord and would remain obligated to the landlord until the old lease expired. The sublet tenant usually accepts the apartment in "as is" condition and does not benefit from any redecorating until the lease expires.

In this case the landlord is more likely to be a party to the sublet because the new tenant would probably want to enter into a new lease with the landlord when the sublet expired, where permitted by law. Landlords generally charge a small fee to allow a sublet, to cover administrative expenses.

Assignment (Reletting)

When tenants must terminate their lease early you may choose to assign the lease (or relet) to new tenants who will finish the remainder of the term. If it takes several months to locate a suitable replacement, the original tenants are still liable and must pay rent, even though they may not be occupying the unit.

Assignment differs from subletting in that once new tenants have signed the lease, the original tenants are fully released from any additional obligation. In some cases, the landlord will ask the replacement tenants to sign a new one-year lease instead of completing the obligation under the old lease. Landlords usually charge a higher fee to accommodate an assignment.

Assignment is, in effect, a termination of one lease and the creation of a new one. Thus, when the old tenants move out you should inspect the apartment for damages and deduct the cost of repairs and redecorating from the security deposit. The original tenants' security deposit is refunded and a new one is taken from the replacement tenants.

Assignment Is Preferable to Subletting

The reasons for this are clear when you think how involved and complicated the situation would be if subtenants had to first contact the original tenants to get repairs and service for the apartment. And if landlords had to enforce the rules and regulations of occupancy with a sublet, they would have to contact the original tenants who may have moved to another state.

With an assignment, you have what amounts to a new lease with new tenants and your dealings with the former tenants are at an end.

Sublet/Assignment Clauses in Standard Leases

Most lease and rental agreement forms address the issue of subleasing and assignments in a similar fashion. State laws generally allow rental agreements to require tenants to obtain the owner's prior consent in order to sublet or assign an apartment. Written permission may be necessary if the lease is in writing.

Owners should not unreasonably withhold permission, and sublease/assignment clauses in form leases normally do not contain any language that would constitute an unreasonable withholding of permission.

The following provisions are fairly common and are considered generally acceptable by both landlords and tenants:

- Residents may be prohibited from transferring their lease interest to a trustee in bankruptcy or for the benefit of the residents' creditors or any other act of bankruptcy or insolvency.
- Owners may reserve the right to rent other vacancies in the premises before consenting to reletting the dwelling unit. [This clause could be considered antagonistic and you can waive the right if the tenants are responsible for finding their own sublessee.]
- Prospective residents may be required to meet the criteria customarily used to evaluate the acceptability of residents for similar dwelling units in the premises.
- Sublet/assignment may be restricted during the last 90 days of the lease term. During this period of time a landlord could require prospective sublessees to sign new, full-term leases.

Obligations and Liabilities

The current tenants usually remain liable for responsibilities under the lease until a new lease is signed. An owner may require financial assurance from the old tenants or the prospective lessees, including advance payment for rent and expenses of reletting. Such expenses might include decorating, repairs, replacements, advertising, commissions and reasonable administrative fees for performing the details involved in this type of transaction.

Unless agreed, owners generally do not have a responsibility to advertise or incur expenses on behalf of the residents or themselves in conjunction with reletting an apartment. A resident who subleases is normally liable to his sublessee for the performance of the owner's obligations under the rental agreement.

A landlord is not directly liable to a sublessee in regards to obligations under the rental agreement and the sublessee is not directly liable to the owner with respect to the resident's obligations, unless otherwise agreed.

Obey State and Local Laws

While some states have given residents a right to sublet or relet, most states honor the rental agreement if subletting or reletting is specifically prohibited. If you are in doubt about your rights in this regard, it's best to check with your local municipality or real estate board on the issue of subletting and assigning leases. Unless your city has a landlord/tenant law, the lease document and specific subletting policies that have been agreed to by the tenant will prevail.

The Relet Agreement

If you agree to relet, execute a relet agreement (exhibit 32) that spells out the terms and conditions of a relet.

The relet agreement gives the tenants the responsibility for finding suitable new tenants for the apartment. Suitable tenants are ones who meet the landlord's usual financial and other requirements, and who are willing to assume the balance of the lease term. The landlord has the right to reject the prospective sublessees on the basis of a credit check.

The form spells out exactly when the old tenants' responsibilities end. Only upon the new residents paying a full security deposit, signing a lease, paying the first month's rent and accepting the keys, are the old tenants given their security deposits back and released from the lease.

The agreement lists the amount of reletting fee (if any) and states the exact day the apartment will be vacated.

It also provides new tenants with two options:

The first is to accept the apartment in "as is" condition, at the same rent and without redecorating or cleaning. In this case you should have the new tenants sign an "as is" letter (exhibit 33), which indicates in writing that the new residents accept the unit in its existing condition.

EXHIBIT 32: Relet Agreement

RELET AGREEMENT

NAME: ______________________________

ADDRESS: ______________________________ APT #: ________

CITY, STATE, ZIP: ______________________________

LEASE EXPIRATION DATE: ______________________________

I am requesting permission to relet my apartment and I understand that the following items must be complied with:

1. I am responsible for my own advertising costs incurred.
2. I am responsible to show the apartment and find the new resident.
3. Lessor has the sole right to accept or reject this resident per their current credit criteria.
4. The reletting resident must pay a full month's rent as security deposit.
5. I will accompany the reletting resident to the office to avoid confusion as to which apartment the applicant is applying for.
6. The new resident will sign a lease and I understand that until the resident has signed this lease, paid the first month's rent on the apartment, and accepted the keys I am not released from my lease. Should this applicant cancel his agreement and fail to complete this transaction, I understand that my lease is still binding.
7. I understand that the reletting applicant has two choices:
   1. To take a lease for the remainder of my term, at my present rent, accepting the apartment "as is" with no decorating or cleaning.
   2. To take a new one-year lease at the new market rent of $____________.
      If this is the case, the apartment will be redecorated for the new resident, and I agree to pay cleaning charges for any cleaning as agreed to in my security deposit agreement. If this form of reletting is used, I agree to vacate the apartment five working days prior to the reletting resident's move-in date.
8. I understand that I will be charged a fee of $____________ for reletting.
9. I will return my apartment keys and my forwarding address to the lessor's office on my move-out date. Under no circumstances will I give a copy of the apartment keys to the reletting resident.
10. I agree to pay rent on the apartment through the new resident's move-in date.
11. I understand that the remainder of my security deposit is refundable provided that I have complied with the above agreements, have no unpaid bookkeeping charges, and I am not in violation of my lease agreement.
12. To move from and vacate the apartment on or before ____________________, 19______, which shall be the cancellation date of my lease.

Accepted by: Lessor:

______________________________ ______________________________

Resident Signature Signature

____

Date

The second option is to sign a new one-year lease at a higher rent. This option provides for redecorating and cleaning the apartment, as with any new lease. In this case, the old tenants agree to leave the apartment a few days before the reletting residents' move-in date, to allow the landlord to prepare for the new tenants.

EXHIBIT 33: "As Is" Letter

Date ______________________

____

____

____

Dear ______________________:

We are glad to welcome you as a new resident in apartment ________.

This letter is to verify that you are accepting the apartment ''as is'' and will not request further cleaning or redecorating for the duration of the lease.

Also, you agree that upon termination of your lease, you will leave the apartment in the same condition to comply with the provisions of your security deposit agreement.

Very truly yours,

Accepted by:

______________________ (tenant)

____

______________________ (date)

In both cases, you should send the old residents a notice to vacate form and inspect the apartment for damage. This inspection should be done in the presence of both old and new tenants, if possible.

The relet agreement also deals with details about return of security deposits, payment of outstanding bookkeeping charges, providing forwarding addresses and return of keys.

Both you and the old residents should sign the relet agreement and you should keep a copy of the form in your permanent files.

Cancellation

When tenants must terminate a lease early they may choose to cancel the obligation rather than take the time to find a suitable subtenant. In such a case, you can agree to cancel the lease.

In a lease cancellation, residents buy out their lease by agreeing to a set of conditions. In return for a fee the landlord takes on the responsibility of finding a new tenant, and fully releases the tenant from any further obligation as of the effective date.

To cancel a lease, execute an agreement to cancel lease form (exhibit 34). If the tenants requested a cancellation rider when they signed the lease (see chapter 4), this form can be used in conjunction with that rider.

Terms and conditions of this agreement require tenants to pay a fee equal to two months' rent. This fee can vary; it is intended to cover the owner's costs of reletting the apartment, including cleaning and redecorating, and to cover the risk of possibly losing a month's rent if you can't find suitable tenants right away.

The form specifies the day the apartment will be vacated, which is also the cancellation date of the lease, and deals with details of returning keys and providing forwarding addresses.

As in any move-out, tenants must leave the apartment in good condition. Send a notice to vacate form and inspect the unit for damages before returning the security deposit.

Return of Possession

However the lease is ended, your goal is the same: You want to regain possession of the apartment in good condition and on time.

EXHIBIT 34: Agreement to Cancel Lease

AGREEMENT TO CANCEL LEASE

FOR AND IN CONSIDERATION of ______________________________ ______________, LESSOR, allowing the undersigned to cancel prior to its expiration, that certain Lease ("Lease") dated______________, 19________between LESSOR and______________________________for an apartment located at ______________________________in______________Illinois, I hereby agree to the following:

1. To pay a sum equal to two months' of Lease rent prior to moving from and vacating the apartment;
2. To promptly return the apartment keys to LESSOR prior to moving from and vacating the apartment;
3. To provide my forwarding address to LESSOR prior to moving from and vacating the apartment;
4. To leave the apartment in a clean condition and free of any and all damages;
5. To move from and vacate the apartment on or before______________, 19,___ which shall be the cancellation date of the Lease.

It is further understood that my security deposit is fully refundable, provided that I have complied with the aforesaid and further provided that there are no unpaid charges of any kind on my account as of the date the Lease is cancelled.

In the event the undersigned is in default under the aforesaid Lease as determined by LESSOR then LESSOR shall have the right to keep and apply the aforesaid cancellation fee toward any damages arising as a result of such default.

The undersigned, as additional consideration for this Agreement, does hereby forever release any claim, cause or causes of action which it may have or which shall arise in the future against LESSOR its officers, directors, employees or agents arising out of the aforesaid Lease.

This agreement shall be null and void if not strictly complied with.

DATED:______________________________

______________________________ Resident Signature

______________________________ LESSOR

______________________________ Resident Signature

Tenants' Rights to Possession

When tenants rent an apartment, they are given and retain possession of the unit throughout the lease term. During the lease term, if tenants are in compliance with the terms of the lease, an owner may not take any action to regain possession except in the case of an abandonment or as otherwise permitted by law.

Even if the tenants are not in total compliance with the lease, an owner cannot take possession of the apartment unit by locking the tenants out, removing part of the dwelling unit (for example, the front door) or withholding services (utilities, water, garbage removal).

Turning Over Possession

When a lease is terminated, tenants must relinquish possession immediately. The tenants do this by removing all personal belongings from the apartment and delivering all keys to the owner.

Usually turning over possession is a routine businesslike procedure. You and the tenants agree to terminate the lease or sublet the apartment; the old tenants move out on the agreed-upon day; and the new tenants move in without a hitch.

However, sometimes things do not go smoothly.

Forcible Detainer

Tenants may fail to return possession by not vacating the unit or not returning the keys. This normally constitutes a forcible detainer, meaning that the owner (or new tenants, if there are any) may initiate eviction proceedings (see chapter 8) and request actual and punitive damages.

Abandonment

Occasionally tenants will abandon an apartment without notice. Sometimes this happens when you are in the process of filing a five-day notice for nonpayment of rent or a termination notice for breach of contract (see chapter 8). If you check the apartment and find it is or appears to be vacant, an abandonment notice (exhibit 35) should be prepared. (Comply with state and local laws governing the posting of notices.) A copy of the form must be posted on the apartment door for ten days. The original is kept in your files.

When the ten-day period has elapsed, you regain full dominion and control over the premises and property and can begin preparing the apartment for rerental.

EXHIBIT 35: Abandonment Notice

____

(OWNER) vs.

____

(TENANT)

____

____

If tenant vacates or abandons the Apartment, ten (10) days non-occupation being deemed an abandonment, or breaches any covenant or agreement in this Lease, TENANT'S right to possession of the apartment shall immediately terminate. The mere retention of possession thereafter by TENANT shall constitute a forcible detainer and if OWNER so elects, but not otherwise, this Lease shall thereupon terminate, but this Lease shall automatically terminate without need of an election by OWNER on any transfer of TENANT'S interest by operation of law, such as TENANT'S bankruptcy or insolvency.

In any such event, the apartment, or any part of it, may be relet by OWNER for such rent and such terms and such period as OWNER may elect without releasing TENANT from any liability under this Lease. On such termination, TENANT shall surrender possession of the Apartment immediately and OWNER or OWNER'S agent shall have full and free license, with or without process of law, to enter and take possession of the Apartment and expel and remove TENANT or any other person who may be occupying the Apartment and to repossess himself of the Apartment as of his former estate. Such entry by OWNER or OWNER'S agent shall not constitute trespass or forcible entry and detainer and shall not cause forfeiture of rents due by virtue thereof, nor a waiver of TENANT'S covenants or agreement in this Lease.

TENANT shall on demand pay all deficiencies if the rent on reletting is not sufficient to satisfy the rent provided in this Lease and, in addition, shall pay all expenses of reletting, including decorating, repairs, replacements and brokerage commissions.

Being duly sworn, on oath (OWNER) ______________________ deposes and says that on the ______ day of ______________, 19______, he (she) served this notice to the TENANT by delivering a copy to the TENANT, or by posting a copy on the main door of the described premises, no one being in actual possession thereof.

STATE OF __________)
)
COUNTY OF __________)

____
Notary

Subscribed and sworn to before me this ______ day of __________, 19______

(Notary seal here)

Abandoned Personal Property

Occasionally tenants will move out and return the keys, but leave behind some personal property. This property must be disposed of properly.

Generally, personal property left in an apartment is considered abandoned if the residents appear to have moved out (except in the case of eviction), and the apartment no longer contains food or clothing. *Abandonment* is a term that has technical meaning in the law and some states have specific statutes defining it.

Your lease form may contain language governing abandoned property and your rights to dispose of same. The general procedure to follow for disposing of the property is as follows:

- Try to contact the residents by telephone through their new number or through the emergency or employment telephone numbers provided on the lease application. If you reach the residents, request that the property be removed from the apartment during the next seven days.
- If the resident fails to claim personal property at the end of the time period, you should make an inventory of the property, noting any damaged items.
- If you reasonably believe that the abandoned property is valueless or of such little value that the cost of storage would exceed the amount that would be realized from sale, or if the property is subject to spoilage, dispose of it immediately.
- If the property is of value greater than the cost of storage, store the property for a reasonable time, not exceeding 60 days. Take reasonable care against loss or damage. You should not feel responsible to the residents for any loss not caused by your negligence. The residents may claim the property during the term of storage by paying for the transfer and storage costs. Property not claimed during the term of storage may be disposed of in any reasonable manner without liability to the owner.

539

8

Rent Collection

Jim Bastl *and his wife Debbie own and manage a six-flat building. The Bastls work about two hours a week on their property. They give one of the tenants a discount in the rent in exchange for maintaining the common areas of the building.*

"I realized at an early age that I would not become wealthy by working for a living. At the same time, I have always known that I can make money as long as someone else is willing to lend it to me. As a computer programmer, I used my analytical ability to search for an investment vehicle that would build wealth without requiring substantial amounts of my own money. After considering all the investment options available today, I found only one where this is not a problem: real estate. Banks will loan up to 80 percent of a property's value.

"Collection of rent has not been too much of a problem, since I am careful in screening my tenants. I buy professional forms and envelopes from an office supply store and send the rent invoice with a return envelope in enough time for the renter to pay the bill. Although a few of my tenants have had to pay late charges, I usually call to see if we can work out the problem."

The Most Important Management Task

Other property management activities that occur once a year (renewal of leases, inspection of apartments, maintaining positive resident relations) are a continuing responsibility. Collecting the rent, however, is a regular, once-a-month task, and in many ways this task is the owner's most important management activity. The rent is your income from the property. Without this income you won't be able to operate and maintain your property.

You should set a policy of when and how the rent should be paid each month, and consistently enforce this policy. Anticipate problems that might arise, i.e., tenants who habitually pay the rent late, the possible need to evict a tenant–and decide ahead of time how you will deal with these eventualities. A lot of stress can be avoided if you plan ahead and deal with these matters in a businesslike way.

Payment Policies

The best policy is to demand that rent be paid in full on or before the first of the month. A more lenient policy is to allow a five-day grace period, which allows tenants to pay the rent any time between the first and the fifth of the month, inclusive, without penalty. Either of these policies might include a provision for a late fee. Whatever policy you establish, the key to enforcing it is to be consistent and not waver from one month to the next or from one tenant to the next.

Payment Procedures

Where To Collect

There are several ways to go about collecting the rent. One is to ask the tenants to bring it to you in person, but residents may object to this unless you live or have an office on the property. Another way is to go to the tenants' apartments on the first of each month. Some owners prefer this method, but it may not always be convenient. The most common procedure is to have tenants mail the rent. To make it easy, you can provide the residents with 12 preaddressed envelopes.

When To Collect

Rent is due at the beginning of any term of one month or less, otherwise rent is payable in equal monthly installments at the beginning of each month. Unless otherwise agreed, rent is normally uniformly apportioned from day-to-day using a 30-day month.

Most leases clearly state that rent is due and payable in full on or before the first day of each month. If your rental agreement doesn't address this issue or if you don't have a written lease agreement that provides that rent is payable in advance on the first of the month, then the rent is payable at the end of the rental period, that is, at the end of the month.

Methods of Payment

The rent is considered paid if it is made by any means or in any manner customarily used in the ordinary course of business. This includes cash, money orders, certified and cashier's checks, etc. It does not include farm animals, produce, food stamps, products or goods, or other personal property.

Payment by check is conditional. If a tenant gives you a check on the first of the month and it is subsequently returned for nonsufficient funds, it is as if that tenant never paid. The owner may require a bad check replaced by cash and all future payments made in cash.

Second-party checks, including payroll checks and/or government checks, should not be accepted. Be sure the residents are told to whom to make out the rent payment checks.

Give a Receipt

A receipt book, which can be purchased in most stationery stores, can be used to receipt all money, including application fees, initial security deposits, rents, credit check fees, partial payments, relet fees, lock-out fees and buy-out fees. Copies of receipts should be placed in the residents' files.

Delinquencies and Late Charges

The lease will indicate when the rent is to be paid, and when it becomes delinquent. If the rent is due on the first of the month, it is considered delinquent on the second (or the fifth, if you allow a grace period). At this point you could choose to immediately file a five-day notice and proceed with eviction. However, unless you want to get rid of the tenants because of other undesirable qualities, you should probably take less extreme action.

Reminder Letter

If the rent is late, you can send the tenants a rent reminder letter (exhibit 36). If it is your policy to charge a late fee as soon as rent becomes delinquent, indicate this on the letter. Otherwise, send a late charge notice (exhibit 37) on the day the late charge goes into effect.

Late Charges

Some form leases have a built-in late charge and most leases at least have a provision allowing it. Depending on the specific lease, the late charge is usually assessed between the sixth and tenth day of the month, but it can be assessed as early as the second day. Certain leases specify the exact amount to be charged; for instance, a charge of $5 on rent paid after the fifth and $10 after the tenth. Without a written provision being stated somewhere in the lease, a late charge cannot be demanded.

The charge should be high enough to discourage habitual lateness, but not so high as to be unreasonable. An exorbitant late charge, say over $25, could possibly be challenged as unreasonable.

There is a valid argument against charging late fees. Although they are intended to encourage tenants to pay rent on time, late fees indirectly give tenants permission to pay the rent late. Tenants feel that it is acceptable to pay late as long as they agree to pay the late charge.

You must decide what is more important to you: getting the rent on time, or getting an additional income from the late fee. If you have enough funds in reserve to make the mortgage payment before receiving the rent, a late charge, if rigidly enforced, can provide additional income.

EXHIBIT 36: Rent Reminder Letter

Date ______________________________

Dear ______________________________:

Our records indicate that your rent is not yet paid. To avoid late fees, please remit your past due rent immediately.

Sincerely,

EXHIBIT 37: Late Charge Notice

Date ______________________________

____

____

____

Dear ______________________________:

Our records indicate that your rent is still not paid. A $2.00-per-day late charge is now in effect. I am sure you will want to take care of this matter immediately.

If I can be of any help to you in this matter, please feel free to contact me at ______________________________.
(Phone Number)

Sincerely,

You can choose to waive the late fee, but by doing so you are excusing the lateness and encouraging it to happen again. If you habitually allow late payments, you can't suddenly change your attitude and begin eviction proceedings when the tenants are late again. If you want to return to the strict terms of the lease, you must first notify the tenants of your intention.

Whether or not you charge a late fee, you should attempt to make personal contact with residents whose rent is outstanding and find out why it is late. Get the residents to set a firm date when the rent will be paid. Remind the residents to include fees for late payment. Start eviction procedures if the residents do not pay on the promised date.

Collecting Late Rent

Most tenants will pay their rent on time or within a reasonable grace period. Some will not. If sending reminder letters or making personal contacts is not effective, you will have to take further action. Typically, you will serve a five-day notice, send a follow-up letter and then begin eviction proceedings.

The Five-Day Notice

In most states, a five-day notice (exhibits 38 and 39) is the first step in processing rent-delinquent residents through the court system. It is usually served on the fifteenth of the month, but you can issue it as early as the second. Don't put off sending a five-day notice just because the residents have promised to pay. Issue the notice anyway; if and when the residents pay, you can tear up the notice.

Be aware that, in effect, this is a *six-day* notice. If you serve the notice on the tenth of the month, you cannot file any further papers in court until the sixteenth.

At the same time that you issue the five-day notice, you can include an explanatory cover letter (exhibit 40).

Filling Out the Notice

Office supply stores that sell legal forms can supply you with five-day notice forms, or you can copy and use exhibit 38. Fill out the form, using your data to correspond with the sample filled-out five-day notice (exhibit 39).

EXHIBIT 38: Owner's Five-Day Notice

OWNER'S FIVE DAY NOTICE

You are hereby notified that there is now due the owner the sum of $ ____________
(1) Rent per month $ ____________, (2) Rent Due from ____________ to ____________
being rent for the premises situated in ____________, County of ____________
and State of Illinois, and known and described as follows, to wit: ____________
____________ together with all buildings, storage areas, recreational facilities, parking spaces and garages used in connection with said premises.

And you are further notified that payment of said sum so due has been and is hereby demanded of you, and that unless payment thereof is made on or before the expiration of five days after service of this notice, your right of possession under the lease of said premises will be terminated.

****Only FULL PAYMENT of the rent demanded in this notice will waive the landlord's right to terminate the lease under this notice, unless the landlord agrees in writing to continue the lease in exchange for receiving partial payment.

To ____________

____________ is authorized to receive said rent, so due.

____
owner

By ____________
Agent or Attorney

Dated this ________ day of ________, 19 ____

FOLD

STATE OF ILLINOIS
COUNTY OF ____________ } SS.

AFFIDAVIT OF SERVICE

____________ (Served by), being duly sworn, on oath deposes and says that on the ________ day of ________, 19 ________ he served the above notice on the tenant named above as follows:*

- ☐ (1) by delivering a copy thereof to the above named tenant, ____________.
- ☐ (2) by delivering a copy thereof to ____________, a person above the age of 13 years, residing on or in charge of the above described premises.
- ☐ (3) by sending a copy thereof to said tenant by certified mail, with request for return of receipt from the addressee.
- ☐ (4) by posting a copy thereof on the main door of the above described premises, no one being in actual possession thereof.

Subscribed and sworn to before me this ________ day of ________, 19 ________

____________ Notary Public

X ____________

*Identify the method of service used by placing a check in the proper box. Sign on the line marked X.

4703 REV

EXHIBIT 39: Completed Owner's Five-Day Notice

OWNER'S FIVE DAY NOTICE

You are hereby notified that there is now due the owner the sum of $ 429.00
(1) Rent per month $ 429.00, (2) Rent Due from 1/1/88 to 1/31/88
being rent for the premises situated in Waterford Park, County of Cook
and State of Illinois, and known and described as follows, to wit: 1234 Main Street, Apt. #201
together with all buildings, storage areas, recreational facilities, parking spaces and garages used in connection with said premises.

And you are further notified that payment of said sum so due has been and is hereby demanded of you, and that unless payment thereof is made on or before the expiration of five days after service of this notice, your right of possession under the lease of said premises will be terminated.

****Only FULL PAYMENT of the rent demanded in this notice will waive the landlord's right to terminate the lease under this notice, unless the landlord agrees in writing to continue the lease in exchange for receiving partial payment.

To Jane Q. Doe
1234 Main Street, #201
Waterford Park, IL 50008

Waterford Park Rental Office
is authorized to receive said rent, so due.

Inland Real Estate Corporation
2901 Butterfield, Oak Brook, IL 60521
Owner

By John A. Dooe
Agent or Attorney

Dated this 12th day of January, 19 8

FOLD

STATE OF ILLINOIS
COUNTY OF Cook } SS.

AFFIDAVIT OF SERVICE

John A. Dooe (Served by), being duly sworn, on oath deposes and says that on the 12th day of January, 19 88 he served the above notice on the tenant named above as follows:*

☒ (1) by delivering a copy thereof to the above named tenant, Jane Q. Doe.

☐ (2) by delivering a copy thereof to ______, a person above the age of 13 years, residing on or in charge of the above described premises.

☐ (3) by sending a copy thereof to said tenant by certified mail, with request for return of receipt from the addressee.

☐ (4) by posting a copy thereof on the main door of the above described premises, no one being in actual possession thereof.

Subscribed and sworn to before me this 12th day of January, 19 88

Notary Public

X John A. Dooe

*Identify the method of service used by placing a check in the proper box. Sign on the line marked X.

4703 REV

EXHIBIT 40: Five-Day Notice Cover Letter

Date ______________________________

Dear __________________________________:

Enclosed is a five-day notice for your unpaid rent. This is a legal notice that you have five days in which to pay your rent. This is a demand for payment.

You are responsible for the apartment for the remaining term of the lease, whether you are occupying it or not, or until the apartment is rerented. Vacating the apartment will not release you from the responsibility of the lease. If you vacate without paying, a judgment will be entered against you that will appear on your credit record.

To avoid additional late charges and legal fees, which the lease states you are required to pay, please pay your rent within the prescribed five-day period.

If we do not receive full payment (Amount now due: $____________, including late fee) by (date) ______________________________ we will proceed with eviction proceedings.

If you have any further questions concerning this matter, please contact me.

Sincerely,

The top part of the five-day notice is filled out before being delivered to the resident. States vary in their requirements of posting and delivering notices. Check with your attorney to make sure the method described below is correct in your area.

The amount indicated as due must be rent only; it should not include late charges, security deposit, repair charges, etc. Write in the amount of one normal month's rent as shown on the resident's lease or extension. If a partial payment has been made, fill in the actual amount of rent still owed.

The rent is considered due for the full month, even if the resident has already paid a partial amount. A month's rent is not considered paid until the full amount is received. The beginning and ending dates of that month must be recorded on the notice.

Other information to record on the top part of the form is the complete name and address of the tenant (enter this in the boxed section "To"); and a complete description of the property, including location (city and county), street address and apartment number.

The bottom part of the five-day notice (Affidavit of Service) is completed after the resident has been served with the notice. Upon delivery, the original copy is filled out according to the sample.

The first line of the bottom section ("Served by") is for the name of the person who actually serves the five-day notice. This individual should be the owner or agent.

The person who served the notice signs the form at the bottom in the presence of a notary public any time prior to the time of filing for court eviction.

Delivering the Notice

The form offers four possible modes of delivery.

The preferred mode of delivery is for the owner to personally serve the notice to the principal adult resident. The notice can also be served to an occupant above 13 years of age or to an individual in charge, such as a babysitter.

Delivery by certified mail is not recommended because the eviction cannot be filed until the proof of receipt has been returned.

It is possible to post the notice on the apartment door (inside the apartment building, not outside, and not under the door). However, if you seriously want to evict the resident, use this method only as a last resort.

Partial Payments

Residents may attempt to pay part of the overdue rent during the period covered by the five-day notice. You do not have to accept a partial payment. You are only obligated to accept the full amount indicated on the five-day notice.

If you want to keep the tenants, it might be a good idea to accept a partial payment; but if you want to evict the tenants, insist on full payment. Accepting partial payments will only delay the inevitable.

If you accept a partial payment, you must serve another five-day notice indicating the balance due.

Follow-Up Action

In most cases a five-day notice will motivate tenants to pay. If not, you will have to take further action. On the sixth day following service of the five-day notice, if the tenants have not given you the rent, a legal action notice letter (exhibit 41) can be issued.

This form lets the tenant know that you are serious about an eviction and it might motivate them to pay. Otherwise if you seriously want to evict the tenant, proceed directly to filing eviction papers.

EXHIBIT 41: Legal Action Notice Letter

Date ______________________

Dear ______________________:

We have referred your delinquent rental account to our attorneys. They will file an eviction suit against you (date) ______________ in the __________ County Circuit Court. They will ask for possession of your apartment, and for a judgment against you for all rent due, plus late charges, attorneys' fees and all costs and expenses involved with this matter. You will be served with a copy of the complaint and a summons to appear in court.

However, if you pay the rent due, plus late fees and other costs (total costs to date: $__________) we will stop the legal proceedings that have been initiated against you. We cannot accept partial payment.

To avoid a forcible eviction by the __________ County Sheriff's Department, possible damage to your credit standing, a judgment and garnishment of wages, and future credit bureau and collection agency action, please phone me immediately at ______________________ and arrange to make payment.

Sincerely,

Eviction

It is a good idea to retain a lawyer to represent you for your first eviction; after that you can probably carry out evictions yourself. The process is generally as follows:

On the seventh day after filing the five-day notice, file eviction papers in county circuit court and obtain a court date, usually in two or three weeks. The court (or possibly you or your lawyer) will serve the eviction papers to the tenants.

Show up for court on the court date. If the tenants do not show up, the judge will order an eviction. If the tenants do show up, a lenient judge may grant an automatic two-week stay to allow the tenants more time to come up with the rent. If the tenants claim hardship (illness, unemployment, small children involved, difficulty finding other housing) the delay may be a month or more.

If the tenants do not pay within the court-decreed stay, you appear in court again, and the judge will enter a judgment against the tenants (monetary award) and order the eviction. Another stay is possible for hardship.

You take the eviction order to the Sheriff's department to set up an eviction date, usually in two or three weeks. Again, these papers are served to the tenants.

Usually the tenants will move out before actual physical eviction; if not, a moving company hired by the Sheriff (and paid for by you) will come and move the tenants out. At this time you regain possession of the apartment.

Clearly this is a long, time-consuming process. A number of filing fees must be paid, even if you do not retain an attorney. If the tenants have decided not to pay, you will lose a month or more of rent during the eviction process.

Attorney fees vary to process an eviction; these fees may be awarded to you by the court.

Collecting a Judgment

Partial Payments

If the resident attempts to pay part of the overdue rent during the period covered by the five-day notice you do not have to accept it. You are only obligated to accept the full amount indicated on the five-day notice.

In general, accept partial payments from tenants you want to keep; and do not accept partial payments from tenants that you want to evict.

After a resident makes a partial payment, you may have to serve another five-day notice indicating the balance due.

After delinquent tenants move out you can begin activities to recover the amount due. Winning in court does not mean that you will automatically be paid. The court may award you a judgment, but you must enforce it. You will probably have to take additional action to collect the funds.

Using a Collection Agency or Attorney

When residents have moved out without notice, or have been evicted, or have damaged the apartment in excess of the security deposit, or moved owing you back rent, the debt can be turned over to a collection agency or attorney.

Depending on the circumstances, it might be better to use a collection agency rather than an attorney. Collection agencies are usually licensed by the state and licenses can be revoked in the event a collection law is violated. Collection attorneys operate on their own and are controlled only by their peers in the bar association.

In either case, it is vital to select a reputable and talented attorney or agency. Collecting bad debts requires special skills and experience and is usually best handled by professionals.

Collection agencies normally work on a contingency basis. They generally charge a percentage of the amount collected as their fee.

Even with the help of a professional collection specialist, you may not always be successful in collecting bad debts from tenants. Thus, you should initiate legal proceedings promptly to minimize potential loss.

A collection agency will need as much information as possible to track down the former residents. You can use the transmittal form (exhibit 42) to forward information to the collections manager.

If possible, obtain the residents' forwarding address before they leave the apartment, for the purpose of forwarding mail or returning the security deposit. It is important to obtain their places of employment in case it is necessary to garnish wages, if permissible by law.

Other approaches that might prove successful in obtaining a forwarding address include recording the license plate number on the residents' car and contacting the Secretary of State, contacting the moving company, calling the old telephone number to see if calls are being referred to a new number and contacting the person listed on the application for notification in case of emergency.

EXHIBIT 42: Transmittal Form

Date: ______________________________

____

____

____

____

Gentlemen:

Enclosed are the necessary documents relating to the EVICTION, POSSESSION, FORCIBLE DETAINER and/or COLLECTION of Accounts Receivable for apartment:

______________ at ____

Names of Residents: ______________________________/______________________________

Monthly Rent: $__________ times ______ months = $______________

Months included: ______________________________________

Other Charges: $__________ for ______________________________ = $______________

SUBTOTAL: = $______________

- -

Attorney's fees: = $______________

Court Costs: = $______________

TOTAL DUE: = $______________

Please send COLLECTION letter first before beginning suit. ________

Please begin suit immediately. ________

Please do not sue—COLLECTION ONLY. ________

Please send letter demanding tenant take remedial action to cure default as listed. ________

Comments: ____

____

Please notify us of any actions taken by tenant as a result of your efforts. We will notify you immediately of any action or receipt of any funds on behalf of the tenant.

9

Insurance

Cathie Moscato *owns a business services company and is married to a school teacher. Two years ago, before getting married, Cathie bought a small six-flat apartment building in the suburbs.*

"I've always believed real estate to be the best investment around. Fortunately, my husband and I live on the property and are able to service the tenants immediately. My business hours are somewhat flexible, which allows me time to maintain a well-kept property.

"A couple of months after I bought the building, there was a fire in one of the top floor units. The fire was discovered at around 2 a.m. by one of the tenants. Although the fire was contained in that one apartment, by the time the fire department extinguished it, there was considerable smoke and water damage throughout the building.

"The fire department's official report listed the cause of the fire as the tenant's careless smoking.

"What could have been a financial disaster turned out to be a minor incident thanks to my independent insurance agent, who counseled me in purchasing the correct insurance for the property.

"Not only did my insurance cover the cost of repairs, but it also covered my loss of rental income during the repair period. My premium payments did not increase because my insurance company won the law suit against the tenant's insurance company, who ultimately paid the claim."

As the owner of an income property, you should carry insurance to protect your investment and its income against catastrophe. The following summary is provided for general information purposes only and is subject to the terms and conditions of your individual policies, which may vary.

Because no two properties are alike, there is no all-purpose insurance policy that will cover all buildings. Instead, the insurance agent will issue a multi-peril package (sometimes called a business-owners' package). This package consists of property and liability insurance, along with a number of endorsements and/or riders.

Property Insurance

The purpose of this coverage is to protect you from loss from damage to your property. There are two types of property to be considered: real property and business personal property.

Virtually all real property, except foundations and underground improvements, is included in the definition of a building under a policy. Most policies define a building as: buildings, structures, additions, fixtures, appliances, permanent equipment and machinery used for the maintenance and service of a building. Some companies include fences and TV antennas, some do not. Piers, wharves, docks, pools and valuable landscaping must be separately insured. Be sure to check what is included in the definition of real property on your policy.

Business personal property includes rental office contents on premises, lobby and recreational room contents, model apartment contents and furnished unit contents.

Limitations or Exclusions

Types of property which might have limited coverage or be excluded from this package of coverage include tenant improvements and betterments, boiler and machinery, leased equipment, money and securities, valuable papers, private collections, landscaping and mobile equipment such as trucks, automobiles, watercraft and aircraft.

Endorsement Options

Endorsements are separate documents attached to policies that modify the policy's original terms.

Agreed-Amount Endorsement

It is practical to establish a fixed value on your real insurable property to which the insurance underwriter will agree in advance. This agreement serves to eliminate coinsurance (see definitions). For superior property, an agreed-amount clause is a means of protecting against the consequence of inadvertent underinsurance in an inflationary environment.

Through this endorsement, a coinsurance clause is superseded and a specified amount of insurance takes the place of a specified percentage of actual cash value (ACV) or replacement cost. Partial losses are paid in full, after the application of the deductible. Total losses are paid to the policy limit.

Inflation-Guard Endorsement

Under this type of endorsement, the property coverage is automatically increased by a specific percentage each month (or quarter) to help meet rising construction and replacement costs.

Ask your agent to include this feature in your policy to prevent future coinsurance penalties or underinsurance.

Replacement-Cost Endorsement

This endorsement eliminates the deduction for depreciation in property valuation at the time of a loss. It is used in lieu of Actual Cash Value (ACV) or depreciated value.

Coverage is limited to either the cost of restoring the property to its original (nondepreciated) condition or the actual cost of repairing or replacing the property, whichever is less.

EXHIBIT 43: Certificate of Insurance Form

SET TAB STOPS AT ARROWS

CERTIFICATE OF INSURANCE

ISSUE DATE (MM/DD/YY): Must be completed

PRODUCER

Name & Address of
Contractor's Insurance Representative

THIS CERTIFICATE IS ISSUED AS A MATTER OF INFORMATION ONLY AND CONFERS NO RIGHTS UPON THE CERTIFICATE HOLDER. THIS CERTIFICATE DOES NOT AMEND, EXTEND OR ALTER THE COVERAGE AFFORDED BY THE POLICIES BELOW.

COMPANIES AFFORDING COVERAGE

COMPANY LETTER **A**	Name of Insuring Company
COMPANY LETTER **B**	Name of Insuring Company
COMPANY LETTER **C**	Name of Insuring Company
COMPANY LETTER **D**	Name of Insuring Company
COMPANY LETTER **E**	Name of Insuring Company

INSURED

Name & Address of
Contractor hired

COVERAGES

THIS IS TO CERTIFY THAT POLICIES OF INSURANCE LISTED BELOW HAVE BEEN ISSUED TO THE INSURED NAMED ABOVE FOR THE POLICY PERIOD INDICATED. NOTWITHSTANDING ANY REQUIREMENT, TERM OR CONDITION OF ANY CONTRACT OR OTHER DOCUMENT WITH RESPECT TO WHICH THIS CERTIFICATE MAY BE ISSUED OR MAY PERTAIN, THE INSURANCE AFFORDED BY THE POLICIES DESCRIBED HEREIN IS SUBJECT TO ALL THE TERMS, EXCLUSIONS, AND CONDITIONS OF SUCH POLICIES.

(Left margin, vertical: These Sections Must Be Completed)

CO LTR	TYPE OF INSURANCE	POLICY NUMBER	POLICY EFFECTIVE DATE (MM/DD/YY)	POLICY EXPIRATION DATE (MM/DD/YY)	LIABILITY LIMITS IN THOUSANDS		EACH OCCURRENCE	AGGREGATE
	GENERAL LIABILITY	These sections must be completed	This date should reflect a date prior to commencement of job.	This date should reflect a date past completion of job.	BODILY INJURY		$	$
	X COMPREHENSIVE FORM				PROPERTY DAMAGE		$	$
	X PREMISES/OPERATIONS				BI & PD COMBINED		$ 500	$500 *2
	UNDERGROUND EXPLOSION & COLLAPSE HAZARD				PERSONAL INJURY			$
	X PRODUCTS/COMPLETED OPERATIONS							
	X CONTRACTUAL							
	X INDEPENDENT CONTRACTORS							
	X BROAD FORM PROPERTY DAMAGE							
	PERSONAL INJURY							
	AUTOMOBILE LIABILITY	*1 Minimum requirement if vehicles are not required for the job			BODILY INJURY (PER PERSON)		$	
	ANY AUTO				BODILY INJURY (PER ACCIDENT)		$	
	ALL OWNED AUTOS (PRIV. PASS.)				PROPERTY DAMAGE		$	
	ALL OWNED AUTOS (OTHER THAN PRIV. PASS.)				BI & PD COMBINED		$ 500	
	*1 HIRED AUTOS							
	*1 NON-OWNED AUTOS							
	GARAGE LIABILITY							
	EXCESS LIABILITY				BI & PD COMBINED		$1,000	$1,000
	X UMBRELLA FORM							
	OTHER THAN UMBRELLA FORM							
	WORKERS' COMPENSATION AND EMPLOYERS' LIABILITY				STATUTORY			
					$ 100 (EACH ACCIDENT)			
					$ 100 (DISEASE-POLICY LIMIT)			
					$ 100 (DISEASE-EACH EMPLOYEE)			
	OTHER				*2 All limits shown are suggested minimums			

DESCRIPTION OF OPERATIONS/LOCATIONS/VEHICLES/SPECIAL ITEMS as relates to job contracted

Your name and trust in which your property is titled should appear here as additional named insured for job described herewith.

CERTIFICATE HOLDER

Your Name
& Address

CANCELLATION

SHOULD ANY OF THE ABOVE DESCRIBED POLICIES BE CANCELLED BEFORE THE EXPIRATION DATE THEREOF, THE ISSUING COMPANY WILL ~~ENDEAVOR TO~~ MAIL 30 DAYS WRITTEN NOTICE TO THE CERTIFICATE HOLDER NAMED TO THE
* ~~LEFT, BUT FAILURE TO MAIL SUCH NOTICE SHALL IMPOSE NO OBLIGATION OR LIABILITY OF ANY KIND UPON THE COMPANY, ITS AGENTS OR REPRESENTATIVES.~~

AUTHORIZED REPRESENTATIVE

This section must be signed

* Have this wording crossed out

Policies will pay on a replacement cost basis only if the damaged property is repaired or replaced at the same premises within a reasonable time after the loss.

Where replacement may take a significant amount of time, you may elect to settle on an ACV basis initially and, after the property has been restored, settle the balance due on a replacement cost basis.

Demolition and Increased Cost of Construction/Contingent Liability Endorsement

The ordinance or law exclusion in most property policies excludes loss from operation of building codes that require demolition of partially damaged structures and mandate superior construction in new or replacement buildings. Demolition coverage, which may be included by endorsement to the standard fire or all-risk policies, provides coverage for the cost of demolition and the loss from that remaining portion of the building which must be demolished when required by local ordinance.

The demolition endorsement is often combined with an increased cost of construction endorsement which affords coverage for the difference in costs between the original damaged construction and the new construction required by current building codes. Ordinances mandating superior construction are common in many cities where fire codes have been changed over the years. Check your local ordinance.

Difference-in-Conditions (DIC) Endorsement

This endorsement can add back coverage for some of the normal exclusions found in most policies. Backup of sewers and drains, wind-driven rain, off-premises power failure and off-premises water damage (example: a break in a city water main resulting in damage to premises) are normal exclusions under the basic fire policy.

Earthquake Endorsement

Coverage for damage from earthquake, and resulting aftershocks within 72 hours, may be provided by endorsements to the standard fire or all-risk policy or by special all-risk forms and DIC policies. Coverage includes damage to excavations, foundations and pilings, which is excluded under the standard fire policy.

Deductibles are generally quite high and rates are determined primarily by location and building construction.

Fine Arts Schedule

Any sculptures, antiques and other art work must be scheduled by endorsements on the policy. Be sure to advise your agent of the existence of these objects if you wish to insure them.

Glass Endorsement

Most apartment package policies limit glass coverage. If there is a large percentage of glass in the makeup of the building structure, additional coverage should be purchased. This may be accomplished by endorsing the apartment package policy or by purchasing a separate policy.

Discuss with the insurance agent any unique types of glass such as stained glass, neon and fluorescent signs and structural glass and lettering or ornamentation thereon. Coverage includes the repair or replacement of frames when necessary.

Loss of Rents Endorsement

This clause provides for reimbursement of rents lost, less any discontinued expense, when the loss is caused by an insured peril under the policy. Try to purchase this coverage on the basis of actual loss sustained within a 12-month period or 100 percent of annual value whenever possible.

Flood

The Federal Flood Program will provide up to $250,000 per building for flood damage when the building is located in a designated flood zone. Your local zoning or building code office will be able to tell you if your property is located in such a zone. This is a separate policy, not an endorsement. Apply for coverage through your insurance agent. The coverage is not effective until a completed application and payment of premium is received by the Federal Flood Program Agency.

Additional coverage may be purchased through a DIC (difference in conditions) policy. You may use the National Flood Program as coverage for the large deductible required under the DIC policy.

Liability Insurance

The purpose of liability insurance is to protect you against a lawsuit arising from some accidental or unintended occurrence. General liability protects against claims arising from premises, products, incidental contracts, libel, false arrest, etc.

The liability portion of a policy generally is written on a comprehensive basis for any occurrence arising out of the ownership, maintenance or use of the premises and for operations which are necessary or incidental to the property such as lawsuits arising out of slips and falls, and certain liabilities assumed under contracts or agreements. The limits are usually combined single limits for bodily injury and property damage liability and range from $300,000 to $1,000,000. Coverage of employee injuries is not included and must be purchased under a workers' compensation/ employers' liability policy.

An annual aggregate limit limits the total amount which will be paid for liability coverage in any one policy year. Many policies in 1987 include a limit for all occurrences within a policy year as well as the per occurrence limit. Be sure to check which limit you have purchased because of this annual aggregate limitation. An umbrella or excess policy purchase will be important to your protection.

Types of Liability Policies

Liability policies are of two types: *claims-made* and *occurrence-based.* Claims-made differs from an occurrence policy primarily in the manner in which coverage is triggered.

Occurrence-based policies cover events that occur during the policy period, and the insurance company is obligated to defend and pay for claims that arise from such covered occurrences at any time in the future, even years later. On the other hand, claims-made policies obligate the insurance company to defend and pay only for those claims made while the policy is in force, and for incidents which occurred on or after the retroactive date (usually the policy effective date). In other words, in a claims-made policy the company will pay claims for any occurrences on or after the retroactive date, and only up until the policy expires.

If your coverage is the claims-made type, yet you want coverage to last for a certain period of time after the policy expiration or cancellation, one option is to purchase an extended reporting period (sometimes called tail coverage) for your policy. This extends coverage to protect against claims that may be made after a policy is no longer in force.

Umbrella or Excess Liability

It is prudent to protect your assets with an umbrella or excess limits liability policy. The policy adds at least $1,000,000 of protection to primary liability policy limits of commercial, auto and employers' liability, and insures many uncovered liability exposures for $1,000,000 or more over a self-insured retention, normally $10,000 or $25,000.

Pollution Liability Exclusion

Effective with the 1986 and 1987 renewals, insurance companies excluded pollution liability coverage from their general liability policies. Older policy forms provided coverage for pollution liability as long as the act was "sudden and accidental."

The new liability insurance, now called *commercial liability policy,* excludes all pollution coverage. The exclusion is built into the policy itself and cannot be removed by endorsement. You should research your property to determine whether or not you have an exposure to pollution liability. If an exposure exists and coverage is desired, a special application and survey must be completed.

There is a growing need for property owners to protect themselves against financial liability associated with environmental damage. Although environmental impairment insurance is available, deductibles and premiums are substantial.

Broad Form Commercial General Liability (CGL)

Broad form commercial includes: contractural, personal injury which includes libel, slander, and false arrest (discrimination or humiliation coverage is included but limited), advertising, premises medical, host liquor, fire legal, incidental medical malpractice, non-owned watercraft, limited worldwide coverage, employees as additional insured, automatic coverage for newly acquired entities and broad form property damage which adds back care, custody and control. Some of these are discussed below; others are defined at the end of this chapter. Your agent can explain how these options apply to your property.

Contractural (Independent Contractors)

You may have occasion to enter into contracts employing others, such as painters, roofers and so on. When the contractor enters your premises or does work on your behalf, she or he may incur or cause injury claims for which you may be held liable. Some of the claims asserted against you by people injured by the contractor are covered by your own policy under the commercial general liability section if your agent has included independent contractors on an "if any" basis.

In some states, if a contractor cannot respond to a workers' compensation claim, the person for whom the injured employee is working (you) may have to respond. Therefore, you should request evidence that the contractor carries liability and workers' compensation insurance, prior to his beginning the job.

This evidence is normally provided in the form of a certificate of insurance and is obtained from the contractor's insurance broker.

Medical Payments

Coverage is automatically provided in the amounts of $1,000 or more per person and $10,000 or $25,000 for all persons requiring medical attention as a result of a single accident arising from owned or rented premises. Some policies exclude payments in behalf of tenants or residents. Liability need not be proven.

Personal Injury

You face risks for claims other than bodily injury or property damage. If you libel or slander someone, invade a person's privacy, commit a trespass or mistakenly accuse someone of a theft he or she can sue you.

Indemnity for certain personal injuries is in the insuring agreement of the commercial liability section of the policy.

Host Liquor

This involves the liability of a host for serving liquor (without charge) to persons already clearly intoxicated and who, while intoxicated, cause bodily injury or property damage to others.

Making Claims

One of the conditions of an insurance policy is that you give prompt notice to the insurer of any accident or occurrence and of any claim or suit brought against you. An occurrence is an incident such as someone falling on your premises or an error which causes loss or injury to a person, or any unplanned event which could give cause to a lawsuit.

If you fail to give reasonable notice, you may be shocked to find that the insurance company's obligations to defend you and pay any claims have been waived. Try to report any notice of a lawsuit the same day it is received.

Notice is normally given by contacting the agent or broker who sold you the policy. To protect yourself, it is wise to give notice in writing and to get written confirmation from the agent acknowledging that your notice has been received and forwarded to the insurer.

Don't attempt to judge whether or not insurance will apply. The report should be made regardless of coverage. If there is a serious question in your mind whether the policy covers the claim, consult your attorney for assistance in giving notice to the insurer. A poorly drafted notice may prompt the insurer to deny coverage rather than to investigate and pay the claim.

Property Claims

Property damage claims should be made promptly. To report property claims use the property loss form provided by your insurance carrier. A sample is included as exhibit 46.

Photos should be taken when damage to your property occurs and you need to make immediate repairs to prevent further loss. It is not necessary to wait for the claims adjuster before you do whatever emergency repairs are necessary to prevent further loss. Be sure to retain any damaged, replaced materials or objects for the adjuster to view upon arrival. Most property policies cover your insured property if you move it to a safer place to avoid loss or further damage.

Liability Claims

To report liability claims use the liability loss report form and the incident report form provided by your carrier to assist you in providing necessary information to the insurance company's claim adjuster. Samples are included as exhibits 44–46.

The incident report is very beneficial in tenant-landlord communications. Using this form to extract information from the tenant or visitor at the time of complaint assures the complainant that proper attention is being given to the incident. The report is then forwarded to the insurance carrier, who responds to the complaint. Some important notes to remember regarding liability incidents are:

- Make no statement admitting liability or authorizing medical treatment.
- Take photos of the area when an accident occurs, prior to proceeding with any necessary immediate repairs. If any machine or object may have been responsible for the accident, preserve it, as is, in a safe place until it can be examined by experts.
- Advise any employees not to discuss the case with anyone until instructed by your claims adjuster or attorney.

Other Types of Insurance

FAIR Plan

In the past, if you were unable to buy insurance for property because it was in a riot-prone or environmentally hazardous urban area, coverage was made available through the Federal Riot Reinsurance Program under the FAIR (fair access to insurance requirements) Plan. This program no longer is federally active, however, in Illinois, it has become a statewide program.

EXHIBIT 44: Incident Report

INCIDENT REPORT

Date: ______________ Time: ______________ Name of Reporting Person: ______________________

Date of Incident: ______________ Time of Incident: ______________ Property: ______________________

Specific Location of Incident: ____
(floor, apt., room, area, address, etc.)

Type of incident: Accident _______ Crime _______ Fire _______ Ambulance _______ Vandalism _______

Mechanical _______ Theft _______ Loss _______ Other ______________________

WHAT HAPPENED? ____

____

____

____

____

LIST INJURIES
OR DAMAGES ____

____

____

LIST PEOPLE
INVOLVED ____

____

PREVALENT CONDITIONS AT TIME OF INCIDENT: ______________________
(weather, lightning, environment, etc.)

____

____

- -

FOR MANAGEMENT USE ONLY

Insurance Notified: ______________________ By Phone: _______ By Mail: _______
(date)

Name of Insurance Agent: ____

Board Notified: _______ Name of Board Member: ______________________

Police Notified: _______ Report Number: ___________ Name of Officer: ______________________

Follow-up Action Required: ____

____

____

EXHIBIT 45: Liability Loss Report

LIABILITY LOSS REPORT

Reported by: ______________________________ Date: ______________

Complex: ____

Date of Loss: ______________

Contact Person: ______________________________ Phone Number: ______________

- -

INJURED PARTY OR DAMAGE TO PERSONAL PROPERTY OF TENANTS, ETC.

Name: ____

Address: ____

Phone Number: ______________________ Work Number: ______________________

Age: __________ Sex: __________ Date of Injury: ______________________

Where Injury Sustained (Address): ______________________________

How Injury Sustained: ______________________________________

____

____

____

____

(If additional space is required, please use reverse side.)

Type of Injury: ______________________________________

____

____

Treating Hospital: ______________________________________

Was Police Department Called? If So, Please Indicate: ______________________

Additional Comments: ______________________________________

____

____

____

____

____

EXHIBIT 46: Property Loss Report

PROPERTY LOSS REPORT

Reported by: ______________________________ Date: ______________

Complex: ______________________________

Date of Loss: ______________

Contact Person: ______________________________ Phone Number: ______________

Location of Loss: ______________________________

Kind of Loss (Fire, Wind, Explosion, etc.): ______________________________

Description of Loss & Damage: ______________________________

____

____

____

____

Estimated Amount of Loss: ______________

Police or Fire Department Reported to: ______________________________

Claimants Name, Address & Phone Number: ______________________________

____

____

____

____

Additional Comments: ______________________________

____

____

____

____

____

____

A building must be otherwise insurable except for its location in a blighted or deteriorated eligible urban area.

You must submit an application for eligibility and may be accepted, conditionally accepted or unconditionally declined. You cannot be declined for reason of environmental hazards in urban areas.

Coverage is generally limited to fire, extended coverage, vandalism and malicious mischief. Maximum limits are $500,000 at any one location.

Tenants' Insurance

As a landlord, you should encourage your tenants to carry adequate personal property and liability insurance.

The landlord has limited liability for injury or damage occurring within the rental portion of the premises. Both landlord and tenant have a duty to take reasonable care in the portion of the premises under their control. For example, if tenant Jones on an upper floor allows his bathtub to overflow and the water drips through the ceiling and ruins rugs in tenant Smith's apartment below, the landlord is not liable, since Smith is in exclusive possession of his apartment. However, the landlord, on being advised, must attempt where possible to aid the tenant suffering the loss by turning off the water.

If a tenant causes a fire, damages are paid by the apartment building owner's insurance company, who could then seek recovery from the tenant's liability policy, thus protecting the good claims record of the building owner. A high and frequent claims record usually means higher premiums for the building owner.

Boiler and Machinery Insurance

Boiler and machinery insurance can be endorsed into many packages or written on a separate policy. Protection includes property damage and legal liability for damage to the property of others in your care, custody and control, and associated defense costs. A large component of the boiler and machinery premium is for engineering and inspection services.

Boiler Coverage

Almost all apartment building policies exclude damage to the insured property resulting from internally caused explosion of boilers and other pressure vessels. Consequently, boiler coverage is needed if the property contains any heating or process boiler or steam generator that operates under pressure. Boilers include hot water boilers, steam boilers and steam piping.

Boiler explosions are rare. However, even one such explosion can be a catastrophic event in terms of potential destruction and injury. A far more common occurrence is the less destructive but still costly cracking, burning, bulging or collapse of boilers and pressure vessels.

One of the most common failures of boilers is the failure of the low-water cutoff, the control that shuts off the burner when the water level is low. Such failure generally results in damage from overheating, and in the case of cast iron boilers, cracked sections. If your insurance policy includes a boiler inspection service, this can be as valuable as the coverage itself.

Machinery Coverage

Machinery coverage provides insurance against damage and loss resulting from the breakdown of machinery on the premises. Machinery includes objects such as air compressors, fans, air conditioners, blowers, pump units, engines, turbines and miscellaneous electrical equipment such as switchboards and other apparatus used for power distribution. This coverage also extends to surrounding property which is excluded under the apartment building package policy.

It is wise to insure only those machines that are extraordinarily expensive and time-consuming to repair or whose function is critical to the entire operation. Again, the insurance company's machinery inspection service can be a valuable component of the insurance policy.

Coverage Options in Boiler and Machinery Insurance

- Repairs and replacement: essentially an elimination of depreciation.
- Extra expenses for the period of restoration.
- Prevention of vacancy and consequential damage.
- Legal liability for bodily injury arising out of an accident covered under the terms of the policy.
- Joint loss agreement (loss adjustment endorsement) should be obtained when you have different insurers for building and boiler and machinery. This means the boiler carrier will settle the loss and subrogate against the property insurer if necessary.
- Business interruption (loss of rents): on a valued daily or weekly indemnity basis. Coverage options include:

Actual loss sustained: The loss of net profit plus specified fixed charges and expenses that continue despite the accident. This loss must be proven. If coverage is on a coinsurance basis, you should obtain a waiver of coinsurance, if possible. Care must be taken in establishing the values.

Valued form: A daily indemnity is specified which is the amount of recovery for each day during which rents are totally suspended. In the case of a partial suspension, a portion is paid based on reduction of current business.

Workers' Compensation

Each state has its own workers' compensation law, whereby all workers suffering injury or illness related to the job are reimbursed for medical costs, lost earnings and rehabilitation costs. Where death occurs, an employee's heirs are entitled to death benefits provided by statute.

If you hire employees such as rental agents, cleaners or maintenance personnel, you must purchase workers' compensation/employers' liability insurance.

Even if you have no direct employees, you still should have voluntary workers compensation/employers liability insurance for those situations where a subcontractor is uninsured or an independent contractor can show employee status. State workers' compensation courts do not always recognize independent contractor arrangements.

The objective of workers' compensation is to indemnify the employee for loss of earnings and expenses. The employer is obligated to pay for the reasonable cost of medical, surgical, hospital and nursing services as required. The injured employee is also entitled to weekly compensation payment for the length of the disability and rehabilitation services. Workers' compensation statutes in all states now include disease.

Every worker injury involving medical treatment or lost time must be reported on the form used in your state. Each state has its own form; copies are available from your local adjuster or agent. For samples of the Illinois, Indiana and Arizona forms see exhibits 47, 48 and 49.

Employers' Liability

A further exposure facing an employer is an action instituted by a third party. This could arise where an injured employee sues and recovers from

EXHIBIT 47: Workers' Compensation Claim Form—Illinois

FORM 45: **Employers First Report of Injury or Illness** PLEASE TYPE OR PRINT

Filing of this report does not affect your liability under the Workers' Compensation Act and is not incriminatory in any sense.

A	*45 / ILLINOIS UNEMPLOYMENT COMPENSATION NUMBER / DATE OF REPORT: MONTH DAY YEAR / CASE OR FILE NUMBER
B	EMPLOYER'S NAME / Is this a lost workday case? ☐Yes ☐No
C	DOING BUSINESS UNDER THE NAME OF / CITY, STATE / ZIP CODE
D	MAIL ADDRESS / CITY, STATE / ZIP CODE
E	EMPLOYER LOCATION IF DIFFERENT FROM MAIL ADDRESS
F	NATURE OF BUSINESS OR SERVICE / SIC CODE / TOTAL NUMBER OF EMPLOYEES AT THE LOCATION WHERE ILLNESS OR INJURY OCCURRED
G	NAME OF WORKERS' COMP. INSURANCE CARRIER / POLICY NUMBER / SELF INSURED YES ☐ ☐NO / COUNTY WHERE INJURY OCCURRED
H	EMPLOYEE'S NAME (LAST, FIRST, MIDDLE) / SOCIAL SECURITY NUMBER
I	HOME ADDRESS / CITY, STATE / ZIP CODE
J	MALE ☐ FEMALE ☐ / MARRIED ☐ SINGLE ☐ WIDOW(ER) ☐ DIVORCED ☐ / BIRTH DATE: MONTH DAY YEAR / NUMBER OF DEPENDENT CHILDREN UNDER 18 AT TIME OF INJURY OR ILLNESS
K	DATE AND TIME OF THE INJURY OR EXPOSURE: MONTH DAY YEAR a.m. p.m. / EMPLOYEE'S AVERAGE WEEKLY EARNINGS $ / LAST DAY EMPLOYEE WORKED: MONTH DAY YEAR
L	JOB TITLE OR OCCUPATION / DEPARTMENT NORMALLY ASSIGNED
M	ADDRESS OF LOCATION WHERE INJURY OR EXPOSURE OCCURRED / CITY, STATE / ZIP CODE
N	DID EMPLOYEE DIE AS A RESULT OF THE INJURY OR ILLNESS? YES ☐ NO ☐ / IF EMPLOYEE DIED AS A RESULT OF THE INJURY OR ILLNESS, GIVE DATE OF DEATH: MONTH DAY YEAR
O	WAS THE INJURY OR EXPOSURE ON THE EMPLOYER'S PREMISES? ☐YES ☐NO / DID THIS INCIDENT RESULT IN: ☐ OCCUPATIONAL INJURY ☐ OCCUPATIONAL DISEASE / Was Employee given Industrial Commission Handbook? YES ☐ NO ☐
P	NATURE OF THE INJURY
Q	PART OF THE BODY AFFECTED (BE SPECIFIC)
R	WHAT TASK WAS EMPLOYEE PERFORMING WHEN ILLNESS OR INJURY OCCURRED?
S	OBJECT OR SUBSTANCE RESPONSIBLE FOR INJURY OR ILLNESS (SOURCE)
T	HOW DID ACCIDENT OR ILLNESS OCCUR (TYPE)?
U	WHAT HAZARDOUS CONDITIONS, METHODS OR LACK OF PROTECTIVE DEVICES CONTRIBUTED?
V	WHAT UNSAFE ACT BY A PERSON CAUSED OR CONTRIBUTED TO THE INJURY OR ILLNESS?
W	HAVE MEDICAL SERVICES BEEN RENDERED TO THE EMPLOYEE? YES ☐ NO ☐ / IS OR HAS THE EMPLOYEE BEEN HOSPITALIZED? YES ☐ NO ☐
X	NAME AND ADDRESS OF PHYSICIAN / CITY, STATE / ZIP CODE
Y	NAME AND ADDRESS OF HOSPITAL / CITY, STATE / ZIP CODE
Z	REPORT PREPARED BY: (NAME—PRINT OR TYPE) / SIGNATURE / TITLE AND TELEPHONE NUMBER

REPORT ALL ACCIDENTS IMMEDIATELY AND SEND ORIGINAL AND 2 COPIES TO:

NOTE: DISCLOSURE OF THIS INFORMATION TO THE INDUSTRIAL COMMISSION IS MANDATORY UNDER IL. REV. STAT. CH. 48, § 138.6. FAILURE TO PROVIDE ANY INFORMATION COULD RESULT IN PROSECUTION. APPROVED BY FORMS MANAGEMENT.

EXHIBIT 48: Workers' Compensation Claim Form—Indiana

State Form 34401

STATE OF INDIANA

Industrial Board Division

FORM No. 24

Employer's Report to Industrial Board of Injury to Employee

Revised March, 1976

State's Number For:	File: ____ Carrier: ____ Employer: ____
Carrier's File No. ____	
(The spaces above not to be filled in by Employer)	

EMPLOYER

(1) Name: ____ (2) I.D.#: ____ (FOR STATE USE ONLY)
(3) Mail Address: Street: ____ (4) City: ____
(5) County: ____ (6) State: ____ (7) Zip: ____
Actual location: (8) Street: ____ (IF DIFFERENT FROM MAILING ADDRESS) (9) City: ____
(10) County: ____ (11) State: ____ (12) Zip: ____
(13) Nature of business: ____

EMPLOYEE

(14) Name: ____
Address: (15) Street: ____ (16) City: ____
(17) County: ____ (18) State: ____ (19) Zip: ____ (20) Tel. No.: ____
(21) Age: ____ (22) Date of Birth: ____ (23) Social Security No.: ____
(24) Sex: ____ (25) Marital Status: ____ (26) Names, ages of all dependents: ____
(27) If a minor, is an employment certificate or permit on file: ____ (28) Length of employment: ____
(29) Regular department: ____ (30) Regular occupation ____
(31) Occupation when injured/exposed: ____ (32) No. of hours worked per day: ____
(33) Days per week: ____ (34) Piece or time work: ____ (35) Wages per hour: ____
(36) Wages per day: ____ (37) Any other compensation: ____ (38) Average weekly earnings: ____

TIME and PLACE

(39) Date: ____ (40) Time: ____ AM/PM (41) Exact address of incident: ____
(42) Was this employer's premises: ____ (43) Department: ____
(44) If in a mine, did it occur on surface, underground, shaft, drift or mill: ____
(45) When and to whom was first report of incident reported: ____

CAUSE OF INJURY

(46) Machine, tool or substance causing injury/illness: (Be specific. If he was using tools or equipment or handling material, name them and tell what he was doing with them.) ____
(47) Kind of power: ____ (48) Part of machine on which accident occurred: ____
(49) Was safety appliance or regulation provided: ____ (50) Was it in use at time: ____
(51) Was incident caused by employee's failure to use or observe safety applicance or regulation: ____
(52) Describe fully how accident/exposure occurred: (Tell what happened and how it happened. Name any objects or substances involved and tell how they were involved. Give full details on all factors which led or contributed to the accident. Use separate sheet for additional space.) ____
(53) State what employee was doing when injured/exposed: ____
(54) Name and addresses of witnesses: ____

NATURE OF INJURY

(55) Date and time disability began: ____ AM/PM (56) Was employee paid in full for this day: ____
(57) Lost Workdays: ____ (58) Has employee returned to work: ____ (59) If yes, what date and time: ____ AM/PM
(60) What wage: ____ (61) What occupation: ____ (62) If no, probable length of disability: ____
(63) Nature and location of injury/illness (describe fully exact location of amputations, fractures and part of body affected): ____
(64) Has employee died: ____ (65) Date: ____

(66) Name and address of physician: ____
(67) Name and address of hospital: ____

(68) Is this an IOSHA Recordable Injury: Yes ____ No ____ IOSHA Case or File #: ____
(69) Employer has compensation insurance with: ____
(70) Date of this report: ____ (71) Firm Name: ____

Signed by: ____ Title: ____
Telephone ____ (TO BE FILED IN TRIPLICATE)

EXHIBIT 49: Workers' Compensation Claim Form—Arizona

EMPLOYER'S REPORT OF INDUSTRIAL INJURY

COMPLETE AND MAIL THIS REPORT
WITHIN 10 DAYS FROM NOTICE OF ACCIDENT
FATALITIES MUST BE REPORTED WITHIN 24 HOURS

Employer must on this form notify his insurance carrier of every injury or disease suffered by an employee, fatal or otherwise which is claimed to arise out of and in the course of employment.
ARIZONA REVISED STATUTES 23-908 & 23-1061

INDUSTRIAL COMMISSION OF ARIZONA
P.O. BOX 19070
PHOENIX, ARIZONA 85005

MAIL TO: (CARRIER NAME & ADDRESS)

FOR CARRIER USE ONLY

FOR OSHA PURPOSES ONLY
OSHA Case No. ______
RECORDABLE INJURY ______
NON-RECORDABLE INJURY ______

EMPLOYEE
1. LAST NAME FIRST M.I. | 2. SOCIAL SECURITY NUMBER | 3. BIRTH DATE
4. HOME ADDRESS (NUMBER & STREET) CITY STATE ZIP CODE | 5. TELEPHONE
6. SEX ☐ MALE ☐ FEMALE | 7. MARITAL STATUS ☐ SINGLE ☐ MARRIED ☐ DIVORCED ☐ WIDOWED

EMPLOYER
8. EMPLOYER'S NAME | 9. POLICY NO. | 10. NATURE OF BUSINESS (MANUFACTURING, ETC.)
11. OFFICE ADDRESS (NUMBER & STREET) CITY STATE ZIP CODE | 12. TELEPHONE

ACCIDENT
13. DATE OF INJURY | 14. HOUR OF INJURY ☐ a.m. ☐ p.m. | 15. DATE EMPLOYER NOTIFIED OF INJURY / / | 16. LAST DAY OF WORK AFTER INJURY / / | 17. DATE OF RETURN TO WORK / /
18. EMPLOYEE'S OCCUPATION (JOB TITLE) WHEN INJURED | 19. CLASS CODE ON PAYROLL REPORT | 20. EMPLOYEE'S ASSIGNED DEPARTMENT | 21. DEPARTMENT NUMBER
22. ADDRESS OR LOCATION OF ACCIDENT CITY COUNTY STATE ZIP CODE
23. ON EMPLOYER PREMISES? YES NO | 24. NATURE OF INJURY (SCRATCH, CUT, BRUISE, ETC.) FATAL? YES NO | 25. PART OF BODY INJURED
26. ATTENDING PHYSICIAN (NAME) ADDRESS (STREET, CITY, STATE & ZIP CODE)
27. IF HOSPITALIZED, HOSPITAL NAME ADDRESS (STREET, CITY, STATE & ZIP CODE)
28. IF VALIDITY OF CLAIM IS DOUBTED, STATE REASON

CAUSE OF ACCIDENT
29. HOW DID ACCIDENT HAPPEN (STATE ALL DETAILS: (USE OTHER SIDE IF NEEDED)
30. SPECIFY MACHINE, TOOL, SUBSTANCE OR OBJECT MOST CLOSELY CONNECTED WITH ACCIDENT
31. WHAT WAS EMPLOYEE DOING WHEN ACCIDENT OCCURED (LOADING TRUCK, WALKING DOWN STAIRS, ETC.)?
32. IF ANOTHER PERSON NOT IN COMPANY EMPLOY CAUSED ACCIDENT, GIVE NAME AND ADDRESS

EMPLOYEE'S WAGE DATA
33. WAS WORKER IN YOUR EMPLOY WHEN INJURED YES ☐ NO ☐ | 34. HOURS PER DAY EMPLOYEE WORKED FROM A.M. ☐ P.M. ☐ THRU A.M. ☐ P.M. ☐ | 35. WAS EMPLOYEE ON OVERTIME WHEN INJURED YES ☐ NO ☐ | 36. NUMBER OF DAYS PER WEEK EMPLOYEE USUALLY WORKED / COMPANY USUALLY WORKS

IMPORTANT ▶ IF WORK LOSS IS EXPECTED TO EXCEED SEVEN CALENDAR DAYS, COMPLETE ITEMS 37 THRU 44
37. DATE OF LAST HIRE | 38. WAS WORKER PAID FOR DAY OF INJURY YES ☐ NO ☐ AMOUNT IF YES $ | 39. WAS EMPLOYEE HIRED FOR PERMANENT EMPLOYMENT YES ☐ NO ☐
40. NUMBER OF MONTHS EMPLOYMENT AVAILABLE DURING THE YEAR MONTHS | 41. GIVE EMPLOYEE'S WAGE STATUS AS APPLICABLE $ PER HOUR ☐ DAY ☐ WEEK ☐ MONTH ☐ | 42. IS EMPLOYEE FURNISHED ☐ LODGING ☐ BOARD ☐ BOTH VALUE $
43. ACTUAL GROSS EARNINGS OF EMPLOYEE FOR THE 30 CALENDAR DAYS PRECEEDING INJURY (EXAMPLE: IF INJURED APRIL 8, GIVE EARNINGS FROM MARCH 9 THRU APRIL 7) $ | 44. DOES EMPLOYEE CLAIM DEPENDENTS YES ☐ NO ☐

IMPORTANT ▶ IF EMPLOYEE IS PAID OTHER THAN FIXED WEEKLY OR MONTHLY SALARY, COMPLETE ITEMS 45 THRU 52
45. IF EMPLOYEE EARNS EXTRA PAY FOR OVERTIME, WHAT IS BASIS OF PAYMENT? PER HOUR | 46. NUMBER OF HOURS OVERTIME CONSIDERED NORMAL PER WEEK
47. GROSS WAGES OF EMPLOYEE DURING 12 MONTHS PRECEEDING INJURY FROM THRU $ | 48. IF EMPLOYEE WORKED LESS THAN 12 MONTHS, SHOW GROSS WAGES FROM DATE OF HIRE THROUGH DAY PRIOR TO INJURY FROM THRU $
49. DATE OF LAST WAGE INCREASE IF WITHIN 12 MONTHS PRIOR TO INJURY | 50. WAGE BEFORE INCREASE $ | 51. WAGE AFTER INCREASE $ | 52. GROSS EARNINGS FROM DATE OF INCREASE THRU DAY PRIOR TO INJURY $

AUTHORIZED SIGNATURE
DATE | AUTHORIZED SIGNATURE | TITLE

NOTE TO EMPLOYER:
1. Mail one copy to the Industrial Commission within 10 days
2. Mail one copy to your insurance carrier within 10 days
3. Keep one copy, for not less than 5 years, as your supplementary record of injuries required by the Federal Occupational Safety and Health Act of 1970.

ICA 04-0101 (Rev. 88)

(THIS FORM APPROVED BY THE INDUSTRIAL COMMISSION OF ARIZONA FOR CARRIER USE)

a legally responsible third party such as the manufacturer of machinery. This third party manufacturer may in turn seek recovery from the employer, contending, for example, that the employer is liable for having negligently maintained the machine or having inadequately trained the employee.

A few work-related injuries do not fall under workers' compensation law. If that is the case, the claim is one of employers' liability, which is part of the workers' compensation policy.

Employers' liability coverage, in contrast to workers' compensation coverage, is subject to a specified limit of liability. This is customarily written at a limit of $100,000 but can be increased to $500,000. It is advisable to have this coverage scheduled on the umbrella or excess liability policy to assure that the higher umbrella limits apply. Some umbrella insurers have refused to insure employers' liability incurred by employee disease; therefore, you should request a higher employers' liability on the workers' compensation/employers' liability policy.

Dealing with Insurance Companies

Begin shopping for insurance coverage at least 60 days prior to the expiration of your current coverage to allow sufficient time to find the best coverage for the lowest premium.

Be sure to provide accurate information about construction and square footage of your building. The premium you pay is partially based on this information. Tell your agent about any improvements or updates, such as new roofing, heating, plumbing and electrical wiring that have been done within the past ten years. This information can reduce your premium as much as 50 percent in some cases.

Coverages are essentially the same throughout the United States, but local variations will apply. Your insurance agent can assist you in choosing your insurance format and assembling an appropriate insurance program.

Rating of Insurance Companies

Your mortgage may require that you obtain coverage from a company with a Best rating of A or A+. This means the company has a superior or excellent evaluation based on its financial condition and operating performance. This is a good idea, as companies may experience financial or service difficulties from time to time. The Best ratings give you some assurance that you are obtaining your insurance from a financially strong company.

Insurance Agents

There are two types of insurance agents: independent and direct writers. An independent agent may represent many different insurance companies, such as Hanover, Kemper, Cigna, Chubb, Fireman's Fund, Travelers, Continental, USF&G and Reliance to name a few. A direct writer normally represents one company, such as Allstate, State Farm or Farmers.

You may wish to obtain quotes from both the direct writer and the independent agent. This will allow you to obtain the most competitive coverage.

Your agent should be insured for errors and omissions, and you should require proof of this coverage. This can be produced in the form of a certificate of insurance. You may have recourse under this coverage if your agent mistakenly fails to provide coverage for which you paid.

Inspections

The insurance company may inspect your property before or after the inception of your policy. If they find conditions and/or physical hazards that will encourage or contribute to a loss on your premises they will issue a notice of recommendations for eliminating or reducing these exposures.

Inspectors from fire, liability, boiler and machinery and workers' compensation insurance companies should be given every cooperation.

Boiler and machinery inspectors (but no others) have the authority to shut down any object that they feel poses an imminent danger.

Respond to an inspector's notice of recommendations by informing your insurer in writing of your intentions to comply with the recommendations, and supply an estimate of the time needed to comply.

Recommendations with which you agree should be carried out, but for those on which there is any question, your objections should be put in writing to the insurance agent. It's a good idea to comply, whenever reasonable, because eliminating or minimizing losses results in direct savings in the long run.

If you do not respond, and a reinspection reveals the same hazardous conditions, the insurer may cancel your coverage within the first 60 days of inception. Coverage will then be more difficult to obtain elsewhere.

The insurer may cancel for reasons of increased hazard by giving the named insured and the mortgagee at least 30 days' advance notice in writing. If possible, negotiate a 60-day or 90-day notice to allow ample time to shop for your next insurance company.

Definitions

All-risk: This term means there is coverage for all perils except those excluded. Be sure to read the exclusions portion of your policy.

Care, Custody and Control: Damage to personal property of others which is in the care, custody or control of the insured is excluded under all standard liability forms. You should purchase a bailee endorsement or policy to cover this exposure.

Bailee: Whenever property is delivered into the custody of a person other than the rightful owner, the person in control of the property becomes the bailee, assuming certain responsibilities for the safety of property in his care.

As a bailee you may store an article for another, or accept packages for your tenants to pick up and/or borrow a piece of equipment. Discuss with your agent your possible bailee exposure.

Certificates of insurance: You should require contractors who do work for you to supply a certificate of insurance in order to limit your liability in case of mishaps. Certificates should show liability coverage for bodily injury and property damage and for workers' compensation/employers' liability. Exhibit 43 on page 160 shows how one sample of a certificate of insurance form looks when completed.

If a suit arises and you cannot provide proof that the contractor had insurance, your policy may pay on your behalf when you are sued. However, your insurance company may then require you to pay a premium for this additional exposure, or may cancel your coverage as a result of this discovery.

Coinsurance: Coinsurance indicates a sharing of the insurance by the insurance company and the insured. The word coinsurance has a more limited and restricted meaning within the insurance business.

The mandatory and minimum amount of coinsurance is usually 80 percent. Illustrating the coinsurance clause by example best explains its meaning and application. For example, a property with an actual cash value of $100,000 must be insured for at least 80 percent of this value of the property, or $80,000.

In this case $80,000 would be the minimum coverage required to avoid penalty in the event of a loss. If the same building is insured for $60,000 in lieu of the required $80,000, it would be insured for only three-fourths of the minimum coverage demanded by the coinsurance requirements. In this instance, a penalty would be imposed should a loss occur.

In the event of a $1,000 loss, exclusive of all deductibles, the insured would receive not $1,000, but three-fourths of the loss, or $750. In the event of a total loss, however, the insured would collect the full face value of the policy, or $60,000. Since the property was valued at $100,000 before the loss, the insured is still penalized for not having insured sufficiently, a $40,000 penalty.

The coinsurance clause is taken very seriously in the insurance business and an insured who does not adhere to its requirements can expect to receive less than full value when faced with a loss.

Deductibles: The use of a deductible means the insured pays the first dollar amount for a loss, as specified in the policy.

Unless changed by endorsement, a standard $100 deductible may apply separately to each building (and its contents), subject to a $1,000 aggregate per occurrence.

Premium dollars can be saved by increasing the deductible. A larger deductible will mean a larger financial outlay in the event of a loss and may mean total responsibility for smaller losses, but it will also result in an immediate savings on the premium.

Deductibles are collected in three different ways:

- **Occurrence:** One fire or other insured loss equals one occurrence and one deductible applies.
- **Per claim:** This applies to every claim filed regardless of number of occurrences. One fire may produce six or more claims and six or more deductibles will apply.
- **Aggregate (either occurrence or annual):** With a $25,000 annual aggregate deductible, the insured retains a maximum of $25,000 of losses in a given year and the insurer is responsible for any additional loss payments in that year.

Physical hazard: This is a characteristic that increases the chance of loss. Some hazards arise from a repaired defect in the property (for example, a broken step); others are inherent characteristics of the property (for example, a building is of frame construction).

Premium: This is money that the insured pays the insurer for coverage of a defined nature. This exchange must take place prior to or at the inception date of coverage; you may be surprised to find you are not insured if a loss occurs prior to premium payment. A large premium can be financed with monthly or quarterly payments by a premium finance company at interest rates close to bank prime rates.

Property values: Insured values reflect not market value but the actual construction cost, that is, the actual cost to rebuild at the time of loss.

Unless specifically endorsed or stated in the coverage form, all property will be valued at actual cash value (ACV) at the time of loss. ACV is defined as the cost to repair or replace the damaged property less an amount for actual physical depreciation. This basis of adjustment may be modified, however, by the attachment of a replacement cost endorsement.

Punitive or exemplary damage awards: Most companies will exclude responsibility for payment of any award for punitive or exemplary damage. Responding to and complying with insurance company recommendations will add to your noticeable effort to provide a safe environment for your tenants and will be beneficial in the defense of suits that may arise.

Self-insured retention (SIR): That portion of a loss that you pay.

Vacancy: This is a condition which exists when there are no furnishings or other personal property in the building. Some insurers consider property vacant when there are no full-time occupants. Most policies contain a clause which suspends coverage when a building is vacant beyond a stated period of time, normally 30 days. Vacancy policies are available, but are very expensive.

10

Maintenance

Andy Chychula *is an emergency medical technician with the local fire department. His 24-hour work shift every three days allowed him time to earn extra income repairing and fixing neighborhood homes. He eventually purchased a three-flat and a five-flat apartment building. Two of his friends involved in real estate finance and brokerage persuaded him to combine his talents and assets with them and buy a larger apartment building. They formed a partnership and purchased a 49-unit apartment building valued at over one million dollars.*

"Apartment property maintenance is the process of allocating human resources, supplies and services to continue the physical operation of a multitenant property. Property maintenance is often confused with property management. Property management focuses on operations of a property as a business concern, while maintenance focuses on the operation of a property as a physical asset.

"The key element of property maintenance is foresight. Trying to save money by avoiding preventative maintenance usually leads to financial loss. Property maintenance should be active, not reactive. An astute property maintenance program will continuously plan ahead and anticipate problems before they occur.

"After all, it's cheaper to repair or replace a bad pipe before it bursts. After it bursts, it's too late. Not only do you have to fix it, but other damages may have occurred to carpeting, plaster and furniture. Worst of all, such disasters cause very bad tenant relations."

Preserving the Asset

A primary responsibility of owning rental property is the preservation of tangible assets. You must safeguard your property from physical damage and loss of income. Beyond keeping the property in good physical condition, a good maintenance program that includes regular upgrades or cosmetic improvements can actually increase the value of your investment.

Owning and operating rental property requires ongoing physical maintenance. Vacant apartments must be cleaned and decorated to make them more appealing and rentable. Broken or worn-out items need to be repaired or replaced. You can either hire a contractor to maintain your property or do it yourself.

Routine maintenance expenses should run about five percent of gross income. As an example, if the gross annual income from your property is $10,000, maintenance expenses may total around $500.00. By setting aside $45.00 a month, you will have enough in reserve for normal anticipated repairs. Having the money handy when you need to get a job done will be less stressful than having to delay a repair until the funds are available.

Good preparation and planning will help keep maintenance problems under control. Preparation includes keeping spare parts, tools and service telephone numbers on the property or in some other convenient location. Preparation also means developing the skills and acquiring the equipment necessary to do the work yourself or developing relationships with good electricians, plumbers, cleaning and decorating contractors and so on.

Repair and Deduct Laws

A comprehensive cleaning and maintenance program will help you fulfill your responsibility to provide habitable living accommodations to your tenants (see chapter 2).

In many states, maintaining habitable premises is mandated by law, and the rules are getting tougher all the time. New state and local ordinances being introduced contain a provision called *repair and deduct.* This ordinance already exists in the landlord-tenant acts of many states. The intent is to force landlords to keep their properties in good condition.

The old general rule was that tenants and landlords could negotiate the landlord's basic obligation to make repairs through mutual agreement. For example, a landlord could require a tenant to maintain everything inside an apartment while the landlord maintained the outer shell of the building and common areas. If a landlord agreed to make repairs and failed to do so, the tenant didn't have much recourse.

Under a repair and deduct ordinance tenants are allowed to have repairs made and deduct the expenses from the rent regardless of any preexisting agreement with the landlord. If a landlord does not maintain the property in habitable condition, the tenant can take action by calling professional contractors to perform the work and deducting the bill from the rent. The only requirement generally is that the tenant give the landlord sufficient notice, usually ten to 14 days.

Even if a municipality has a repair and deduct ordinance, an owner and tenant may still agree in writing that the tenant is to perform specific repairs, maintenance tasks or minor remodeling providing: First, the agreement is entered into in good faith and is not for the purpose of evading the obligations of the owner; second, the agreement does not diminish the obligations of the owner to other residents; third, the terms and conditions of the agreement are clearly and prominently disclosed and fourth, the consideration for such agreement is specifically stated.

Renting As Is

Some landlords rent apartments "as is," and require tenants to decorate and upgrade. In this way, the landlords save money and tenants can decorate the apartments to their specific tastes. But most tenants don't want to invest their own money and time improving someone else's property. Also, you may get a tenant who wants purple walls with a dragon mural. If you allow tenants to do their own decorating, you should limit colors of paint and wallpaper patterns.

There is another drawback to renting an apartment as is. Few prospective renters can visualize how a shabby-looking apartment can be transformed with new carpeting, freshly decorated walls and a thorough cleaning job. Thus, good tenants will be reluctant to rent an apartment as is; you may have to allow a big deduction on the rent.

Upgrading

From time to time you will have to spend money to upgrade an apartment. Upgrading includes replacing aging appliances, worn-out carpets and outdated lighting fixtures; perhaps remodeling a kitchen or bathroom. Upgrading should be planned for and done on a regular schedule. It is better to replace a refrigerator before it breaks down on a hot Sunday in July.

Sometimes you will upgrade an apartment for an existing tenant, at or before lease renewal time; other times you will make these improvements in order to make the apartment attractive for a prospective tenant.

The decision of whether to repair or replace is based on economics, and some upgrading can be put off. However, a malfunction in an essential appliance such as heat, air conditioning, stove or refrigerator requires immediate action.

The decision to upgrade is based on several factors.

Consider the market for rental units in your location. If the demand is strong you may not have to do any upgrades, but if the market is weak, you may need to invest in some improvements to remain competitive and attract renters.

Look realistically at the overall condition and physical appearance of the unit. Check for worn-out shades, draperies or blinds; stained or torn carpeting and flooring; broken, deteriorated or severely outdated appliances, light fixtures or plumbing fixtures. Perhaps the apartment needs a total rehab. Good tenants will expect and demand the apartment be in like-new condition before they move in. Existing tenants also deserve an attractive, well-maintained unit.

Decide how much money can be invested in upgrades compared to how much the rent can be increased to amortize these expenses. Suppose you put $2,000 of improvements into an apartment that is currently renting for $400 a month. If rents are increased six percent a year for the next three years, the additional income would be only $915. To amortize a $2,000 expense over three years, rent would have to be increased 13 percent per year. At a six percent rent increase, it would take almost seven years to pay off the cost of improvements.

The easiest practical way to determine how much can be spent on improvements is to work backwards from the projected rent increases. If the $400 apartment has a ten percent rent increase per year for the next five years, the additional income would amount to $2,928. Deducting a conservative figure for inflationary operating expenses of two percent per year, approximately $2,432 would be available for necessary improvements for the five-year period.

Doing Your Own Maintenance

If you want to perform your own routine maintenance tasks you will need tools and equipment. Consider purchasing this basic list of items:

Cleaning Supplies

- canvas trash bag with shoulder strap
- straw broom
- whisk broom
- dustpan
- plastic trash bags
- mop and mop wringer
- sponge mop
- wooden pick-up stick with pointed end
- wide floor broom
- shovel
- rags
- buckets
- 6″ and 12″ squeegees
- handy box carrier
- three-foot stepladder
- toilet brush
- floor cleaner and wax for hardwood floors
- steel wool
- furniture polish
- scouring powder
- all-purpose cleaner (powder and/or liquid)
- spray deodorizer
- spray wall-tile cleaner
- sponges
- five gallon paint bucket
- scrub brush
- spray bottles
- razor blade scraper
- spray window cleaner
- liquid floor wax and applicator
- wax stripper
- metal polish
- toilet-bowl cleaner (liquid or crystal)
- spray oven cleaner
- drop cloths

Basic Tools

- claw hammer
- Phillips screwdriver
- metal files or rasps
- channel-lock pliers
- needle-nose pliers
- wire stripper
- putty knives
- razor knife

black electrical tape
electric continuity tester
flat-head screwdriver
awl or punch (ice pick)
regular pliers
Vise-Grip pliers
wire cutters
20-foot tape measure
paint brushes
paint roller
razor scraper
flashlight (plastic cover to avoid electrical contact)
pipe wrenches
wood saw and hacksaw
spirit level
crescent wrenches
electric drill

Preparing a Vacant Apartment for Rental

Vacant apartments must be in good rentable condition when they are shown to prospective residents. The preparation process for vacant apartments consists of possible upgrading, surface cleaning, painting and thorough cleaning and maintenance. Use the apartment make-ready checklist (exhibit 50) as a guide to prevent overlooking or forgetting an item.

Surface Cleaning

Vacant apartments should be cleaned as soon as possible after the old tenants move out. This initial cleaning includes removing all the trash, wiping down the appliances and countertops, sweeping and vacuuming the floors and cleaning the windows. Once the vacant apartment is clean, you can show it to prospective tenants even if it still needs painting and repairs.

Minor Repairs

Inspect vacant apartments, using the pre-inspection checklist (exhibit 23). You will usually see a number of things that need repair or replacement. Some common maintenance items are:

broken or loose doorknobs on cabinets and closet doors
loose closet shelving or rods
loose shower rods, towel bars and hooks
leaky faucets or toilets
clogged faucet aerators

EXHIBIT 50: Apartment Make-Ready Checklist

Property ______	Unit ______
Unit Size ______	Date to be Occupied ______
Inspected by ______	Date ______

CHECKLIST	INSTRUCTIONS (C) clean (P) paint (R) repair (RPL) replace
Check all plumbing (toilets, faucets, pipes). Check for leaks, pressure, etc.	
Check all appliances for proper operation, bulbs, etc.	
Check all hardware (doorknobs, hooks, rods, locks, catches, etc.)	
Check all windows and screens (tracks, locks, operation, cracks, tears, etc.)	
Check all walls, ceilings, baseboard (holes, cuts, nail pops, seams, woodwork trim).	
Check all floors (cleaned and waxed, carpet rips, shampoo, vacuum).	
Check bathrooms (cleaned tubs, toilets, walls, vanities, mirrors, medicine cabinets, sinks, towel bars, toilet paper holders, soap dishes polished).	
Check all closets (shelves, lights, floor, doors).	
Check all thresholds for cracks, dirt, loose screws.	
Check all other doors (warping, rubbing, cracks, squeaks, etc.).	
Check all vents, registers (dirt, operation).	
Check heating and air-conditioning for proper operation (filters, thermostats, etc.).	
Check all kitchen cabinets (doors work, cleaning, peeling, etc.).	
Check all lighting (new bulbs, switches, cleanliness, hanging properly).	
Check for chips or cracks in sinks, counter-tops, appliances.	
REPLACE THESE MISSING ITEMS	
CLEANING DATE	
PAINTING DATE	
MAINTENANCE DATE	
FOLLOW-UP INSPECTION DATE	
NEW CARPETING DATE	

clogged drains
burned-out light bulbs
broken electrical switches or outlets
blown electrical fuses
torn window screens, shades and blinds
broken windowpanes
torn or missing wall or floor tiles in kitchens and baths
doors that stick: entrance, bedroom and bathroom
dirty heating and air-conditioning filters

Most items listed above can be repaired with the tools suggested earlier. Replacement parts can be purchased in most hardware stores. Inspect the apartment personally to determine if you can restore the broken items yourself before calling in professionals.

Painting

The next step in getting a vacant apartment ready is painting. Although you may decide to hire a professional painter, you should know the basic process of painting an apartment. The task is divided into three steps: preparation, painting and cleanup.

Preparation

Remove all nails, screws, anchors and so on and fill all holes with matching plaster. Patch holes five inches in diameter and smaller following directions on the package. Holes larger than five inches will need a section of drywall or plaster lath inserted before patching.

Remove electric switch plates and outlet plates. If walls are very dirty, scrub them. Do not try to paint over dirt. Seal water marks, grease marks, crayon marks and so on with a product designed for this purpose. Scrape loose paint.

Painting

Paint the entire apartment with one coat of flat white latex paint, including ceilings, walls, closets, doors, frames, windows and trim, if applicable. Use semigloss paint in kitchens and bathrooms. (Some people prefer to use semigloss paint for trim, as well.) Use brushes for trim and rollers for walls and ceilings. Extension poles make ceiling painting easier. Use drop cloths to facilitate cleanup.

Cleanup

Replace the switch plates and outlet plates. Remove all paint splatters on countertops, cabinets, appliances, floors and woodwork. Scrape paint smears off windows. Clean paint out of bathtubs and sinks. Sweep up paint chips on the floors.

Final Cleanup

When the apartment is painted and all repairs have been completed, it can now undergo a final cleaning. Follow these procedures for a comprehensive cleaning program:

Kitchen

To clean the oven: Take out any removable oven parts and put them in the sink to soak. Spray the oven with oven cleaner (if it is not self-cleaning). Follow directions on the package; oven cleaners are corrosive. Some oven cleaners take a few minutes to work, others must be left overnight.

Using an all-purpose cleaner, wash the outside of the range: top, front, sides and doors. Clean the countertops and interiors and exteriors of cabinets and drawers. Clean the interior and exterior of the refrigerator. Defrost it if necessary. Clean the dishwasher inside and out. Vacuum and scrub the range hoods and vents.

By this time the oven cleaner will have had time to act. Clean the oven, following directions on the package. Clean and replace the oven parts.

Using scouring powder, clean the sink and faucets.

Finally, wash the wall tile and scrub the floor.

Bathroom(s)

Put bowl cleaner in the toilet, following the instructions on the package.

Spray and clean the shower tile walls with a product designed for this purpose.

Using an all-purpose cleaner, clean the medicine cabinet, vanity, light fixtures, walls and toilet bowl.

Using scouring powder and a spray cleaner, scrub sink and tub and chrome fixtures. Vacuum and scrub exhaust vent.

Finally, scrub the floor.

Closets

Vacuum the shelves, doors and tracks; scrub if necessary.

Lighting

Clean the light globes. Replace bulbs as needed.

Heating and air conditioning

Clean or replace filters in heating and air-conditioning units. Vacuum, wipe or scrub the units if necessary.

Windows

With a spray window cleaner, clean interior window panes (also exterior, if possible). Clean trim and tracks; make sure windows open and close freely. Use a razor scraper to removed dried paint on glass surfaces.

Floors

Sweep and/or vacuum all hard-surface floors and carpeting. For tile floors, mop with all-purpose cleaner and apply liquid wax. For hardwood floors, clean and wax with products designed for hardwood floors. Use a wax finish that minimizes slippery surfaces.

Carpet Cleaning

Carpet cleaning is the last step in apartment preparation. This job is often performed by outside contractors, but the best results are obtained with a process that employs water extraction equipment.

If you decide to do the job yourself, follow the instructions that accompany the carpet-cleaning equipment. Prespotting heavily stained areas will improve the final result. Do not use too much shampoo. This is a common mistake, and it makes the job of rinsing the carpet next to impossible.

When you've finished, cover the wet carpet with an absorbing paper that is available at most hardware stores. If no one will be entering the apartment for a few days, you can omit the paper and let the carpet dry in the open air.

After the carpet dries, vacuum it to pick up any residue. At this point the apartment should be ready for new tenants.

Using Outside Contractors

Certain maintenance functions are best handled by outside contractors. You may have to hire a contractor for snow removal, landscaping, garbage removal, roofing, painting (interior and exterior), tuckpointing, pest control, carpet cleaning, electrical, plumbing, heating and air-conditioning repairs and so on.

Compile a list of recommended service companies for various types of mechanical problems, including plumbers, electricians, heating and air-conditioning contractors and appliance repairers. If you cannot get a recommendation for a particular job, look in the yellow pages and take a chance with a company that can give you a reference list of satisfied customers.

Some owners of small apartment buildings hire a local janitor, possibly someone who lives nearby, to perform daily or weekly housekeeping tasks. Inquiries of neighbors and property owners in the area may result in a few good recommendations.

When using an outside contractor, refer to the contractor guidelines (exhibit 51).

Condominiums

The governing association of a condominium may have a maintenance staff that can perform routine maintenance tasks, charging the owner for time and materials. Association rates are usually less expensive than calling in an outside contractor and the property's maintenance personnel are generally better prepared to deal with problems particular to your building.

Pest and Insect Control

Almost every apartment building will have problems with pests and insects from time to time. The most common nuisance is the cockroach; others are mice, rats, ants and termites.

Pest control is best left to professional exterminators. At the first sign of trouble, have the building treated, and set up a regular schedule of follow-up treatments. If tenants see that you have a regular extermination program, they will not panic if they see an occasional cockroach.

EXHIBIT 51: Contractor Guidelines

CONTRACTOR GUIDELINES

The following was prepared to inform you of our procedures and expectations regarding your business relationship with us.

INSURANCE

All contractors that perform work on our property are required to carry appropriate insurance coverage. A certificate of insurance must be provided before work begins. See the attached page for the specific coverage required.

PROPOSALS

Proposals, when required, should be submitted to the appropriate individual. The proposal must be as specific as possible containing the job address, description of work, type of materials to be used, any warranty/guarantee information, and the dollar amount. If specific payment terms are required they should be specified (see also payment terms).

PURCHASE ORDERS

Prior to starting any work you must get a purchase order or purchase order number. The purchase order should contain all pertinent information regarding the job. You will receive the white copy for your records. All correspondence regarding a job must contain the purchase order number.

INVOICES

All invoices should be sent directly to ____.
Invoices must contain the following information:

1. Job Address
2. Purchase Order Number
3. Description of Work as per the Purchase Order
4. Dollar Amount

PAYMENT TERMS

Immediately upon completion of work you should send in your invoice. It will be processed and payed within 30–45 days upon completion and acceptance of work and upon receipt of invoice.

If you do not receive payment in 45 days, provided there are no discrepancies, you should contact us at ________ ____.

QUALITY OF WORK

All work is expected to be done, according to specifications, in a professional and workmanlike manner in accordance with accepted practices.

WORK AREAS

Upon completion of work or at the end of each work day the work area must be left clean or in the same condition it was prior to the work starting.

DAMAGE TO PROPERTY

In the event that your company causes any damage to any property, personal or otherwise, your company will be held liable and be expected to resolve the matter immediately.

EXHIBIT 51: Contractor Guidelines *(Continued)*

EXTRAS

Any extra work not included in the original price must be approved in advance, in writing, prior to the commencement of such extra work.

KEYS

If you must use a key to gain access to a work area you will be required to sign for the key. All keys must be returned at the end of each work day.

DISCREPANCIES

If there are any discrepancies regarding the terms and conditions of the services rendered you are expected to resolve them immediately.

BUSINESS CONDUCT POLICY

The intent of the policy is to preclude the development of any situation or relationship which might compromise good business judgment or create or appear to create the image of unethical practices. Accordingly, this policy prohibits our company's employees, or their family members, accepting gifts, loans, or use of accommodations from anyone with whom we do business. Gifts of inconsequential value may be accepted in circumstances where such minor gifts are of customary industry practices.

INSURANCE REQUIREMENTS FOR CONTRACTORS

All contractors that do work for us must have a certificate of insurance on file.

The requirements are as follows:

General Liability	$100,000 minimum
Property Damage	50,000 minimum
Workmens' Compensation*	100,000 minimum
Auto Liability & Property Damage	100,000 minimum

*The only people exempt from Workmens' Compensation are sole proprietors and partners and corporate officers.

All policies must contain the following clause:

Cancellation: Should your policy be cancelled before the expiration date, the issuing company will endeavor to mail ten (10) days written notice to the certificate holder, but failure to mail such notice shall impose no obligation or liability of any kind upon the company.

The certificate must be mailed to:

____

____

____

____

Any questions regarding this should be directed to ______________________________
at ______________________________.

Thank you.

____

There are several things you and your tenants can do to help control pest problems; however, these practices are not a substitute for a good, ongoing, professional pest-extermination program.

Caulk cracks and openings around windows, foundations, drains and pipes to prevent pests from entering the building.

Enforce good housekeeping and sanitation practices: Garbage and trash must be covered, and removed promptly; kitchens should be scrubbed regularly to minimize grease buildup; debris and junk should be thrown out—even accumulated newspapers can harbor pests.

When screening prospective tenants, try to find out if their old building had roaches; if so, the roaches will probably move in with the tenants.

Cutting Costs

Often the difference between a positive and negative cash flow is simply a matter of prudently monitoring controllable expenses. Your biggest costs are usually fixed: mortgage payments, real estate taxes and insurance. There isn't too much you can do about these costs except to file a tax protest or refinance the mortgage.

Other expenses, such as utilities and maintenance costs, can be substantially reduced. For example, if you are paying for common-area lighting, you can install timers to turn off the lights during the day. If you pay for heat, air conditioning and hot water, installing programmed thermostats and timers can control the output and keep costs down.

Make sure all mechanical equipment is in peak operating condition. Boilers and air conditioners will run more efficiently if you have them inspected and adjusted annually.

Always be on the lookout for more ways to cut costs. Are you paying for certain routine services that you or one of your tenants can perform? Can you make some of the minor repairs or do your own painting?

Use the cost-cutting checklist (exhibit 52) for suggested ways to save money on maintenance.

EXHIBIT 52: Cost Cutting Checklist

General

Bring in utility companies to explain present rate structure and revise to the most favorable rate.

Heating/Air Conditioning

Check boiler efficiency.

Maintain the boiler regularly to insure the highest efficiency.

Lower daytime and nighttime thermostat settings for heat. (Follow local ordinances.)

Clean radiators and air registers.

Repair all leaks.

Reduce water temperature in hot water systems.

Check operation of automatic controls.

Balance heating system.

Check operation of all electric heating units.

Install indoor/outdoor controls.

Tune up heating plants.

Install flue restrictors.

Reduce air-conditioning and/or heat in unoccupied units.

Keep doors closed as much as possible when the heating and air conditioning is in operation (specifically service and fire doors).

Leave thermostat on a desired temperature rather than adjusting it all the time.

Maintain thermostat controls for heating public areas at not more than 68° from October to April.

Increase moisture in air to increase tenant comfort and at the same time reduce use of heating fuel.

Check out motors and pumps on heating systems for cleanliness; investigate the possibility of using a lower wattage motor.

Keep air filters clean, change them often.

Do not block registers or ducts.

If the building has window air-conditioning units and a central heating furnace, cover or close the floor or sidewall registers and low return air grills while air-conditioning is on.

With a forced-air system, keep the return-air grills and warm air ducts clean.

If laundry facilities are available in the building, keep dryer lint filter clean.

Eliminate humidity controls for all but certain circumstances.

Insulation

Install heat-absorbing and heat-reflecting glass to reduce heat from direct sunlight by 40 percent to 70 percent.

Repair broken glass.

Repair window putty.

Replace caulking.

Adjust door closers.

If feasible, redo roofing and sidewalls to provide insulation.

Use storm windows and doors or double pane glass to reduce the loss of heat.

Waterproof foundations to minimize heat loss.

Install weather stripping and caulking to seal cracks around windows and doors.

EXHIBIT 52: Cost Cutting Checklist *(Continued)*

Electricity

Reduce lighting levels.

Clean bulbs and fixtures.

Investigate the most efficient light sources that can provide the illumination required:
- High pressure sodium vapor (most efficient)
- Metal Halide
- Fluorescent
- Mercury
- Incandescent (least efficient)

Replace two 60-watt lamps with one 100-watt to save 12 percent of previous usage and provide the same amount of light.

Put reflective covers or backers on fluorescent lights to maximize light refraction.

Reduce hall lighting to minimum safe levels.

Reduce exterior lighting (around building and parking areas) by removing every other bulb.

Repaint dark-colored areas (lobbies, halls) white to increase reflected light.

Install photocells in place of electric timers.

Install fluorescent light in place of incandescent.

Locate refrigerators away from heating equipment and direct sunlight.

Keep refrigerator coil surfaces clean to provide maximum cooling.

Notify tenants to defrost their refrigerators when frost in the freezer compartment is about ¼ inch thick.

Water

Reduce water temperature in water heater.

Repair leaks.

Check boiler water level.

Check combustion efficiency of boiler.

Ask utility company to check the efficiency of the hot water tanks being used.

Instruct tenants to use cold water when operating a garbage disposal. This solidifies the grease, reduces hot water usage and cuts down on maintenance.

Insulate pipes so that less energy will be wasted in running until it "warms up."

Repair dripping faucets.

Investigate use of smaller water-saving nozzles and spray heads on water fixtures to increase pressure but reduce total gallons of water used.

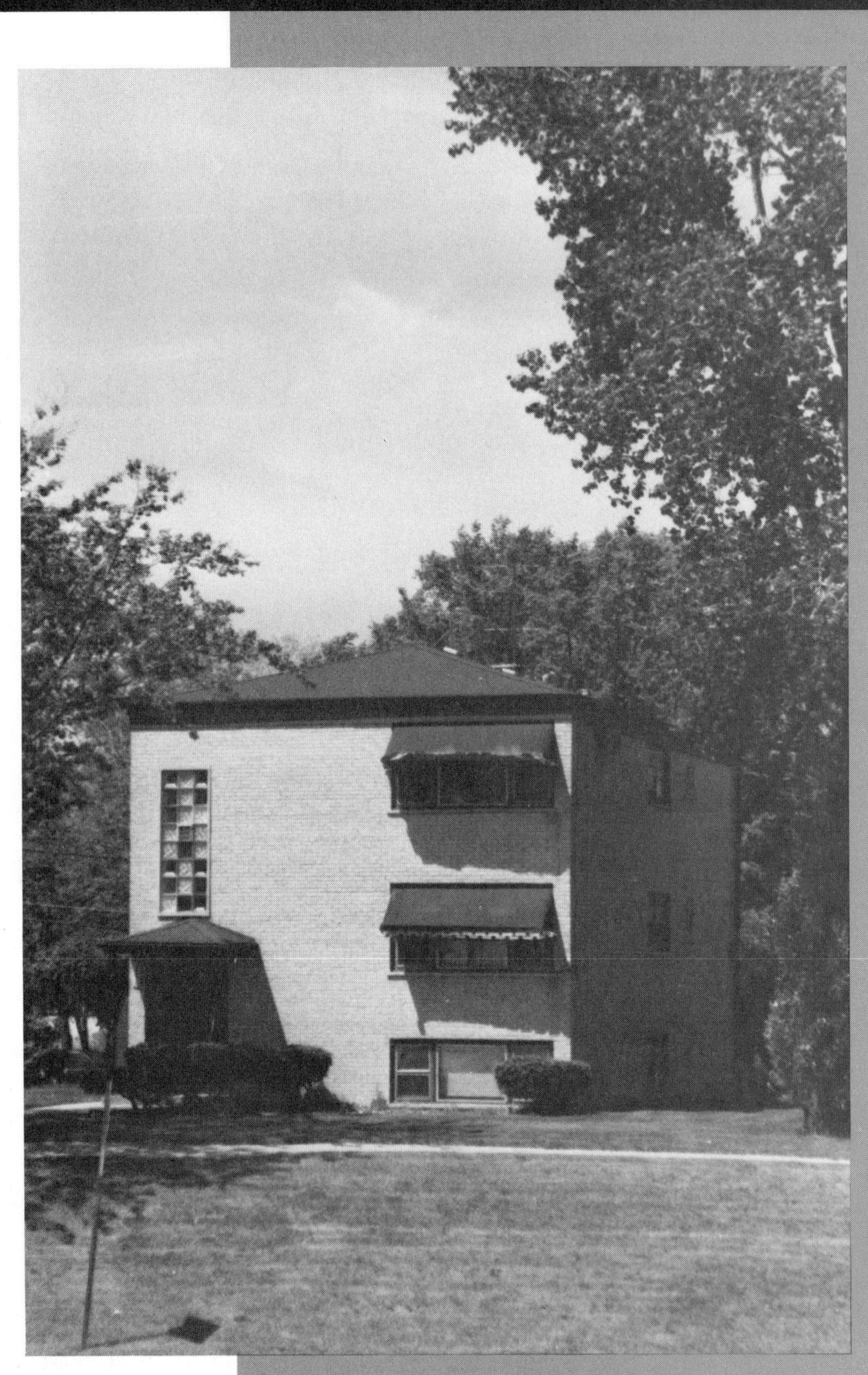

11

Property Taxes

Carole Bilina *is employed as an assistant director in a social service agency. Her position entails writing, public relations and administration. Carole, with her mother/partner, owns and manages two 6-flat buildings. Her mother resides in one apartment; Carole in another; and they share the management tasks together.*

"In 1976, we bought our first property in a neighborhood known as Uptown at a time when the area was generally perceived as being less than desirable. The decision to pioneer was based strictly on economics. Uptown was one of the few communities we could afford and we gambled the area would improve in time. Two years later we acquired a second building in a nearby area known as East Ravenswood.

"In the beginning, the area was so bad you wouldn't want to live there, but we did much of the property rehabbing work ourselves. As work progressed, and as the neighborhood improved, we attracted better tenants. Our communities steadily got better over the years, bringing increases in property values and equal increases in property taxes.

"When we discussed rehabbing the Uptown building, we planned on saving the exterior work until last. Our hope was to avoid triggering a sequence of events that would result in our property being prematurely reassessed because of improvements. Another factor we considered was the quadrennial reassessment and the date it was due. If we could schedule the cosmetic work for completion after the reassessment, we might minimize the tax increase for another four years.

"Regardless of our efforts to minimize increases, property taxes have gone up each year. Fortunately we have offset these increases with equal increases in rents. Our renewal letters to tenants cite taxes as one of the major reasons we have to increase rent. As far as paying the bills, we escrow money each month for taxes and insurance with our bank and they actually pay the bill, although now I think it would be better to earn interest on the money and pay the bills ourselves."

The basic principles contained in this chapter are followed throughout the country. Most of the material, however, specifically details the Illinois property tax system. Where there are differences between Illinois and other states, it has been noted. All exhibits pertain to Cook County, Illinois.

How To Read a Tax Bill

The following discussion is intended to help you understand how your tax bills are calculated. Local laws may vary; consult your local tax office. See exhibit 53, How to Read a Tax Bill.

EXHIBIT 53: How To Read a Tax Bill

EXAMPLE
$240,000
12 UNIT APARTMENT BUILDING

Assessed Valuation (33.33%)	$80,000
Equalization Factor (1976)	1.4153
Equalized Value	$113,224
Tax Rate	× 8.785%*
Tax Bill	$9,946.73

*For each $100 of Assessed Valuation.

COMPUTE YOUR OWN TAX BILL

Assessed Valuation	$
Equalization Factor	×
Equalized Value	$
Tax Rate	× %
Your Tax Bill	$

Market Value

The assessor, or assessor's appraiser, has the responsibility of determining a market value for each property in a jurisdiction (county, township, borough or parish). The market value of a property is the price the property would probably sell for in a competitive market. If there has not been a recent sale of a property comparable to yours, the assessor uses other methods to determine a market value.

One method that would be used—especially on newer or special-use buildings—is the cost approach, which determines the current cost of replacing the improvements, less depreciation from all causes, plus the value of the land.

Another method, used for income-producing property, is the income approach, which establishes the value by capitalizing the income the property produces or is expected to produce.

Once the market value is decided, the assessed value can be determined.

Assessed Value

The assessed value is a percentage of the market value. It varies between states, within a state and/or by type of property, and can be 100 percent of the market value. In Illinois, the percentage used to determine the assessed value for residential rental properties is 33⅓ percent of the market value. Therefore, an apartment building purchased for $150,000 would have an assessed value of $50,000. In Cook County, which consists of Chicago and a few surrounding suburbs, there is one exception to this. Any apartment building with six units or less has an assessment value of 16 percent. Thus, a $150,000 six-flat located in Cook County would have an assessed value of $150,000 times 16 percent, or $24,000.

Equalization Factor

When the assessor determines market value and takes the proper percentage of that amount and computes an assessed value, the state injects a multiplier called the state equalization factor. This factor varies between counties. Many states outside Illinois do not have an equalization factor so the following would not apply.

According to the State of Illinois, the purpose of the multiplier is to make assessed values equitable between the counties. Comparable properties located in comparable areas in different counties should have approximately the same value. In an effort to keep the state factor, or multiplier, at one (1.00), a township may apply its own factor that covers only that township. However, a township factor does not preclude the state from applying a factor also.

Tax Rate

Once you have an equalized assessed value, the tax rate (or in many states the millage rate) is determined. Local taxing bodies add up assessed values on all properties in their jurisdictions. The total operations budgeted amount is divided by the total assessed value base to determine the tax or millage rate. Multiplying the equalized assessed value by the tax or millage rate gives you your total taxes due (tax bill).

Are You Over-Assessed?

A property could be over-assessed (or under-assessed) even though the assessors have done their jobs properly.

Assessors have many properties to assess at any given time; they tackle this problem by using a mass appraisal approach. The assessor takes comparable properties in comparable areas and places comparable market values and, therefore, comparable assessed values on them. Since the assessor is not inspecting properties for their unique features, the values they place are almost always inexact. An individual appraisal is much more accurate for determining market value because it focuses on the unique characteristics of the property.

When purchasing property, it is generally a good idea to allocate a portion of the purchase price for personal property that should be shown on the closing statement. Personal property is taxable in many states, but not in Illinois. If below-market financing is involved, the selling price may be inflated and, if so, it should be adjusted downward to reflect the effects of the financing. The assessed value should not indicate a market value higher than what was paid for the property after the adjustments for personal property and financing.

There may be comparable properties near your property that are assessed lower than your building. You will need photographs of these properties when you go in to the assessor with this information. The assessor may lower your assessed value or raise the assessed value on the comparable properties.

When using an income approach (rental property), keep in mind that assessors employ guidelines in determining normal operations of a property. They follow these guidelines when looking at vacancies, percentage of taxes to gross possible rent and percentage of expenses to gross possible rent. For example, in Cook County the real estate taxes should not exceed 25 percent of gross possible rent. In the rest of Illinois, the guideline is 15 percent of gross possible rent. For vacancies and expenses, guidelines vary with the neighborhood and size of the property.

If your vacancies or expenses are higher than the guidelines it is up to you to prove that these problems should be considered in assessing the property and are not due to poor management. Assessors do not have to lower the value on a property simply because the owner or manager is not doing an adequate job. Be ready to justify and support your claims, especially major, unexpected and necessary expenses. Be ready to give reasons why you are experiencing vacancies.

Anything that causes major damage to the property, such as flood, fire, tornado and so on should be brought to the attention of the assessor. Any problem with the property that would have a negative effect on value should be documented.

Valuation and Tax Rate Protests

In many states, property is reassessed every year. In Illinois, however, Cook County reassesses one quarter of its properties each year. The year that a property is scheduled to be reassessed is called the *quadrennial.* However, the taxpayer may file a complaint in any and every year and the assessor can reassess the property in nonquadrennial years.

In Cook County, the taxpayer files a complaint (exhibit 54) with the assessor's office. You do not need legal representation. The assessor's office has all the forms and you supply whatever documentation is relevant to your case. The assessor then renders a decision.

If you are dissatisfied with this decision, you can proceed to the Cook County Board of Tax Appeals. From this point forward in Cook County, you must have legal counsel. Your attorney would file a petition with supporting documentation and argue the case (exhibit 55).

EXHIBIT 54: Real Estate Assessed Valuation Complaint

198__ REAL ESTATE ASSESSED VALUATION COMPLAINT
ASSESSOR OF COOK COUNTY

TYPE OR PRINT ALL INFORMATION

ASSESSOR'S COMPLAINT NO. ____________ PHONE NO. ________

Township ____________

NAME OF OWNER/LESSEE ____________ ADDRESS ____________ CITY ____________ ZIP CODE ________

IDENTIFICATION OF REAL ESTATE

One set of forms (3 copies) must be prepared for each Docket Number

PROPERTY ADDRESS ____________ CITY ____________ VOL. ____________ MAJOR CLASS ☐

PERMANENT INDEX NUMBER ☐☐ - ☐☐ - ☐☐☐ - ☐☐☐ - ☐☐☐☐
AREA SUB-AREA BLOCK PARCEL UNIT

☐ Proration or multi-parcel complaint
☐ ☐ ☐ to ☐ ☐ ☐

STATE OF ILLINOIS }
COUNTY OF COOK } SS

☐ Residential ☐ Commercial / Industrial ☐ Vacant ☐ Apartment 7 or more units

Undersigned Complainant, being duly sworn, deposes and says: (1) That he is the owner/lessee of the above described property, (2) That an alleged over-assessment has occurred and is based on the following facts:

(DESCRIBE BRIEFLY) ____________

(3) That any documents, records or other evidence offered in support of this complaint by the undersigned, his attorney or other representative, are true, accurate and pertain to the above described property.

Year Purchased ________ Purchase Price ________
Estimate of fair cash market value of land and Building as of January 1, 198__; $ ________

____
Owner/Lessee

____
Accepted by

STATE OF ILLINOIS }
COUNTY OF COOK } SS.

____________, on oath states: (1) He is the Representative of record for the Owner/Lessee and has knowledge of matters covered by this affidavit and has read the rules of the Assessor of Cook County. (2) He has not directly or indirectly solicited employment by the Owner/Lessee and knows of no solicitation of said Owner/Lessee by any person that has resulted in the employment of the affiant.

Representative
I (We) hereby appear on behalf of the above complaint.

____
Representative

Name ____________ Date ____________

Address ____________ Tel. No. ____________

City ____________ State ____________ Zip ____________

FOR OFFICE USE ONLY

Form 4818 Rev. '75

EXHIBIT 55: Real Estate Assessed Valuation Complaint—Appeal

1986 REAL ESTATE ASSESSED VALUATION COMPLAINT

THE BOARD OF APPEALS OF COOK COUNTY

TYPE OR PRINT ALL INFORMATION. PLEASE COMPLY WITH BOARD RULES AND REGULATIONS IN FILLING OUT THIS FORM.

Name of Appellant ______

Address of Appellant ______

City ______ Zip ______ Phone No. ______

LOCATION AND IDENTIFICATION OF REAL ESTATE

Address ______ City ______ Township ______

Description of Property: ______

Year Purchased ______ Purchase Price $ ______ Improvements made since Purchase:

______ Cost of Improvements $ ______

Owner's Estimate of FAIR CASH MARKET VALUE of Land and Building(s) combined as of January 1, 1986. $ ______ The undersigned Appellant states that the above described real estate is OVERASSESSED by the Assessor of Cook County for the year 1986 because:

______

______

Was an Appeal made to the Assessor for 1986? ____ Yes ____ No.
Was an Appeal made to the Board of Appeals for 1985? ____ Yes ____ No.
Was a reduction granted by the Board of Appeals for 1985? ____ Yes ____ No.
What was a 1985 Board of Appeals complaint number (master if known)? ______

The undersigned states that he has read the above complaint, has personal knowledge of the contents thereof, and the same is true in substance and in fact.

______
Signature of Appellant, or Attorney

ATTORNEY'S CERTIFICATION: I, ______
ATTORNEY'S NAME (PRINTED OR TYPED) FIRM

______, certify that I have obtained
FIRM ADDRESS CITY PHONE

from ______ (1) explicit
APPELLANT TITLE OR POSITION

authorization to file this 1986 assessment complaint and (2) the appellant's assurance that I am the only attorney so authorized.

______
Signature of Attorney CODE NO.

NOTICE TO APPELLANT: You will be notified by mail of the time and place of your hearing. You must be prepared at that time to present any evidence you have in support of your claim. Please see the Rules of the Board of Appeals for the information which must be provided. All appellants are strongly encouraged to submit at least one photograph of their property's exterior. If the property is held in a trust, a disclosure of all the beneficial owners of the trust, signed by the trustee, must be filed at the hearing.

B.A. Form R.E. No. 1

TAXPAYER'S COPY

COMPLAINT NO.

Received & Checked by:

List in ascending order all Permanent Index Numbers of related parcels of the property owned by Appellant.

	PERMANENT INDEX NUMBER	VOLUME
1.		
2.		
3.		
4.		
5.		
6.		
7.		
8.		
9.		
10.		
11.		
12.		
13.		
14.		
15.		
16.		
17.		
18.		
19.		
20.		
21.		
22.		
23.		
24.		
25.		

EXHIBIT 55: Real Estate Assessed Valuation Complaint—Appeal *(Continued)*

BOARD OF APPEALS

Cook County, Illinois

1986

IMPORTANT NOTICE

1. This Board of Appeals complaint form with attached carbon copies should be filled out and signed. Two copies (the yellow and pink) must be filed with the Board of Appeals at its offices. The third copy (white) is for your records. The Board cannot accept responsibility for complaints forwarded by mail.

2. All items on the complaint form must be filled in with complete and correct information. If the particular property in question consists of two or more permanent index numbers, then all numbers should be listed on the right hand side of the complaint form. Failure to fully complete this form may render your complaint void.

3. A properly completed and correct complaint form must be filed within the time specified in the official publication of the Board of Appeals for the township in which the property is located, as provided by the Illinois Statutes prescribing the time for filing of complaints. The Board will not accept any complaint filed after the official closing date for the township.

After the Board of Tax Appeals, your attorney can file a specific objection complaint (SOC) and/or a certificate of Error (COE) (see exhibit 56). To file an SOC for the current year, the taxes must be paid on time, in full and under protest. Also, a complaint must have been filed for the prior year's taxes with the Cook County Board of Tax Appeals, which was discussed above. Since an SOC is a lawsuit, it must be drafted by your legal counsel. No form is provided by the courts. The Circuit Court of Cook County will approve or disapprove the SOC.

When a certificate of error is filed for the current year, an assessed valuation complaint must be filed with the Assessor of Cook County for the upcoming year. The Board of Tax Appeals must approve the COE, so if they denied relief for the current year, they probably will not approve the COE. Therefore, your attorney would also file an SOC, which does not need approval of the Board of Tax Appeals.

In Illinois counties other than Cook, the system is different. You do not need an attorney to proceed with the complaint beyond the assessor's office. After the Assessor, you can file a complaint with the Board of Review. If needed, you can then file with the Property Tax Appeal Board (PTAB). The PTAB is run by the state and handles complaints from all over the entire state except Cook County. Even though you don't need an attorney, you should hire one for this step in the appeal process, unless you are very knowledgeable.

In many states the appeal process is similar to the Illinois system, excluding Cook County. The names for the review boards vary between states as do the forms and the rigidity of the rules for filing. In many areas, the assessors or appraisers are willing to work with a taxpayer to determine the value of the property before formally issuing a notice. By working with the assessor in this manner, you may be able to avoid the appeal process altogether. Check with the local office and/or with other taxpayers familiar with the appeal process in your area to determine the best course of action. Other sources of information that should be helpful are listed under Resources at the end of the book.

In Illinois when you pay taxes under protest you are claiming that the tax rate is excessive. This means that the taxing districts have overbudgeted and you have paid too much in taxes because the tax rate on your bill is too high. Paying taxes under protest is of benefit only if at least one law firm in your county analyzes the budgets of the various taxing districts and files in court for refunds based on the analyses.

There are law firms that specialize in doing this work in Cook County and several other counties surrounding Chicago. In these counties an attorney pays the taxes on your behalf, on time and in full, but under protest.

The process can sometimes be very long, possibly ten years or more in Cook County, before you receive a refund. The actual procedure for paying under protest consists of merely filling out a protest form (exhibit 57) and submitting it with your tax bill and check at the time of payment. In some areas there may also be a small fee.

Some other states also allow for payment under protest. Check with your local office for further details.

For More Information

If you have questions but aren't quite ready to hire an attorney, there are several organizations that you can contact. One is the Illinois Property Assessment Institute (IPAI), 707 North East Street, Bloomington, IL 61701, (309) 828-5131. Other states also have their own state organizations. Another is the International Association of Assessing Officers (IAAO), 1313 East 60th Street, Chicago, IL 60637-9990, (312) 947-2069. There is also the Institute of Property Taxation, 122 C Street NW, Suite 200, Washington, DC 20001, (202) 347-5115. These organizations offer classes and materials concerning property taxation at reasonable fees. The Illinois Department of Revenue also has some helpful materials at a reasonable fee. Taxpayers in other states should call their own state offices to determine what materials are available and which department offers it.

If you don't have time to learn about property taxes, retain an attorney. Look for one who is established in the field; preferably one who works almost exclusively in the field of property taxes and has a reputation for being honest, reliable and imaginative.

EXHIBIT 56: Application for 1985 Certificate of Error

APPLICATION FOR 1985 CERTIFICATE OF ERROR

TOWNSHIP: ____________________

VOLUME: ____________________

PERMANENT INDEX NUMBER: ____________________

COMPLAINT DOCKET NUMBER: ____________________

PROPERTY CLASS: ____________________

NAME: ____________________

ADDRESS: ____________________ CITY: ____________________

TELEPHONE NUMBER: ____________________ ZIP CODE: ____________________

(CIRCLE ONE) CERTIFICATE OF ERROR: ____________________

IBM ERROR WRECK

BOARD-UP OCCUPANCY

EXCESSIVE VALUATION 2–41 OTHER

DEPUTY'S SIGNATURE: ____________________

DATE OF REQUEST: ____________________

ADDITIONAL DATE REQUESTED: ____________________

FIELD CHECK: YES _______ NO _______ C. OF E.: ISSUED _______ DENIED _______

REASON REFUSED: ____________________

____________________ DATE: ____________________

IMPORTANT
THIS IS AN APPLICATION ONLY

YOU WILL BE NOTIFIED BY MAIL AS TO THE DISPOSITION OF THIS APPLICATION FOR CERTIFICATE OF ERROR. ALL INQUIRIES BY PHONE CAN BE MADE BY CALLING THE C/E DEPARTMENT AT 443-5327.

EXHIBIT 57: Taxes Paid Under Protest

County Collector of Cook County
Chicago, Illinois

Dear Sir:

Pursuant to Section 194 of Revenue Act of 1939, as amended, payment is herewith made under protest of the amount indicated below on the 198__ general taxes extended against the real estate described by Volume and Permanent Real Estate Index Numbers of your Collector's Warrant Books and records for said year appearing below on attached hereto and made a part hereof.

Payment of the second installment herewith and payment of the estimated first installment are made under protest to the extent of 100% of the total tax for the year.

This payment shall be applied to the taxes of all taxing bodies ratably, subject to a refund of 100% of the entire tax, protest is made to the tax rates levied on the following grounds: the taxes and rates are in excess of the limits fixed by law; the limits were improperly scaled; the appropriations and levies were passed, published and itemized contrary to law; the statutes under which the levies were made are unconstitutional; the levies were not filed with the County Clerk at the time or in the manner prescribed by law; the levies were duplicated; the levies were not for legal purpose; all or a portion of each of the taxes levied are excessive, fraudulent and void, as will be more fully specified in the objections filed to the 198__ Collector's application in the Circuit Court of Cook County.

And this payment is accordingly made under protest.

Received: NAME OF TAXPAYER:

COOK COUNTY COLLECTOR ADDRESS:

VOLUME	TOWN	PERMANENT REAL ESTATE INDEX NUMBER	ESTIMATED FIRST INSTALLMENT	AMOUNT OF SECOND INSTALLMENT	TOTAL TAX PAID UNDER PROTEST

12

Accounting

Ronald Fliss *is a full-time, self-employed accountant and a part-time real estate investor. He has purchased several condominiums that he rents with the option to buy. He believes that renters take better care of the property if they have an option to own it.*

"I like to have my tenants take care of their own units and call me only when major problems arise. For the most part, the lease-option arrangement allows me to treat them as owners.

"I visit the units monthly to collect rents, observe conditions and determine how the tenants are doing. If there is something wrong, I want to know before it becomes serious.

"I believe that good record-keeping on each condo is essential. I keep a ledger book with pages on each property, recording income and expenses that occur monthly. Keeping records indicates how each property is doing financially and serves as a basis for reporting to the IRS.

"Tenant relations are usually friendly. I try to find good, responsible people to rent my units and treat them as friends. I believe people respond better to consideration than to general rules. There are times, however, when I must be firm in a situation to force proper compliance with the agreement. It takes some experience to know when to be cordial and when to be firm.

"I believe that if tenants feel they are in a well-kept, desirable property, they will really try to maintain that situation by paying rent on time, observing condo rules and being fair with the owner-landlord."

Bookkeeping

The bookkeeping for your rental property can be as simple or sophisticated as you like. However, the type of accounting system you use will depend greatly on the size of your income portfolio. A personal computer or computer service company may be helpful if you operate over 24 units. On the other hand, a simple receipts-disbursements bookkeeping system is adequate for managing a few units.

The Internal Revenue Service requires that taxpayers be able to substantiate rental income and expenses reported on their tax returns. By using a bookkeeping system such as the one illustrated in this chapter, you will not only satisfy IRS requirements but also determine your cash flow or deficit on a month-by-month basis.

Operating income property is a business and just as in any other business you will want to make intelligent decisions based on sound economic reasoning and facts. Maintaining adequate records will enable you to monitor the expenses of your property, allowing you to determine if any of the expenses can be reduced, thereby increasing your cash flow.

Your accountant will be able to prepare your tax return more easily if the history of the past year is readily available. Funds received and cash disbursed as part of a business need to be treated with a little more sophistication than your personal checkbook transactions. Even if your accountant or computer service bureau keeps your records, you need some knowledge of bookkeeping.

Using a Ledger To Produce a Monthly Financial Statement

Checking Accounts

The IRS does not require that you maintain a separate checking account for each building you own (unless the property is not owned by you personally; for example, owned by a partnership), but keeping separate accounts facilitates the record-keeping. By keeping the cash receipts and cash disbursements separate from your personal transactions, it is much easier to prepare the monthly operating statement because all of your transactions are in one checking account.

If you are using a separate checkbook for each building and the building account does not have sufficient cash to pay a certain bill, you will have to put your personal funds into the checkbook. If you have to do this, be certain to indicate in your checkbook where the money came from; for example, "transfer from personal checkbook." Later, when the building checkbook has sufficient cash, you can write a check reimbursing yourself from the building account.

Rent Schedules

As you receive the monthly rental checks, deposit them into the appropriate building account checkbook. Next, record the rental receipt on a rent schedule (table 1) for the appropriate building. By recording this when you receive the rent, you can determine at a glance which tenants still owe you money. As your number of units increases, this rent schedule becomes very important; without it you might overlook a nonpaying tenant due to the high number of units you own. Your rent schedules function as a cash receipts journal.

Record cash disbursements in the building checkbook when they occur. At the end of each month, complete the cash disbursements journal (table 2). Record each month on a new sheet. Keep all sheets for your accountant to review at year-end.

To prepare the monthly cash disbursements journal, go through the building checkbook, recording each disbursement by check number, payee and description. In the sample journal (table 2) six columns are used for types of disbursements (mortgage, supplies, utilities and so on). The building and the number of checks written each month will determine the number of columns you will need to record the transactions. Thirteen-column accountant's worksheets, which can be purchased at most office supply stores, are recommended.

TABLE 1: Rent Schedule

Building Location or Name ______________________________ 19______

Security Deposit	*Tenant Name*	*Apt. No.*	*Jan.*	*Feb.*	*Mar.*	*Apr.*	*May*	*June*	*July*	*Aug.*	*Sept.*	*Oct.*	*Nov.*	*Dec.*	*Total*
$350	Smith	1	$ 350												
400	Jones	2	400												
375	Adams	3	375												
375	Johnson	4	400												
	Total rents		$1,525												
	Plus laundry income		50												
	Total income		$1,575												

TABLE 2: Cash Disbursements Journal

Building Location or Name ____________________ For the Month of ______________, 19______

Check Number	*Payee*	*Mortgage Payment*	*Supplies*	*Utilities*		*Office Supplies*	*Other*
				Gas	*Water*		
101	Citizens Mortgage	$1,250.00					
102	Ace Supply Store		$10.98				
103	Utility Co.—Gas			$192.72			
104	Water Company				$39.41		
Cash	Smith Hardware		10.00				
105	Ace Supply Store		17.33				
106	All-Office Supply Store					$22.00	
		$1,250.00	$38.31	$192.72	$39.41	$22.00	

Cash Disbursements Journal

If you pay cash for a supply or service instead of writing a check, get a receipt and indicate on the receipt what type service was performed or supply purchased. You can then reimburse yourself from the building checkbook for the cash you spent, or on the cash disbursements journal write *cash* in the check-number column. Attach all receipts to each month's cash disbursements journal. By doing this, you will leave an "audit trail" and, should you ever have to substantiate the building operation numbers, all of the paid receipts will be attached to the appropriate month's disbursements journal.

Operating Statement

At the end of each month, tally the income and expenses from your journals and enter the figures on the cash-flow statement (table 3). The operating statement shows a summary of activity during the month and is broken down by line items.

TABLE 3: Cash-flow Statement

Building Location or Name ______________________________ 19______

Cash Receipts (table 1)	*Jan.*	*Feb.*	*Mar.*	*Apr.*	*May*	*June*	*July*	*Aug.*	*Sept.*	*Oct.*	*Nov.*	*Dec.*	*Total*
Rent	$1,525.00												
Laundry	50.00												
Other													
Total Receipts *(a)*	$1,575.00												
Cash Disbursements (table 2)													
Mortgage payment	$1,250.00												
Accounting													
Advertising													
Cleaning and maintenance													
Insurance													
Legal													
Repairs													
Supplies	38.31												
Real estate taxes													
Utilities													
Electric	192.72												
Gas													
Water	39.41												
Scavenger													
Landscaping													
Snow removal													
Wages and taxes													
Carpeting													
Appliances													
Office supplies	22.00												
Other *(describe)*													
Total disbursements *(b)*	$1,542.44												
Net Cash Flow (Deficit) (a − b)	$ 32.56												

Line Item Definitions

Cash Receipts

Rents: all monies received as rent, not including security deposits or other deposits. Security deposits received from tenants are not considered income for tax-reporting purposes. It is a good idea to maintain these in a separate checkbook (or an interest-bearing account) until the tenants vacate the units. If you use some or all of the security deposit to pay for past-due rent or damages to the apartment, then at this time it becomes taxable to you.

Laundry: income received from laundry equipment.

Other: Such items as application fees, late fees and credit-check fees.

Total cash receipts equals total of above items.

Cash Disbursements

Mortgage payment: principal, interest, tax escrow and insurance escrow. Get an amortization schedule from your lender for your mortgage payments. Using the amortization schedule you will be able to record each month's principal and interest payments. If your real estate taxes and insurance are included in your monthly mortgage payments, the lender can also provide you with the specific amounts.

Accounting: fees paid to accounting companies or individual accountants for services rendered.

Advertising: signs, print ads, promotions, printing of fliers and so on.

Cleaning and maintenance: labor only, does not include supplies.

Legal: fees paid for legal services.

Repairs: parts and labor for appliances, electrical, plumbing, air-conditioning and heating, including do-it-yourself maintenance or contractor work.

Supplies: cleaning, janitorial, maintenance and so on.

Landscaping: service contract or new purchases.

Snow removal: service contract.

Wages and Taxes: administrative and janitorial.

Carpeting: new purchases.

Appliances: new purchases.

Other: miscellaneous.

Total cash disbursements: total of above expenditures.

Net cash flow or deficit from property: total cash receipts less total cash disbursements.

Analyzing and Using Operating Statement Data

To further refine your operating statement, determine the rental income and other items on the operating statement on a per-unit basis. You do this by dividing each income and expense category by the total number of units in your building. You can use this information to determine relationships that may help you increase your cash flow.

Past operating statements provide historical data for preparing your annual budget and detail important information that is useful when you purchase more investment property.

For example, suppose you own a four-flat apartment building with utility costs of $14 per unit. You are considering purchasing a 12-flat. By using information from your other properties, you can project a per-unit utility cost for the building you are considering buying.

However, do not arbitrarily use the data without giving thought to the details of the potential building. For example, if your four-flat building is gas heated and the 12-flat building for sale has electric heat, the heating costs are not comparable.

You can put this information onto a personal computer using an electronic spreadsheet (for instance, Lotus 1-2-3). In addition to per-unit totals, income and expenses can be expressed as a percentage of gross rents and other values such as vacancy-loss comparisons of the properties.

Maintaining good records makes preparing your tax return easier and helps you analyze your building operations on a monthly and annual basis.

When you are ready to sell your real estate investment you'll have information readily available to show a potential buyer.

Effects of 1986 Tax Reform Act

The Tax Reform Act of 1986 has significantly changed real estate as an investment. Real estate experts believe it will be good for real estate in the long run. The following information only touches the surface of the changes affecting real estate. Contact your own tax advisor for a more in-depth analysis of how this tax law affects you personally.

Active Owners

The Tax Reform Act eliminated most tax shelters associated with real estate investments. However, the revisions did leave a substantial portion available to active owners who make less than $150,000 per year in earned income.

Owner-operators of income property who have less than $100,000 per year in earned income can still deduct up to $25,000 for depreciation and operating losses to reduce their taxable income from all sources. The $25,000 tax loss is phased out in stages for income over $100,000, up to $150,000. If your adjusted gross income stays below $100,000, you could purchase several properties before reaching the $25,000 limit. The picture is even brighter for existing rental properties because of the effect the tax bill is having on rents. The elimination of tax incentives for builders has caused a sharp reduction of new apartment units on the market. This will result in increased rents as the demand for rental units is unfulfilled.

Passive Owners

Many of the tax benefits for passive real estate investments have disappeared, but the following advantages still exist:

- Limited Liability: The mortgages are non-recourse (only the specific property is at stake), and you have no personal responsibility for any bills or operating expenses.
- Professional Management: A professional management company handles all of the day-to-day concerns. A passive investor enjoys worry-free ownership.

Depreciation

Depreciation is defined as the allocation of a cost of an asset to the periods benefited in a rational and systematic manner. What this means to you is a noncash deduction on your tax return.

For example, suppose you purchased a four-unit apartment building for $150,000, of which $30,000 is allocated to the land. Land is a nondepreciable asset, so the higher the land allocation, the lower the amount remaining that you can depreciate. The building value is then $120,000, and, for simplicity's sake, let's assume you depreciate this using the straight-line method for a period of 30 years. You can then deduct the $4,000 from your rental income as an expense, but you did not pay $4,000 in cash. On your tax return, you would claim a deduction of $4,000 for depreciation expense. This is what is meant by a noncash expense.

The Tax Reform Act of 1986 increased the life over which you would depreciate the building from 19 years to 27.5 years (31.5 years for commercial property). In addition, you are now required to use the straight-line method of depreciation as opposed to using an accelerated method, which was used in the past. This amount of depreciation expense you can claim each year on your investment.

Prior to 1981 most residential property used a depreciable life schedule of from thirty to forty years. In 1981, the Economic Recovery Tax Act (ERTA) was passed. It was intended to stimulate the economy out of a recession. This tax reform decreased the time in which you could claim depreciation from 40 to 15 years. Also, you could elect to use an accelerated method, which increased your depreciation expense even more.

In 1984, in an attempt to reduce the national budget, Congress passed the Deficit Reduction Act (DRA), which increased the time from 15 to 18 then 19 years.

Clearly, our tax laws are continually changing, and it is very possible that we will experience more tax reform in the near future.

Active vs. Passive Income

There are three different types of income and they are reported differently on your tax return. Wages are earned income; dividends and interest are considered portfolio income; and real estate investment is classified as passive income.

In general, if you own the building personally (as opposed to a limited partnership investment), you will be able to deduct any losses you may incur against your other income. For example, you earn $50,000 from your job and your apartment investment has a $10,000 loss (remember depreciation is a non-cash expense, so it is not unusual to report a loss on your tax return). You would be able to deduct the $10,000 rental loss on your tax return, in effect decreasing your W-2 income from $50,000 to $40,000. Depending upon your individual tax bracket, this could save you up to $3,850 in taxes.

Congress has limited the deduction you can claim from real estate losses to a maximum of $25,000. So, if you have more than $25,000 in passive losses, you cannot deduct any amount over the $25,000 limit. Also, if your income is over $100,000, you start to lose 50 percent of the loss until at $150,000 of income you cannot deduct any losses from your building. These nondeductible losses become "suspended" losses, to be used when the property is sold. You do not lose these rental losses; it merely becomes a difference in timing—changing from a current deduction to a deduction that will decrease your gain on the sale of the property in the future.

Prior to 1987, when you sold an investment for a gain and it met certain conditions, 60 percent of the gain could be excluded from your income. If you were in the 50 percent tax bracket, by having long-term capital-gains income (sale of stock, for example), you would pay an effective tax rate of only 20 percent on the gain instead of your usual 50 percent rate.

Beginning in 1987, the capital-gains exclusion is no longer available. However, for 1987, long-term capital gains will be taxed at a maximum rate of 28 percent, rather than a maximum rate of 38½ percent for other types of income. For tax years 1988 and later, there is no difference between the capital-gains rate and other tax brackets. All income will be taxed at a maximum rate of 28 percent.

For tax years beginning after 1987, two tax rates for individuals, 15 percent and 28 percent, are prescribed by law. These rates apply to both calendar-year and fiscal-year individuals for post-1987 tax years. In addition, the law effectively creates a third rate of 33 percent for 1988 (and later tax years), which applies to individuals whose taxable income reaches beyond certain levels. The purpose of this 33 percent tax rate is to phase out the tax benefits flowing to high-income taxpayers from the 15 percent rate and from the taxpayers' personal and dependency exemptions.

Alternative Minimum Tax

The alternative minimum tax, or AMT, is like a separate set of rules for determining your tax liability. Its purpose, as the name implies, is to ensure that taxpayers who have tax preference income, deductions or credits will pay at least a minimum tax. Tax preference items are given special treatment under the regular tax laws, so it was possible for taxpayers to take advantage of this special treatment and avoid paying any federal income tax. Congress deemed this unfair, so it implemented the concept of a second tax system to make sure that taxpayers who benefited under the regular tax laws would not escape taxation altogether. The taxpayer would pay the greater of the regular income tax or the AMT.

The alternative minimum tax concept is not new with the most recent tax law change, but its scope is increased so that more taxpayers will be subject to this tax than in the past. The more common tax preferences a real estate investor will encounter, or has encountered in the past, are the excess of accelerated depreciation over the straight-line method and the 60 percent long-term capital-gains exclusion.

The long-term capital-gains exclusion was eliminated in 1987. However, Congress added the following as tax preferences: Passive losses deducted against earned or portfolio income is not allowed for AMT purposes. The entire gain is considered in calculating the alternative minimum taxable income.

As mentioned earlier, in the past most taxpayers did not need to concern themselves with the alternative minimum tax provisions because it affected so few. However, with the current tax law, many new taxpayers will be subject to this tax because of its far greater scope.

The above discussion on the new tax law and how it affects you, the real estate investor, is a brief overview. The new Tax Code itself is approximately 2,000 pages with a Technical Corrections portion increasing the tax-law effects. To fully understand how the new law affects you and your investments, seek the help of qualified tax professionals.

Conclusion

Property management can be divided into five main functions: public relations, administration, financial controls, marketing and operations. Almost everyone will be more adept in certain areas than in others. Someone who has good communication and public relations skills may not be so competent in financial or administrative tasks; a person who enjoys bookkeeping and maintenance tasks may not be good at renting apartments or tenant relations.

How you spend your time as a landlord will depend on the condition of your property and the status of the rental market. If your building needs upgrading and rehabbing, you will devote most of your attention to maintenance. A newer property probably will require less time for operations and more time for public relations or marketing. You will spend more time on marketing in a soft rental market, and more time on financial controls at tax-preparation time.

When you own a residential-income property, you will have to pay attention to all five functions, and with experience, you will become comfortable with them. It certainly is permissible, however, to hire someone to perform the tasks that you prefer not to do. A good business person knows when and how to delegate authority, and managing a rental property is a business.

The Landlord's Handbook was planned as a reference book to make the tasks of managing property easier and more rewarding. We suggest you read the whole book, then keep it at hand and when problems arise, use the index and table of contents to locate the section that pertains to the issue at hand. Remember that many of the general guidelines reflect national laws, and a landlord always should take specific state and local laws into consideration.

The handbook highlights the elements of property management and provides the reader with enough information about major issues to make the job of management easier and less time-consuming. This book is not intended to be an exhaustive resource on maintenance, advertising, accounting and so on. These subjects already are discussed in detail in other books, which a landlord should read.

More editions of the handbook are planned: a college edition and subsequent expanded editions based on input from our readers. If you would like to see certain topics expanded or shortened, please contact the communication department at Inland Real Estate, 2901 Butterfield Road, Oak Brook, Illinois 60521 or call (312) 218-8000. Your comments and suggestions would be gratefully appreciated and acknowledged.

Resources

Apartment & Condominium News, Relocation Consultants Inc. of Chicago, 660 Industrial Drive, Elmhurst, Illinois 60126, (312) 279-1423; one-year subscription.

"Explanation of Tax Reform Act of 1986," P. L. 99-514, by CCH Tax Law Editors, Commerce Clearing House, Inc., 4025 W. Peterson Ave., Chicago, Illinois 60646.

"Journal of Property Management," Institute of Real Estate Management, 430 N. Michigan Avenue, Chicago, Illinois 60611, (312) 661-1930; one-year subscription.

"Landlord-Tenant Relations Report," CD Publications, 8555 16th Street #100, Silver Spring, MD 20910.

"Metro Chicago Real Estate," Law Bulletin Publishing Company, 415 N. State Street, Chicago, Illinois 60610, (312) 644-7800; one-year subscription.

Milin, Irene and Mike, "How to Buy and Manage Rental Properties," Simon and Schuster, 1968.

Wik, Philip G., "How to Buy and Manage Income Property," Prentice-Hall, 1987.

Index